Pensions, Savings and Capital Flows

Pensions, Savings and Capital Flows

From Ageing to Emerging Markets

Helmut Reisen
OECD Development Centre, Paris, France

IN ASSOCIATION WITH THE ORGANISATION FOR
ECONOMIC CO-OPERATION AND DEVELOPMENT

Edward Elgar
Cheltenham, UK • Northampton, MA, USA

© Organisation for Economic Co-operation and Development 2000

Published by
Edward Elgar Publishing Limited
Glensanda House
Montpellier Parade
Cheltenham
Glos GL50 1UA
UK

Edward Elgar Publishing, Inc.
136 West Street
Suite 202
Northampton
Massachusetts 01060
USA

A catalogue record for this book
is available from the British Library

Library of Congress Cataloguing in Publication Data

Reisen, Helmut.
JK   Pensions, savings and capital flows : from ageing to emerging markets /
Helmut Reisen.
   'In association with the Organisation for Economic Co-operation and
Development'
   Includes index.
   1. Pension trusts—Investments. 2. Old age pensions—Finance.
3. Savings and investment. 4. Capital market. 5. Cash flow. 6. Monetary
policy. 7. International finance. I. Organisation for Economic
Co-operation and Development. II. Title.
HD7105.4.R45 2000
332.67'314—dc21   99–049040
                                                            CIP

ISBN 1 84064 308 0 (cased)

Printed and bound in Great Britain by MPG Books Ltd, Bodmin, Cornwall

Contents

Figures and Tables

Preface

In 1998, the world witnessed the strongest financial panic since the Great Depression. With virtually all emerging-market assets on fire sale, these are very hard times for those who defend the gains from global capital mobility. And yet they are real. The potential benefits of global financial integration are nowhere stronger than for funded retirement savings. The ageing member countries of the Organisation for Economic Co-operation and Development (OECD) can avoid part of their demographic problems by investing in the younger developing countries, while the latter can also spread some of their idiosyncratic risks, derived from higher exposure to country-specific shocks, by investing some of their pension assets in the OECD area. The author of this book, Helmut Reisen, who heads the research division 'Global Interdependence' at the OECD Development Centre, has been a much-noted proponent of these mutual benefits.

Nevertheless, he has not ignored the concerns which the growing financial integration between OECD and non-OECD countries has been feeding on both sides. The fast developing-country growth that some see as creating global capital shortages will actually provide the solution to the problem, since sustained growth tends to boost domestic savings. This does not necessarily imply that savings should not be targeted: Asia did not wait for growth to stimulate savings but actively promoted them. Mr Reisen summarizes how that can be achieved through monetary and fiscal policy; perhaps surprisingly, pension reform does not necessarily stimulate the national saving rate.

When a country is visibly engaged in promising economic reform, investors try to get a claim on the economy, giving at times rise to excessive capital inflows. While one of the essays in this book shows that the sovereign credit rating industry has the potential to help dampen excessive flows with timely negative announcements, the major policy problem will rest with the authorities of the recipient countries. Mr Reisen's essays provide valuable assistance for their decision how much to accept and how much to resist of these inflows, and how to manage the economy and the banking system to avoid painful financial instability. Emerging markets will only then be able to improve OECD pension returns in the 21st century if

they catch up with OECD levels of corporate profitability and if they reduce their vulnerability to the currency crises witnessed in the 1990s.

Ulrich Hiemenz
OECD Development Centre

The author would like to thank Terri Wells for her painstaking efforts in formatting the book.

Part 1

Pension Investment

Pension Investment

The first part of the collection brings together a number of papers that essentially build the case for the pension-improving benefits of global asset diversification. The benefits of portfolio diversification are particularly present in the case of fully-funded pensions. Ageing industrial countries can escape part of the demographic problem by investing in emerging markets, while poor countries can diversify away some of their idiosyncratic risks stemming from higher exposure to country-specific shocks by investing some of their pension assets in industrial countries. Such diversification benefits notwithstanding, pension funds are still heavily invested into home assets, in particular in the non-OECD area. The gradual erosion of that home bias that we are now already observing for OECD assets will have tremendous implications for global capital flows.

The first essay, originally published jointly with Bernhard Fischer in 1994 as OECD Development Centre Policy Brief No. 9, draws partly on my 1994 Amex Bank Review Prize Essay 'On the Wealth of Nations and Retirees'. In this essay, the principal argument for investing part of the OECD pension assets in the developing world is based on modern portfolio theory which promises a free lunch – higher risk-adjusted returns – for any portfolio currently underinvested in foreign assets. The argument has been criticized on the grounds that the low return correlation between OECD and emerging stock markets which is required for the free lunch to materialize will not stay that low once retirement savings are seriously invested overseas. This criticism, however, ignores the important differences with respect to maturity, structure and policy harmonization between the two country groups. Moreover, it ignores differences in ageing profiles between the OECD and non-OECD areas, which can be exploited by foreign investment.

In the absence of foreign pension investment into younger economies, what should we expect to happen to the capital returns on funded pensions once the OECD baby boomers have started to retire? As the labour force declines, the existing capital stock becomes oversized relative to the labour force. The change in relative factor proportions reduces the rental return on capital relative to wages; this effect is reinforced if fully-funded pensions indeed stimulate savings. Simultaneously, the prior phase of asset

3

accumulation would give way to a long period of asset decumulation, as the baby boomers start to draw on their pension assets to finance their retirement. Clearly, therefore, a fully-funded pension scheme is bound to get under stress by population ageing, very much like an unfunded scheme. But the funded pensions, unlike the unfunded schemes, can partly beat demography in an open economy. The asset decumulation during the retirement period will not be confined to home assets, but to emerging-market assets that still will be benefiting from net pension contributions of the underlying younger population. And capital returns, unlike in a closed economy, will not be lowered by a declining labour force, but by the world capital market and the demand for capital by the younger non-OECD area.

The second essay, co-authored by John Williamson, was prepared at the request of the Ministry of Finance of the Republic of Chile and presented to the conference 'Pensions, Privatization and Macroeconomic Policy' early in 1994 in Santiago de Chile, organized by Salvador Valdés-Prieto of the Catholic University of Chile. The sheer size of pension assets and the uniform investment behaviour of pension fund managers led Chile's authorities to worry about their impact on the foreign exchange market and the domestic bond market, if the local pension funds were free to invest abroad. The essay argues, by contrast, that such concerns are misplaced. Since the diversification of pension assets fosters stock market integration rather than interest linkages, it does little to limit short-term monetary sovereignty.

The third essay was originally presented at the 1996 Annual Meeting of the American Economic Association, at the suggestion of Estelle James from the World Bank. Subsequent drafts acquired a fairly different look, due not least to generous and excellent comments from anonymous referees of the journal *World Development*. The essay argues that the new pension funds in Latin America (and other emerging markets) stand to benefit from international diversification, just like the funds located in OECD countries. But there will not be a free lunch for a pension fund in a developing country: diversifying into developed markets will reduce risk, at the cost of lower returns. This is a price worth paying for funds whose pension beneficiaries are poor and thus cannot tolerate much risk. *The Economist* (15 March 1997), devoting its Economic Focus Page to my paper, summarized it aptly: low returns, happy returns. Moreover, restrictions of foreign investment by developing-country pension funds can hardly be justified on grounds of financial-development externalities: the home bias generally observed in pension fund investment should translate into sufficient potential demand for domestic financial assets so as to deepen markets and the institutional infrastructure. A case for initial localization requirements, however, can be derived from the fiscal costs of moving from

unfunded to fully-funded pension systems if a rise in domestic interest rates due to fiscal illusion and domestic tax collection costs is important.

The fourth essay was prepared for an expert meeting held by the OECD Committee on Financial Markets on 7–8 July 1997. The essay emphasizes the demographic impact on stock market valuation which is shown to be significant along with more conventional determinants such as interest rates and wage inflation. The favourable support on valuations from the strong baby boom cohorts in OECD countries is predicted to be reversed from the next decade, as US funded pensions cease to be a source of net savings. This is likely to support a shift of OECD-based assets into the emerging stock markets where favourable demographic trends will continue well into the year 2050.

1. Pension Fund Investment: From Ageing to Emerging Markets[*]

AGEING POPULATIONS AND GROWING PENSION ASSETS[1]

The rich world's ageing population will inevitably intensify pressures that can be expected to stimulate strong growth in private funded pensions (and other means of private old-age maintenance), both inside and outside the OECD area. Unfunded, earnings-related pension schemes could be reasonably well sustained under the demographic conditions of the immediate post-war decades. Increasingly, though, as the baby-boom generation starts to retire, a dwindling cohort of tax-payers will have to support an increasingly old population, as Figure 1.1 exemplifies for the five major OECD economies (the G5).

Figure 1.1   Old age dependency ratios: ratio of people aged 65 or older to people aged 15–64

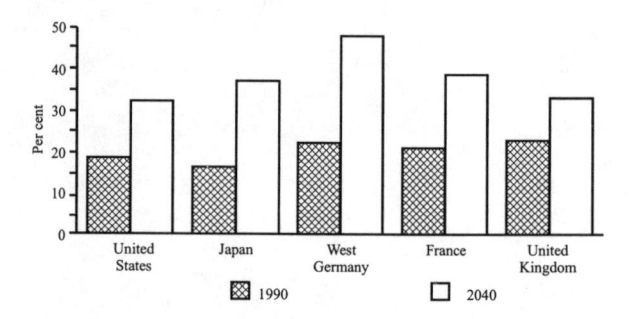

Source: Hagemann and Nicoletti (1989).

---

[*] Originally published as OECD Development Centre Policy Brief No. 9, Paris, 1994.

The demographic time-bomb imposes some most unpleasant arithmetic on unfunded state social security systems:

- *Public finances* will come under ever growing pressure from the scale and financing requirements of public pension schemes. Public debt in almost every country is much larger than is generally documented when pledged state pension benefits and future pension contributions are factored in. Recent simulations (van den Noord and Herd, 1993) have estimated the gap between the present value of contributions and pension payments. As shown here for the G5 (Table 1.1, first column), the gap runs from 43 per cent of GDP in the United States to 216 per cent of GDP in France. Further increases in public borrowing to finance these gaps would raise public debt ratios in OECD countries to probably unsustainable levels. To close the deficits of the state pension system with the level of benefits unchanged, current contribution ratios (second column) will either have to be raised successively under the current pay-as-you-go (PAYG) schemes (third column) or they will have to be immediately raised to balance the present value of net public pension liabilities (fourth column). Alternatively, the pensionable age has to be raised significantly to net out pension liabilities. None of these alternatives can appeal to policy makers.

- *Employment creation* will be strongly discouraged under the scenario presented above. Unemployment in the OECD area is concentrated among those with low skills and low potential earnings. *The OECD Jobs Study* (1994) finds that rising social security contributions, both by employers and employees, have significantly contributed to low-skilled unemployment since the late 1970s. Because of ceilings on social security contributions, and due to real-wage resistance resulting from minimum wages, rising employer's contributions depress labour demand especially for low-income jobs. It goes without saying that the required rise in contribution ratios shown in Table 1.1 would further dampen the prospects for job creation. The rise would also reduce labour supply as it further stimulates the desire to work tax-free in the black economy or, alternatively, discourages entry or return to the workforce. Finally, the policy option to raise the pensionable age is also clearly at odds with the current need to lower the high incidence of unemployment on young labour market entrants.

- *Economic performance* of those countries will be badly damaged where contribution ratios are raised further to balance net public pension liabilities. Where little has been put aside into funded pensions, rising

Pensions, Savings and Capital Flows

social security taxes will cut more and more deeply into profits (or wages). Simulations undertaken by the Dutch Central Planning Bureau (cited in Mortensen, 1993) suggest for Europe (EU) a rise in contribution rates from 15 per cent of gross wages in 1990 to 26 per cent in 2040 under current PAYG schemes. Ageing countries with unfunded pension schemes will lose out to those countries which, thanks to demography or funding, impose lighter welfare costs on businesses.

Table 1.1 Balancing net public pension liabilities (per cent of 1990 GDP)

	Memorandum items		Required changes		
	Estimated net pension liabilities[a]	Contribution ratios in 1990	in contribution ratios		in pensionable age (years)[d]
			PAYG[b]	Funding[c]	
United States	43	5.9	4.4	1.1	4
Japan	200	5.7	6.8	4.3	9
Germany	160	6.6	6.2	3.6	11
France	216	9.2	5.5	4.0	8
United Kingdom	186	6.3	4.8	3.5	12

Notes:
a. Accrued and future pension liabilities, less existing assets and future contributions. The estimation is based on several assumptions which relate, among other things, to the real discount rate (4%), the typical retirement age (60), entitlement (40 contribution years for a full pension), the old age dependency ratio (see Figure 1.1), as well as constant eligibility, employment and transfer ratios.
b. Maximum increase in contribution when pension expenditure peaks (in most cases around the year 2030).
c. Once-and-for-all increase in contribution from 1990 on.
d. Baseline pensionable age is 60.

Source: van den Noord and Herd (1993).

Those who defend the status quo – the prevalence of public PAYG schemes – maintain that higher labour market participation, more immigration, and rising productivity provide enough potential to pay for the old. They are likely to be wrong. To be sure, with high unemployment, in particular in Europe, there is a lot of potential to put people back to work, thus contributing towards the pensions required by the elderly. It is hard to

envisage, however, ways to change current PAYG schemes so as to avoid their detrimental impact on employment creation presented above, in particular when they remain funded from payroll taxes. Certainly, immigration can help improve the age pyramid, but it must be massive to compensate demographic trends. France, for example, would need one million immigrants year by year to balance the financial requirement set by the 300 000 who will retire each year from 2005 to 2020 (Kessler, 1993). Finally, what can we reasonably expect from future rises in productivity? It would be heroic to venture predictions in this notoriously uncertain area of economics. It is safer to predict, however, that our children – should they be more productive and richer than we are today – will be unlikely to agree to see their income taxed to the extent required (recall Table 1.1). They would try to avoid and evade taxation, if necessary even by emigrating – leaving the old alone.

In particular in the European Union (EU), private funded pension schemes have seen their development hampered by mandatory and generous PAYG pension schemes, which at present account for some 90 per cent of basic and supplementary pension benefits in the EU. Deferring any longer the required overhaul of the pension system will only complicate the unavoidable reform effort since the elderly will account for an increasingly higher share of votes in the elections. But to safeguard public finances, jobs and performance,[2] expert reports – such as the Mortensen Report (1993) and the World Bank (1994) – recommend unanimously the same option: funded pension schemes have to be phased in – now!

Fully-funded pension funds have so far been important (as a percentage of financial assets and GDP) in only a handful of OECD countries, such as the United States, the United Kingdom, the Netherlands and Switzerland (see Table 1.2). Nevertheless, at the end of 1992 funded pensions in the OECD area alone had already assets of almost $6 000 billion under their control. Taking into account country-specific demographic trends and the likely trends for asset appreciation and contributions, Davanzo and Kautz (1992) project an increase in OECD pension assets at an annual growth rate of over 10 per cent. US and British pensions are expected to grow at a slower rate because of their relative maturity. Continental Europe, still largely unfunded, and Japan, ageing most rapidly, will see their pension assets grow at higher speed. We can thus expect OECD pension funds to manage assets worth more than $12 000 billion by the year 2000.[3] Pension assets will dominate investment trends and capital flows around the world.

The demographic and economic pressures will not only stimulate strong growth in private funded pensions, they will also create incentives to seek maximum returns on pension fund assets. According to the European Federation for Retirement Provision, every 1 per cent improvement in

pension funds' investment returns will reduce employers' costs by 2 to 3 per cent of the payroll. The World Bank (1994) estimates that funded schemes have to yield a real rate of return 2 to 3 percentage points higher than the growth of real earnings, if the contribution rate is not to rise above 15 per cent to cover a replacement rate of 40 per cent of the final salary. The need for high returns on pension assets implies a need for global diversification. Pension fund managers can reap big diversification benefits – an improved combination of risk and return – by investing on the emerging stock markets of the younger economies.

Table 1.2   Pension fund assets in 7 selected OECD countries, 1992

	Total US$ bn	thereof: private US$ bn	Total as a percentage of GDP	Foreign asset share, percentage of total
United States	3 315	2 265	56.4	4.6
Japan	728	362	19.8	8.2
United Kingdom	644	544	61.9	28.0
Netherlands	242	147	75.5	13.8
Canada	230	108	40.9	9.2
Switzerland	188	125	78.2	7.7
Germany	114	85	6.4	4.3
Total OECD	5 740			

Sources: InterSec Research Corp., London Representative Office, European Federation for Retirement Provision (as reported in *The Guardian*, 5 October 1993). OECD, *Main Economic Indicators*, September 1993.

The ageing world is thus likely to buy a stake in the superior growth prospects of the younger economies, mostly by way of stock-market investment. Pension money is relatively stable money (reflecting pension schemes' stable liabilities structure). Provided they remove barriers and bottlenecks on their own, the young capital-hungry countries can count on long-term money to flow in, giving microeconomic benefits (such as risk-sharing and lower capital cost) without much in the way of macroeconomic costs (lower monetary autonomy to target inflation and the real exchange

rate). The shift of pension money from ageing to emerging markets can thus benefit both the young recipient nations and the retirees in the greying economies.

What is needed to make such vision come true? This Policy Brief aims at identifying the appropriate policy responses in both OECD and non-OECD countries. It will first present the mutual benefits to both OECD and developing countries which can be exploited by shifting a fraction of OECD pension assets towards the emerging stock markets. Such a shift is likely to raise the risk-adjusted return on OECD pension assets and to provide the receiving countries with relatively stable foreign equity investment. The Brief then proceeds to identify the barriers that currently prevent a larger diversification of OECD pension assets to the emerging stock markets. Localization requirements for pension fund investment in several OECD countries and the investors' concerns about emerging stock market illiquidity and default risk are most important in that respect. Before deriving policy suggestions how best to remove such barriers, the Brief provides an investment scenario for the potential shift of OECD pension assets to the emerging stock markets.

THE MUTUAL BENEFITS OF GLOBAL PENSION INVESTMENT

Benefits for Ageing OECD Countries

It is little understood that even fully-funded pension schemes will not escape demographic pressures if their assets remain invested in ageing economies alone. Funded pension schemes, unlike earnings-related schemes, can beat demography, however, by serious asset diversification into younger economies. Pay-as-you-go schemes, by contrast, are locked into the ageing economy. The mean return of portfolios is likely to be raised through investment in emerging markets as long as GDP growth in the OECD remains substantially below that of many non-OECD countries. Stock-market capital gains cannot outpace GDP growth in the longer run: share prices cannot rise faster than the dividends which give them their value, nor can dividends rise faster than the profits from which they are paid. Profits in turn can scarcely rise faster than the economy, as that would mean shareholders winning consistently at the expense of someone else. Investment in high-growth developing countries thus promises higher returns than in slow-growth OECD countries, as long as the market is less than perfectly efficient at arbitrating away such differences.

For any portfolio currently under-invested in foreign assets (as a percentage of world stock market capitalization) there is the prospect of a free lunch: international diversification can lower risk by eliminating non-systemic volatility without sacrificing expected return; alternatively, it will raise the expected return for a given level of risk. Risk is reduced by investing in markets which are relatively uncorrelated with the investor's domestic market. International diversification reduces risk faster than does domestic diversification because domestic securities exhibit stronger correlation as a result of their joint exposure to country-specific shocks. An international portfolio provides some insurance against losses originating, say, from a domestic wage push or a decline in the country's terms of trade.

From the perspective of the globally diversified pension fund, investment into the emerging markets promises a much improved risk–return profile. Emerging stock markets are defined by the International Finance Corporation (IFC) as those markets with potential for growth in size and sophistication. The IFC data base now covers 25 countries[4] and more than 1 400 stocks. The market capitalization of these emerging stock markets topped the $1 600 billion mark in 1993, representing almost 12 per cent of world stock market capitalization, up from 4 per cent in 1984. The emerging stock markets have become a distinct asset class for global investors: Malaysia, South Africa, Korea and Taiwan are among the world's top fifteen markets in terms of market capitalization, far ahead of many OECD markets. To be sure, as events of the first half of 1994 demonstrated, these emerging stock markets are risky – riskier as a group than the developed stock markets. What matters to the globally diversified investor, however, is not the local systemic risk but, rather, the contribution of the emerging markets to the riskiness of his total portfolio. The biggest diversification benefits that the emerging markets have offered in the past to the global investor have resided in the low (and at times negative) correlation of returns yielded between the emerging stock markets themselves and vis-à-vis the developed stock markets (see, for example, Divecha *et al.*, 1992). By contrast, OECD stock markets are already highly integrated, with monthly returns displaying correlation coefficients on the order of 50 to 90 per cent. A key question for investors is whether stock markets in Asia and Latin America will continue to display low correlation with those in the industrialized countries (Mullin, 1993).

Figure 1.2 suggests that diversification benefits from investing into Asia and Latin America have been left intact, in spite of the massive equity flows of the early 1990s into these regions. The Figure describes the diversification opportunities for two five-year periods: 1985–89 (when portfolio flows were small) and 1989–93 (a period of heavy equity flows to emerging markets). The diversification benefits derived from investing into

the emerging markets are exhibited by calculating the risk and return of a global portfolio, when varying proportions of the IFC composite index are stirred into a portfolio which initially has a 0 per cent share of IFC stocks, and only comprises stocks from the developed countries with the country mix weighted by stock market capitalization. During 1989–93, a portfolio passively invested in industrial countries alone would have yielded around 7.5 per cent per year (annualized monthly returns), with a risk almost twice as high at 14 per cent, measured by the standard deviation of these returns. An investment of up to 22 per cent during that period in emerging markets would have reduced (rather than increased) risk for the industrial-country investor, by almost two percentage points. Note that the risk-reduction achieved by investing in the emerging markets would have been somewhat lower in the preceding five-year period (1985–89) when capital flows to the emerging markets were still small. This evidence contradicts the hypothesis that the 1990s period of heavy equity flows to developing countries raised the correlation between OECD- and developing-country stock markets, and implies that the benefits from diversification of OECD pension assets into the emerging markets remain. Differences between emerging markets and OECD markets with respect to the exposure to country-specific shocks, the stage of economic maturity and the harmonization of economic policies suggest that the 'diversification free lunch' will not be depleted quickly. Only when the share of IFC stocks in the global portfolio is greater than 22 per cent, does the proposition that higher returns can only be obtained at the price of higher volatility become confirmed.

Figure 1.2   Efficient frontiers: IFC composite vs developed markets
(% share of IFC in total portfolio)

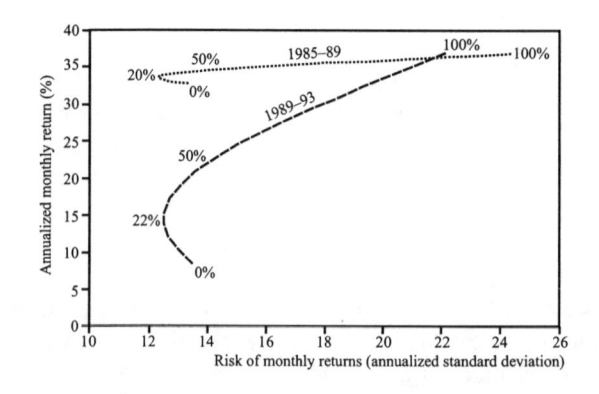

Source: Emerging Markets Factbook, 1990 and 1994, International Finance Corporation.

During both five-year periods considered in Figure 1.2, the emerging stock markets outperformed the developed markets. Investment in emerging markets would thus not only have reduced risk, but would also have increased the annual return. For example, a shift from zero to the risk-minimizing 22 percentage share of emerging market stocks would have raised the annualized return of the global portfolio from 7.5 to 15 per cent.

Benefits for the Recipient Emerging Markets

To the extent that economic development requires a long period of permanent (as opposed to temporary) capital inflows, pension funds seem a particularly suitable vehicle for such inflows. In contrast to managed funds (country and mutual funds) and to private domestic and foreign investors who switch assets rapidly in the search for short-term returns (Gooptu, 1993), pension funds (like life-insurance companies) can be taken as a risk-averse group interested in participating in long-term investment. Pension funds are usually not forced to withdraw their assets suddenly due to a short-term demand for funds. Moreover, unlike money-market funds and bond houses, pension funds are primarily interested in foreign equity investment; since the diversification of pension funds fosters stock market integration rather than interest linkages, it carries little macroeconomic cost in terms of limiting short-term monetary sovereignty (Reisen and Williamson, 1994). Most importantly: pension assets, being huge and long-term, are best suited to absorb, pool and thus reduce risk; the cost of risk capital will be lowered and the level of risk-taking in developing countries will be enhanced; that is, pension funds' investment can stimulate investment and growth.

An obvious advantage of attractive stock markets is the increased availability of private portfolio inflows. Increased foreign equity investment can further enhance confidence in host countries and stimulate the return of flight capital. Provided these flows do not substitute for other forms of external finance or domestic savings, they will result in higher domestic investment. In addition, private equity inflows can improve the mix and risk profile of external finance as they do not create debt, imposing a lower leverage on the recipient countries. Allowing an increase in risk-sharing and risk absorption, equity flows can result in a higher level of risk-taking which may fuel additional investment. Finally, the expansion of a domestic equity market triggered by capital inflows opens up additional sources of funds for companies with sufficient market presence internationally. Such equity flows may also be encouraged by establishing foreign depository receipts to be sold in foreign markets (such as the American Depository Receipts).[5] This leads not only to additional funding but also to an

improvement of the reputation and a broadening of the investor bases. The engagement of foreign investors in emerging markets can help to reduce capital costs for domestic firms. The increase in foreign demand for local stocks will *ceteris paribus* increase the equity prices which lower the cost of capital and encourage new equity issues and raise investment.

The market presence of foreign investors may enforce the discipline of corporate management through more competitive selection for corporate control. By imposing a higher degree of control over the investment behaviour of companies through continuous monitoring of their share prices and thereby of the implied possibility of merger and takeover, foreign investors can contribute to more efficient investment. In addition, open equity markets may emerge as an important alternative to debt-based external finance for developing countries by reducing firms' vulnerability to earnings declines and interest rates. Unlike debt service, common stock dividends can be adjusted with some discretion. At the macroeconomic level, developing countries' vulnerability to interest rate increases can be equally reduced by relying more on equity finance than on excessive debt accumulation. Finally, for developing countries which are pursuing comprehensive privatization of state-owned enterprises a well functioning stock market is essential for facilitating efficient valuation and allocation of the national assets among local and foreign assets.

An important condition for a stock market to fulfil its allocative role is its informational efficiency. The efficient market hypothesis postulates that the prices of the securities traded in the market act as if they fully reflect all available information and react immediately and in an unbiased way to new information. Cornelius (1993) has recently examined the efficient market hypothesis for the six largest and most active emerging markets, namely India, Korea, Malaysia, Mexico, Taiwan, and Thailand. He found that money-supply changes could be used to improve forecasts of changes in stock prices which implies that profitable trading rules could be established. These results cast doubt on the ability of these emerging markets to channel funds into the most productive sectors of the economy. Cornelius presumes that to the extent that legal and institutional reforms would increase the speed at which information is disseminated, further gains in the efficiency of capital allocation were likely to occur. This process is certainly enforced to the extent that foreign investors increase their engagement in emerging markets.

The extent to which the growth of stock markets in developing countries can contribute to the efficiency of the financial system and help enhance investment is difficult to assess. While a positive relationship between economic growth and stock-market development has been observed for some countries it is uncertain, however, whether stock-market development

supports growth or whether growth induces an enlargement of stock markets. What lessons can be drawn with regard to securities markets and economic growth from industrial countries? Observations over the 1970–85 period reveal that retentions were the most important source of finance although there were some marked variations in self-financing ratios across industrial countries (Mayer, 1989). Bank loans were the most important source of debt financing while newly issued equity played a minor and historically a declining role in financing investment. But in no industrial country did companies raise a substantial amount of finance from securities markets although small and medium sized firms were considerably more reliant on external finance than were large firms. One might conclude from these observations that securities markets have made little contribution to industrial finance and economic growth.

This conclusion has been challenged by information gathered by the IFC on the corporate financial structures of nine developing countries (Singh and Hamid, 1992). The evidence established by the IFC study reveals differences in the pattern of corporate finance in developing versus developed countries. First, retentions are a more important source of finance in developed than in developing countries. Internal finance ratios in the sample developing countries never reach the respective averages of the developed world. Second, external equity also plays a more important role in the financial structures of developing countries than in developed countries. Moreover, the importance of equity appears to be rising in developing countries, whereas it is falling in the developed world. The implication of these findings would be that broader, deeper and more efficient securities markets are essential to provide the funds that firms need in order to grow.

Due to the multiple interlinkages with other financial-market segments the widening and deepening of stock markets in developing countries cannot be achieved without a comprehensive approach to the financial system as a whole. For example, securities market participants rely heavily on bank credit to ensure liquidity in these markets. Actors in the primary and secondary markets need access to bank credit lines to support prices immediately after the initial issue, to hold undistributed securities and to manage settlement delays or failures. Therefore, the creation of securities markets in an economy with a weak banking sector will unduly increase systemic risk. Furthermore, an active government securities market is a possible precursor of corporate fixed-income markets and the development of a functioning market for equities. Finally, broader financial-system reforms may also create new sorts of domestic institutional investors such as private pension funds and mutual funds which are likely to create demand for securities issues of all types on their preferred investment assets. This

discussion suggests that the development of direct securities markets is complementary to the development of bank-based systems, not an alternative as is often suggested in the literature.

BARRIERS TO GLOBAL PENSION INVESTMENT

Explaining the Home Bias of Pension Assets in OECD Countries

A look back at Table 1.2 (fourth column) reveals that most OECD pension funds are little invested abroad. Even where pension funds have diversified into foreign assets more seriously – in the United Kingdom, Ireland and Belgium – their foreign assets shares stay way below the global portfolio as suggested by portfolio theory. Why have OECD pension funds failed to exploit the risk-reducing benefits of global diversification[6] and remained so parochial?

Table 1.3 tells us that the diversification of pension-fund assets has been limited, in particular in most of continental Europe, by localization requirements and by requirements of currency matching[7] (which force funds to align the currency mix of their assets with the currency mix of their pension commitments). Only in Australia, Ireland, Luxembourg, now in Spain, and in the United Kingdom are there no governmental limits to foreign investment; in the Netherlands and in the United States non-public pension schemes are also free to invest (generally, a 'prudent man' rule applies). Another group of countries imposes portfolio restrictions that can be qualified as 'medium'; the group includes, among others, Canada, Japan and Switzerland, all countries with important pension assets. Foreign asset holdings are severely restricted in Germany and the Scandinavian countries, either by way of ceilings or currency-matching requirements. Tight restrictions are mirrored by a low proportion of foreign assets in the portfolio of pension funds. The experience in the United Kingdom, where pension funds already accounted for an important proportion of personal savings and of GDP when capital controls were dismantled in 1979, suggests that pension funds will diversify globally once restrictions have been lifted (Reisen and Williamson, 1994). Freed in their portfolio choice, UK pension funds invested almost exclusively in foreign equities, withdrawing funds from illiquid real estate and low-return government bonds at home. The foreign asset share of UK pension funds rose to 15 per cent in 1985, up from 7 per cent in 1979; in 1994 it stood at around 30 per cent.

'Prudential concern' is often cited as a major motive for imposing government restrictions on investment by pension funds, both home and

*Table 1.3   Regulatory constraints on foreign investment by pension funds in
            selected OECD countries, 1994*

Level of restrictions	Country	Ceiling	Matching requirements
Loose	Australia Ireland Luxembourg Netherlands[a] Spain United Kingdom United States[a]	None	None
Medium	Belgium	Location in Belgium	Not applicable
	Canada[a]	20%	None
	Japan	30%	80%
	Portugal	40% (only EU)	None
	Switzerland	30% (global) 25% (equities) 30% (debt instruments) 5% (real estate) 20% (foreign currency)	None
Tight	Denmark	'Small proportion' stipulated 60% minimum in domestic debt	80%
	Finland	5% (foreign currency)	None
	Germany	60%	100%
	Sweden	5–10%	None
	Norway	0	Not applicable

Notes:
a. Applies only to private pension funds. France and Italy are not included, because private funded pension schemes are almost nil.

Source: OECD; the classification of the level of restrictions is based on the author's judgement.

abroad. Foreign investments come under particular scrutiny in some countries, because of deficiencies in information about local business and financial conditions, including regulatory standards for the issuance of securities, settlement risk, transfer risk and default risk. But these are risks which can be dealt with by the market; other motivations for government restrictions on foreign investment play a role. These motives are not pronounced in public, because they closely resemble those for the more

'classical' capital controls, which have been officially dismantled in most OECD countries. Governments still see pension funds:

– as a captive market for absorbing government debt;

– as a vehicle for retaining domestic savings at home; and

– as a means for retaining government control over the allocation of large financial resources towards ailing banks, target industries and other 'priority' areas.

Home bias of pension assets can also be observed in countries where regulatory limitations have been relaxed. Pension funds do not only seek to maximize return, but they also worry about the real purchasing power of their assets. To be sure, long-term deviations from purchasing power parity (PPP) mainly due to currency fluctuations have been widely observed. Pension funds may seek a currency exposure comparable to the imported proportion in the basket of goods consumed by the typical pensioner. Investors in small countries should thus hold a higher share of foreign assets than investors in large, more self-sufficient countries (which moreover provide more potential for domestic diversification benefits than do small mono-structured economies). The argument ignores, however, that currency risk gets partly diversified away in a well-built portfolio, or can be hedged.

Table 1.4 Suggested and actual foreign portfolio shares as a percentage of total pension assets, 1993

Country	Global portfolio[a]	Consumption basket[b]	Actual
United States	63	14	8
Japan	76	9	9
Germany	96	34	5
United Kingdom	90	34	30

Notes:
a. Neutral weighting of foreign equities from Morgan Stanley Capital International world equity index.
b. Imports (cif) as a percentage of private consumption.

Sources: The Economist; International Monetary Fund; InterSec Research Corp.

Table 1.4 suggests that pension fund managers seem more to seek stable purchasing power for pension assets than to reach portfolio shares along world market capitalization as postulated by modern portfolio theory. Where they are, unlike in Germany, free to invest, foreign holdings correspond already (UK, Japan) or are approaching (US) the country's import share in private consumption.

A high share of bonds (and cash instruments) held in the portfolio of pension funds will also tend to lower foreign exposure. An examination of in-house investment guidelines of largely unconstrained pension institutions in Australia, the Netherlands, Switzerland and the United Kingdom recently found a tendency to allocate foreign investments mostly into equities, rather than real estate and bonds (Coote, 1993). This is not surprising. Over the long run, equities have performed higher real returns than any other broad asset class; the diversification benefits derived from equities are higher than those from bonds, as well, since covered interest parity holds across most OECD economies while stock-market integration is still less than perfect.[8] Nevertheless, several factors favour high bond holdings (and thus lower foreign exposure):

– First, pension funds have to align the mix of their asset holdings to the structure of their liabilities. The definition of retiree benefits (nominal vs real, defined-contribution vs defined-benefit) and the maturity structure of receipts thus feature prominently among the determinants of portfolio investment. Mature pension funds, particularly if they are at risk of actuarial insolvency, will shy away from instruments that entail currency risk and potential capital loss, and instead will prefer domestic bonds. A conservative asset allocation, however, is induced in several OECD countries by accounting rules that impose penalties for temporary deficits and by restrictions on overall equity holdings.

– Second, a track record of high real returns on domestic bonds and loans, such as observed in Germany and the Netherlands (Davis, 1993), may seem to justify a conservative asset allocation in favour of domestic bonds. The growing integration of capital markets, however, makes superior inflation-adjusted bond returns increasingly unlikely, raising the shadow costs of regulation that locks pension funds into domestic fixed-income instruments.

Finally, pension fund investment to the emerging markets may well be restrained by the 'benchmark' orientation of pension fund managers. As long as the emerging stock markets are under- or not represented in the benchmarks, investment in these markets will lead to (positive or negative)

tracking errors. Pension fund managers will avoid investing into emerging markets because, in the absence of appropriate benchmarks, such investment will constitute a personal downside risk as long as these other funds try to track the benchmark.

Whatever the motives for pension funds' home bias, this bias is very costly. Only irrational expectations about the level of returns on domestic securities can possibly justify the dominance of domestic securities in portfolios. Tesar and Werner (1992), comparing actual portfolios with the value-weighted world portfolio for 'risky' assets, find that investors are consistently more optimistic about the returns on the domestic market than they are about investment in foreign markets. Most 'optimistic' are German investors who think that the expected return is 420 basis points higher in Germany than what the world market portfolio would indicate – the return differential needed to justify the observed degree of home bias in German investment portfolios.

Host Country Barriers

The home bias of pension assets observed in many OECD countries is obviously not only explained by regulations in investor countries alone – host country barriers matter at least as much. A survey of market experts and participants revealed as most frequently cited impediments to institutional investing in emerging markets the perceived riskiness of these markets, limited information on these markets and illiquidity problems arising from smallness of markets; surprisingly, inflow restrictions in host countries did not appear to be a crucial factor (Chuhan, 1994). Table 1.5 confirms this impression by comparing the regions' global market weights with those where foreigners are free to invest (investible index). The table shows Latin America and other emerging regions to be more open than Asia. Yet, in 1993 Asia received the bulk of cross border equity inflows to the emerging stock markets (which totalled a net amount of $52 billion).

Nevertheless, there are still some extreme cases where formal inflow restrictions may simply prevent foreign equity portfolio investment. Some countries are still completely closed to foreign investment. Direct foreign ownership restrictions can also take the form of certain sectors being closed for foreign investment or direct equity participation limits. Another group of direct barriers to portfolio investment is exchange and capital controls that affect investment in and the repatriation of dividends and capital from emerging markets. Discriminatory tax treatment may also prevent foreigners from investing. (How best to dismantle capital controls, is put forward in Fischer and Reisen, 1993, 1994.) Only to a certain degree can these

restrictions be circumvented. Instead of investing directly, foreign investors may put their funds in global depository receipts (GDRs) or American depository receipts (ADRs) which are traded on principal stock markets, in particular on the New York Stock Exchange (NYSE). Restrictions can be side-stepped by investing in other, more open markets with close ties to the chosen economy. Discriminatory tax treatments are avoided by investing via a country that has more favourable bilateral tax treaties. In general, however, restrictions on portfolio capital inflows have been gradually relaxed with an acceleration of this process occurring in the 1990s. The most difficult task remains to assure instititutional investors on sovereign risk and stock market illiquidity.

Table 1.5 Stock market investibility and equity inflows, 1993

	Stock market weights		Share of net equity flows
	Global	Investible	
Asia	63.7	42.5	57.7
Latin America	31.1	48.8	38.4
Other emerging markets	5.4	8.7	3.8

Sources: IFC, *Emerging Markets Factbook 1994*; Baring Securities, *Cross Border Capital Flows*, 1992/93 Review.

A central concern not only for institutional investors is sovereign country risk, reflecting political and economic instability. Sovereign risk involves threats of nationalization, expropriation, application of price, wage and exchange controls but more implicit socio-political hazards may also arise, for example, from a very uneven income distribution and/or weak political institutions. The importance of political and economic stability in attracting foreign portfolio flows is underlined by a set of preliminary empirical tests attempting to identify the factors that determine the ability of countries to tap into global portfolio equity flows (Walter, 1993). These tests reveal that growth and trading volume in emerging markets are strongly linked to a cluster of macroeconomic and policy variables.

Most institutional investors are concerned that every shift of their large portfolio will move prices against them in an illiquid market. This may explain why larger institutional investors may prefer to avoid the equity markets of smaller countries unless they decide to move into markets under a 'buy and hold strategy'. Indeed, illiquidity in some emerging markets can be severe with individual stocks sometimes not trading for weeks at time.

As a consequence, the investor becomes locked in and executed trade produces extraordinary price movements. These features are frequently attributed to the following characteristics of emerging stock markets: small size, high market concentration, small volume of trading, small number and small size of listed companies, and small number of active traders. Although these characteristics have prevailed in stock markets at their infant stage there are meanwhile a number of emerging markets where the turnover ratio (i.e. the ratio of value traded over capitalization) is comparable to that prevailing in mature markets and where the concentration ratio (i.e. the share of market capitalization held by the 10 largest companies) is on average not higher than the average of developed markets. In addition, the number of domestic companies listed in emerging markets has increased, in particular in countries with comprehensive privatization programmes. However, the market capitalization as a fraction of GDP of many emerging markets is still small.

Thin markets, being characterized by low numbers of transactions per unit of time, tend to increase the volatility of asset prices. The volatility of a speculative market may feed back on its size, in the sense that the high liquidation risk implied by very volatile prices can keep potential entrants out of the market (Pagano, 1989).

Other market frictions which are critical determinants of international investor interest include high information costs, inefficient price-discovery processes, lack of efficient local securities clearance and settlement systems, stamp duties, high fixed commission rates, lack of market transparency and the absence of hedging techniques. Perhaps the most important requirement for a positive attitude of foreign investors is an adequate information system. However, publicly available sources of accurate, reliable and honest information are still scarce in most developing countries. Lack of information, the absence of adequate accounting standards, and reluctance to make balance sheets and profit- and loss-accounts available to investors probably constitute the most severe obstacles to capital market development even in the more advanced developing countries.

A last set of barriers to private capital inflows has to do with the legal, regulatory and supervisory environment, which is weak in many emerging markets. The legal system should provide a framework for the enforcement of property rights or financial contracts which is particularly important for financial markets. Because of the intertemporal nature of exchange the very existence of securities markets relies on the rules protecting the rights of debtors and shareholders and on the rights of individuals to own and trade these rights. Another more specific contribution that the legal system can make to the development of capital markets is to define and enforce penalities on securities fraud. Effective prosecution of violations of

securities laws increases confidence in the markets and encourages foreign investor participation.

Institutional investors often miss an adequate regulatory and supervisory framework for a viable securities market that protects investors, promotes public confidence and guarantees market discipline. Particularly in low-income countries important elements of such a framework (UNCTAD, 1993) are often notoriously absent, such as:

– prudential standards to establish capital adequacy requirements (along international standards), safekeeping of securities, financial reporting requirements for intermediaries as well as a system for monitoring and enforcing such requirements;

– prescriptions to protect investors from market manipulations and lack of transparency including information disclosure, clarity of contractual relationship and strict fiduciary responsibility; and

– organizational rules to provide for the establishment and operation of stock exchange, clearing houses and market information systems, based on the concept of private market organizations (such as stock exchanges).

THE POTENTIAL FOR PENSION FUND INVESTMENT INTO EMERGING MARKETS

The year 1993 may be remembered as when OECD pension funds started to diversify seriously their assets into the so-called emerging markets. While by the end of 1992 pension funds had less than 0.2 per cent of their total asset portfolios invested there (Chuhan, 1994), first evidence by research consultants Greenwhich Associates and InterSec Research reports UK pension funds to have raised the emerging market share in total assets to 2.0 per cent and US pension funds to 0.7 per cent by end 1993. It is likely that these very recent trends will continue for a while.

Table 1.6 compares the small amounts invested by OECD pension funds in the emerging markets in 1992 with an estimate of their potential investment by the year 2000. Although the difference between the tiny pension fund investment in 1992 and our estimates for 2000 is striking, it has to be emphasized that our scenario is based on fairly cautious assumptions.

First, market observers agree that total OECD pension assets will grow rapidly; the estimate by Davanzo and Kautz (1992) that they will swell to

$12 trillion is in line with other forecasts. Second, our scenario assumes that the trend for global diversification of OECD pension assets will lead to a 20 per cent average share held abroad, a sum of $2 400 billion. Third, we assume that these foreign pension assets will be neutrally weighted along country shares in world stock market capitalization. On the trends established during the period 1980–93, we predict the total emerging market share in world stock market capitalization to reach 14.7 per cent by the year 2000, compared with 11.9 per cent in 1993. Neutral weighting would then imply that OECD pension funds invest 2.9 per cent of their assets, or $353 billion, in the emerging stock markets. Again based on trends established during 1980–93, we expect the emerging stock market capitalization to reach $8 200 billion by the year 2000; the $353 billion predicted to be invested by OECD pension funds would thus represent about 4 per cent of the emerging stock market capitalization.

Table 1.6   A pension fund investment scenario

Year	1992[a]		2000[b]	
	$ bn	(%)	$ bn	(%)
Total OECD pension assets	5 750	(100.0)	12 000	(100.0)
Invested in emerging markets of which:	12	(0.20)	353	(2.9)
Asia	6	(0.10)	235	(2.0)
Latin America	4	(0.07)	101	(0.8)
Other emerging markets	2	(0.03)	17	(0.01)

Notes:
a. Estimates about total OECD pension assets are from InterSec Research Co.; the emerging stock market share of the assets is based on Chuhan (1994). The allocation to Asia, Latin America and other emerging markets assumes neutral weighting within the emerging market allocation according to the *IFC Global Composite Index* in 1992.
b. The estimates of total OECD pension assets are based on Davanzo and Kautz (1992). The allocation of these assets to and between the emerging markets assumes (a) that 20 per cent are held abroad and (b) that foreign assets are neutrally weighted. The underlying stock market capitalization weights for the year 2000 have been computed from out-of-sample predictions based on linear OLS regressions for the emerging market shares during the period 1980–93, as given in various issues of the *IFC Emerging Stock Market Factbook*.

Based on the assumptions outlined above, we predict Asia, especially as a result of China's and India's stock market growth, to capture the bulk of the emerging market investment by OECD pension funds, 2.0 per cent of their total assets ($235 billion). Latin America would receive 0.8 per cent (c. $100 billion) and the other emerging markets 0.1 per cent ($17 billion).

Should our scenario materialize, this would imply net equity flows from OECD to emerging markets of annually $40 billion to raise the emerging market investment of OECD pension assets to the predicted level. Whether our scenario has a chance to materialize, however, crucially depends on its two important assumptions: that OECD pension funds will continue to diversify globally up to the assumed foreign asset share of 20 per cent, and that these foreign assets will indeed be neutrally weighted instead of being concentrated in OECD countries.

Following the successful example set by Chile, Singapore, Malaysia and Korea, more and more developing countries are now establishing their own fully-funded pension schemes. To insure the retirees against country-specific risks, developing-country funds will increasingly invest their assets abroad. Consequently, *net* foreign assets related to pension funds will be smaller than indicated by the gross asset positions estimated in Table 1.6, with a corresponding smaller net capital flow from North to South. In equilibrium (after the home bias of pension assets has been deleted), net pension-related capital flows to developing countries will be reduced by the superior growth of their pension assets and will be stimulated by the relative growth of their stock market capitalization.

IMPLICATIONS FOR REGULATORS

The rapid ageing of the rich-country populations can be expected to stimulate strong growth in fully-funded pensions and create incentives to seek maximum returns on pension fund assets. The need for high returns implies a need for global diversification of pension assets. Pension managers can reap big diversification benefits – an improved combination of lower risk and higher return – by investing on the emerging stock markets of the younger economies. There is a massive potential for pension-driven capital flows from the OECD to the developing countries, matching the capital needs of the young recipient economies with the need for high returns of the rich and ageing OECD countries.

In order to realize the mutual benefits of shifting OECD pension assets from ageing to emerging markets, policy makers will have to remove important regulatory and market barriers. The challenge for regulators in OECD countries is to free pension assets so that they will be able to seek the

best mix of risk and return. The costly home bias of OECD pension assets will only be corrected when policy makers, in particular in most of Continental Europe, remove localization requirements and requirements of currency matching. A helpful step would be to bring pension funds and life insurance companies under the discipline of the OECD Codes of Liberalisation. Pension funds should strongly lobby for the deregulation of investment constraints, in particular those militating against investment in countries where demographic trends are more favourable than at home. Fund managers should then raise the emerging-market share in their portfolios, with a focus on those markets where low price-earning ratios suggest unexploited opportunities. This will require an adequate representation of the emerging stock markets in the performance benchmarks relevant to the pension industry.

The challenge for policy makers in the young nations is to remove legal and market barriers to pension fund investment in order to reassure institutional investors about sovereign risk and stock market liquidity. The most difficult task seems to assure institutional investors on sovereign risk and stock market liquidity. A convincing demonstration by young nations that they have a strong commitment to respect property rights permanently is their openness; during the 1980s, it was the threat of being cut off from the benefits of trade integration which prevented outright default by highly indebted countries.

Regulators in young nations also need to foster the deepening of domestic stock markets in order to deal with the illiquidity concern of institutional investors. Encouraging companies that are already listed to issue more stocks and/or firms to be listed at the stock market is – at least in the short-run – a difficult task. A review of the impact of the tax system on the equity supply may lead to measures by authorities to reduce the cost of equity issues and to reduce distortions (such as interest subsidies and exchange-rate risk guaranties) that enhance the attractiveness of borrowing relative to the further issuance of equity. As more active trade in stock markets may provide an incentive for companies to issue more stocks, reducing capital gains taxes and avoiding double taxation of capital gains may make equity purchases and therefore issues more attractive.

Important sources to increase the supply of new stocks are the privatization of public sector companies and bringing privately held companies to the market. Privatization of state-owned enterprises was indeed the major source of new equity supply in recent years, especially in Latin America, and more recently, in Central and Eastern European countries. In many developing countries the scope for privatization is far from being exhausted. With more companies listed and their share holdings disbursed among the local population, stock markets will gain in depth and

breadth and also become more attractive for foreign investors. With buoyant market conditions where prices stand at a significant premium to book values, it might also be easier to persuade family owned companies to issue stocks although this advantage has to be weighted against the loss of management autonomy and the implications on taxable income.

While it is by means of an issue in the primary market that firms raise capital, the development of the secondary market is of equal importance. The greater the liquidity in the secondary market and the greater the information to participants, the more efficient will be the price discovery process in that market for claims in a firm. A liquid secondary market also increases the range of potential primary market investors by improving the maturity transformation role of the market.

Domestic institutional investors can and do play a very important role in capital market development by making information available, increasing market liquidity, lowering transactions costs, facilitating market participation by the general public, helping businesses raising capital, making privatization possible, playing a role in corporate monitoring and attracting foreign investors. They thus fill the gap in the supply of long-term finance that exists in most developing countries, as well as facilitating the privatization of state-owned enterprises and promoting greater dispersion of corporate ownership. The gradual accumulation of privately-managed pension funds does encourage the development of capital markets and its required regulatory framework.

NOTES

1.   This Policy Brief partly draws on Reisen (1994).
2.   The switch from PAYG to funded pensions entails a rise in long-term institutional savings and further beneficial, but more controversial effects, such as a strengthening of domestic securities markets, improved capital allocation, non-inflationary and long-maturity finance for investment, lower returns on equity and lower interest rates (Davis, 1993 and Kessler, 1993).
3.   This estimate is in line with a recent (unspecified) estimation by InterSec Research Corp., a US pension consultancy, which predicts rich-world pension assets to grow to US$9 800 billion by the year 1998 (see *Herald Tribune*, 24–25 September 1994).
4.   In Latin America: Argentina, Brazil, Chile, Colombia, Mexico, Peru, Venezuela; in Asia: China, India, Indonesia, Korea, Malaysia, Pakistan, Philippines, Sri Lanka, Taiwan, Thailand; in Europe/Mideast/Africa: Greece, Hungary, Jordan, Nigeria, Poland, Portugal, Turkey, Zimbabwe.
5.   Two disadvantages of foreign depository receipts have to be borne in mind, however. First, from the perspective of a global investor, investing into depository receipts is less attractive than direct investment on emerging stock markets to the extent that the former display a higher correlation of returns with OECD stock markets. Second, foreign depository receipts do not directly contribute to the development of emerging stock markets.
6.   Preliminary evidence for 1993, however, suggests that pension funds have crossed borders at an unheard of rate, for example raising the foreign share of US pension assets from 4.6 to 8.0 per cent in that year alone.

7. The regulatory constraints imposed on life-insurance companies are generally quite similar (in some countries even tighter) to those displayed for pension funds in Table 1.3.
8. To be sure, international diversification should cover both stocks and bonds. Efficient portfolios made up of only equities display a higher risk for the same level of return than efficient portfolios made up of both stocks and bonds (Solnik and Noetzlin, 1982).

REFERENCES

Chuhan, P. (1994), 'Are Institutional Investors an Important Source of Portfolio Investment in Emerging Markets?', *World Bank Policy Research Working Paper*, No. 1243, Washington, DC.

Coote, R. (1993), 'Self-Regulation of Foreign Investment by Institutional Investors', OECD/DAFFE/INV(93)18, mimeo.

Cornelius, P. (1993), 'A Note on the Informational Efficiency of Emerging Stock Markets', *Weltwirtschaftliches Archiv*, Vol. 129, No. 4, pp. 820–828.

Davanzo, L. and L.B. Kautz (1992), 'Toward a Global Pension Market', *The Journal of Portfolio Management*, Summer, pp. 77–85.

Davis, E.P. (1993), 'The Structure, Regulation, and Performance of Pension Funds in Nine Industrial Countries', *World Bank Policy Research Working Paper*, No. 1229, Washington, DC.

Divecha, A., J. Drach and D. Stefek (1992), 'Emerging Markets: A Quantitative Perspective', *The Journal of Portfolio Management*, Autumn, pp. 41–50.

Fischer, B. and H. Reisen (1993), *Liberalising Capital Flows in Developing Countries: Pitfalls, Prerequisites and Perspectives*, OECD Development Centre Studies, Paris.

Fischer, B. and H. Reisen (1994), 'Financial Opening. Why, How, When', *Occasional Papers*, No. 55, International Center for Economic Growth, San Francisco.

Gooptu, S. (1993), 'Portfolio Investment Flows to Emerging Markets', WPS 1117, The World Bank, Washington, DC.

Hagemann, R.P. and G. Nicoletti (1989), 'Population Ageing: Economic Effects and Some Policy Implications for Financing Public Pensions', *OECD Economic Studies*, No. 12, Spring, pp. 51–96.

International Finance Corporation (IFC) (1994), *Emerging Stock Markets Factbook 1994*, Washington, DC.

Kessler, D. (1993), « Retraites en Europe : quel avenir ? », *Risques*, No. 15, juillet-septembre, Paris.

Mayer, C. (1989), 'Financial Systems, Corporate Finance and Economic Development', in R. Glenn Hubbard (ed.), *Asymmetric Information, Corporate Finance and Investment*, Chicago.

Mortensen, J. (1993), 'Financing Retirement in Europe', *CEPS Working Party Report*, No. 9, Brussels.

Mullin, J. (1993), 'Emerging Equity Markets in the Global Economy', *Quarterly Review*, Federal Reserve Bank of New York, Summer, pp. 54–83.

OECD (1994), *The OECD Jobs Study: Facts, Analysis, Strategies*, OECD, Paris.

Pagano, M. (1989), 'Endogenous Market Thinness and Stock Price Volatility', in *Review of Economic Studies*, Vol. 56, pp. 613–622.

Reisen, H. (1994), 'On the Wealth of Nations and Retirees', in R. O'Brien (ed.), *Finance and the International Economy*, 8, The Amex Bank Review Prize Essays, Oxford University Press, Oxford, pp. 86–107.

Reisen, H. and J. Williamson (1994), *Pension Funds, Capital Controls, and Macroeconomic Stability*, Technical Paper No. 98, OECD Development Centre, Paris.

Singh, A. and S. Hamid (1992), 'Corporate Financial Structures in Developing Countries', *IFC Technical Paper*, No. 1, Washington, DC.

Solnik, B. and B. Noetzlin (1982), 'Optimal Asset Allocation', *Journal of Portfolio Management*, Autumn, pp. 11–21.

Tesar, L. and I. Werner (1992), 'Home Bias and the Globalisation of Securities Markets', *NBER Working Paper*, No. 4218, Cambridge, MA.

UNCTAD (1993), *Foreign Portfolio Equity Investment and New Financing Mechanisms in Developing Countries: Current Issues and Prospects*, Report by the UNCTAD Secretariat (TD/B/WG.1/11), Geneva.

van den Noord, P. and R. Herd (1993), *Pension Liabilities in the Seven Major Economies*, OECD Economics Department Working Papers No. 142, OECD, Paris.

Walter, I. (1993), 'Emerging Equity Markets. Tapping into Global Investment Flows', in *ASEAN Economic Bulletin*, Vol. 10, No. 1, pp. 1–18.

World Bank (1994), *Averting the Old Age Crisis: Policy Options for a Greying World*, A World Bank Policy Research Report, Washington, DC.

2. Pension Funds, Capital Controls and Macroeconomic Stability*

INTRODUCTION[1]

It is well known that high capital mobility introduces an important constraint on macroeconomic policy. The question therefore arises as to whether free international investment by pension funds might have a macroeconomic cost that needs to be weighed against its presumed microeconomic advantages in terms of permitting retirees to enjoy the benefits of international diversification (an improved combination of risk and return). If so, the further question arises of whether a novel form of exchange control – e.g. a requirement that foreign investment by pension funds be allowed only when there is equal inward investment by foreign pension funds – might help to overcome the macroeconomic costs without losing the micro gains.

This paper starts with an analysis of the impact of a small country opening up its stock (equity) market for investment from abroad, focusing on the question of the extent to which this will constrain macroeconomic policy. It then proceeds to examine the investment strategies of, and the restrictions imposed upon, privately-managed pension funds in the OECD area. This is followed by a discussion of UK experience after the liberalization of capital controls in 1979.

The paper then turns to normative issues. We argue that since the diversification of pension funds fosters stock market integration rather than interest linkages, it does little to limit short-term monetary sovereignty. We conclude that the case for regulating this form of capital mobility is weak once a country has got to the point where it does not need to fear a major net loss of savings. The remainder of the paper discusses various techniques by which the foreign investment of pension funds could be regulated, were our main conclusion regarding the pointlessness of such regulation to be rejected. For example, one possibility would be to limit domestic pension

* Originally published as OECD Development Centre Technical Paper No. 98, Paris, 1994; and in S. Valdés-Prieto (ed.), *The Economics of Pensions: Principles, Policies, and International Experience*, Cambridge (UK): Cambridge University Press, 1997, pp. 227–250.

funds to portfolio swaps with foreign pension funds. We also discuss whether there is a case for transitory controls on pension funds while the size of their portfolios is growing particularly rapidly.

THE IMPLICATIONS OF STOCK MARKET INTEGRATION

A classic result of the international monetary theory developed by Robert Mundell in the 1960s states that high (strictly speaking, perfect) capital mobility and fixed exchange rates preclude the use of monetary policy to stabilize the economy (Mundell, 1968, chapter 18). To express the same point in another way, a way that has been made familiar in the debate on European monetary integration: fixed exchange rates, free capital mobility, and monetary independence constitute an 'impossible trinity'. Note that in this context a 'fixed exchange rate' does not mean just an unalterably pegged exchange rate: it includes also an exchange rate whose value is determined by the authorities, even if subject to a crawling peg and guided by a target for the real exchange rate.

However, as shown in later sections of this paper, pension funds invest primarily in stocks (equities) rather than the bonds that are hypothesized to be perfect substitutes in the Mundell-inspired literature. Standard macroeconomic models do not contain a stock market[2] (despite the fact that in some countries a larger part of personal wealth is held in the form of equities than of bonds), so that one cannot simply appeal to familiar results to understand the implications of stock market integration. We therefore attempt to think through the implications from first principles. With apologies to those economists who find such informality aesthetically offensive, we do this without constructing a formal model.

The interesting case to analyse is that in which capital mobility would be perfect in the conventional sense, i.e. bonds are perfect substitutes, but for the continued existence of capital controls.[3] The question is then what effect the elimination of controls on cross-border flows of equity capital would have on a country's monetary independence.

Consider the simplest possible model, in which arbitrage between the bond and stock markets equilibrates rates of return in the two markets. The bond market is conventionally modelled as trading short-term assets with a known nominal interest rate r, while the rate of return on equities consists of the sum of the dividend yield and capital gains. Let dividends per share be d, let the price of a share be e, assume perfect foresight, and use a hat to denote a rate of change. Then perfect arbitrage between the two markets implies:

$$r = d/e + \hat{e}/e.$$

If the right hand side is equated to the equivalent expression for the world market, and that is in turn equal to the foreign rate of interest r^*, then arbitrage through the equity market would indeed ensure the equality of domestic and foreign interest rates, i.e. it would result in the loss of monetary sovereignty.

Now ask whether the assumptions needed to establish that result constitute a useful first approximation to reality. Ask in particular whether it is sensible to assume perfect foresight in the rate of change of share prices, given that the theory of portfolio diversification that is used to explain and guide equity investment is based on *inability* to foresee changes in share prices correctly. The answer is clearly that it is not useful even as a first approximation, and the implication is that one should not expect to find arbitrage equating yields between equity and bond markets. It follows immediately that linking equity markets should not be expected to equate interest rates or, therefore, to eliminate monetary sovereignty.

Of course, one should still expect that opening the equity market will have an impact on aggregate demand unless this is deliberately prevented by the central bank. Consider the case in which both inflows and outflows of equity investment are liberalized. Suppose that this results in a net inflow of equity investment.[4] This will bid up the value of the stock market, producing a positive wealth effect and a lower cost of capital, both of which will tend to increase demand. In order to hold the exchange rate constant, the central bank will have to supply more domestic money to the foreign buyers of stocks, which they will of course pass on to the domestic sellers. If the central bank wishes to hold the money supply (or, indeed, aggregate demand, in either real or nominal terms) constant, it will have to increase the interest rate. The result will be contrasting movements in the expected return on equities (lower) and on bonds (higher); thus the possibility of sterilizing the impact of an inflow of equity capital indeed depends upon arbitrage between the equity and bond markets not being too high.

The final part of this theoretical section examines what difference the existence of equity-capital mobility makes to the response of an economy to various shocks. It is again assumed that equity capital is the only form of capital that is internationally mobile. The shocks that we examine are (a) a tightening of monetary policy, and (b) a decreased desire to hold local equities as a result of less optimistic expectations of their future yield.

Consider first the impact of a tighter monetary policy. The higher interest rate on bonds must be expected to depress the local equity market as well, which will raise holding yields and thus attract an inflow of equity capital from abroad. This will tend to limit the effectiveness of monetary policy,

just as does any other form of capital mobility. The imperfection of arbitrage between bond and equity markets will, however, limit the extent to which monetary policy is undermined.

Consider next the impact of a portfolio shock in the form of a sudden decrease in the desire to hold local equities, say as a result of a downward reevaluation of the likelihood of future earnings growth in the domestic economy. It is of crucial importance to specify also *whose* expectations undergo revision. There are three possibilities: foreigners, local investors, and both.

A pessimistic revision of expectations by foreigners obviously has no impact on the domestic economy in the case where there is no capital mobility.[5] When there are foreign holdings, attempted liquidation of those holdings will drive the stock market down; since domestic holders do not by assumption share the pessimistic reevaluation that initiated the sales of stock, they will buy up shares from the foreigners who will use their receipts to buy foreign exchange, thus placing pressure on the reserves and/or the exchange rate, depending on the exchange-rate regime. If the central bank attempts to defend the exchange rate and sterilize the impact on the money supply, it will have to reduce interest rates, thus aggravating the loss of reserves but diminishing the decline in the stock market. Mobility of equity capital is in this case destabilizing.

If local investors revise their expectations downward but foreigners do not, then the fall in the stock market will tend to induce additional inward investment that will limit the size of the stock market decline relative to the case of no capital mobility. Reserves will rise, and even a central bank that tried to stabilize might decide not to sterilize this inflow as the increased money supply and lower interest rates would tend to offset the negative impact on demand of a lower stock market. Mobility of equity capital is in this case unambiguously stabilizing.

However, both of the above cases seem rather unconvincing, at least as responses to 'a disappointing political development, a sudden decrease in the price of the main exportable good or an increase in the price of the main importable good' (Corbo and Hernández, 1993, p. 5). A more neutral assumption would be that the expectations of both foreign and local investors undergo a similar downward revision. In that case there is no reason why there would be any capital outflow: the stock market will decline to the degree needed to persuade investors as a group to continue holding the existing stocks, but that will involve no net sales by foreigners. (This assertion needs to be qualified to the extent that a group of domestically-based market-makers automatically increase their portfolios in a declining market, but this can surely not be a major factor.) Indeed, the impact of a given downward revision of expectations will be *less* in the case

where portfolios are internationally diversified, because that part of domestically-owned wealth that is invested abroad will be protected against the capital loss from the fall in the domestic stock market. (See Gavin, 1991a, for a rigorous demonstration of this proposition.)

INVESTMENT STRATEGIES OF PENSION FUNDS IN THE OECD AREA

Individual wealth in the OECD area is increasingly managed by institutional investors. Fully-funded, privately managed pension funds have so far been important (as a per contagia of financial assets and GDP) in only a handful of OECD countries, such as the US, the UK, the Netherlands, Switzerland, Canada and Australia (see Table 2.1). Elsewhere, private funded schemes have seen their development hampered by the scale of state social security pension provision (Davis, 1992). State social security in the OECD mostly provides a compulsory, indexed, defined-benefit, and unfunded pension scheme. However, ageing populations, with a rising proportion of retirees, will further strain existing social security systems. Policymakers are thus faced with the unappealing choice of either decreasing benefits or increasing social security taxes. At the same time, the need to tackle unemployment is exerting strong pressure to control labour costs.

These pressures can be expected to stimulate strong growth in private funded pensions and create incentives to seek maximum returns on pension fund assets (Davanzo and Kautz, 1992). According to the European Federation for Retirement Provision (see *The Guardian*, 5 October 1993), every 1 per cent improvement in pension funds' investment returns will reduce employers' costs by 2 to 3 per cent of the payroll. The need for high returns on pension assets implies a need for global diversification. Pension assets will dominate investment trends and capital flows around the world.

Before we examine how pension funds *actually do invest* their assets, it is useful to spell out how pension funds *should invest* to maximize return for given risk. Modern portfolio theory (see, for example, Solnik, 1988) and its major tool, the capital asset pricing model (CAPM), hold that the world market portfolio is the optimal term portfolio in a fully efficient and integrated international capital market. For any portfolio underinvested in foreign assets (as a percentage of world market capitalization) there is the prospect of a free lunch: international diversification can lower risk by eliminating nonsystemic volatility without sacrificing expected return.[6] Alternatively, global diversification will raise the expected return for a given level of risk. The diversification benefits consist of reduced risk, usually measured by the annualized standard deviation of monthly returns,

by investing in markets which are relatively uncorrelated (or even negatively correlated) with the investor's domestic market. International diversification reduces risk faster than domestic diversification because domestic securities exhibit stronger correlation as a result of their joint exposure to country-specific shocks. International diversification should cover both stocks and bonds; efficient portfolios made up of only stocks display a substantially higher risk for the same level of return than efficient portfolios made up of both stocks and bonds (Solnik and Noetzlin, 1982).

Table 2.1 Pension fund assets in 17 selected OECD countries, 1992

	Asset size, US$ bn			Asset mix	
	Total	thereof: private	Total as % of GDP	Foreign asset share % of total	% of funds invested in emerging markets
United States	3 315	2 265	56.4	4.6	n.a.
Japan	728	362	19.8	8.2	n.a.
United Kingdom	644	544	61.9	28.0	78
Netherlands	242	147	75.5	13.8	56
Canada	230	108	40.9	9.2	n.a.
Switzerland	188	125	78.2	7.7	8
Germany	114	85	6.4	4.3	0
Sweden	81	0	33.0	1.0	n.a.
Australia	67	34	23.3	14.6	n.a.
France	41	n.a.	3.1	1.9	n.a.
Denmark	40	21	28.1	4.0	2.9
Ireland	16	n.a.	32.8	35.0	n.a.
Italy	11	n.a.	0.9	4.1	n.a.
Norway	6	4	5.3	0	0
Spain	5	n.a.	0.9	1.0	n.a.
Belgium	4	n.a.	0.2	31.1	n.a.
Portugal	2	n.a.	2.4	3.2	n.a.
Total OECD	5 740				

Sources: InterSec Research Corp., London Representative Office; European Federation for Retirement Provision (as reported in *The Guardian*, 5 October 1993); OECD, Main Economic Indicators, September 1993.

Since OECD stock markets are already highly integrated,[7] their monthly returns display correlation coefficients on the order of 50 to 90 per cent. By contrast, stock markets in Latin America and Asia still display negative or very low correlation with those in the industrialized countries. Note, however, that equity returns in those developing countries that have opened their markets to foreign portfolio investment have become more closely correlated with the returns in developed markets in recent years, with coefficients around 40 per cent (Mullin, 1993). Of course, investment in

emerging markets not only reduces risk, it is also likely to raise the mean return of portfolios.

Growth in the OECD has proved to be and is expected to remain substantially below growth in many non-OECD countries. Through 1994, the OECD (1993) predicts growth to average 2.7 per cent in the OECD area, 6.9 per cent in the so-called dynamic Asian economies, and 6 to 7 per cent in both Argentina and Chile. Stock market returns cannot outpace GDP growth in the longer run: share prices cannot rise faster than the dividends which give them their value, nor can dividends rise faster than the profits from which they are paid. Profits in turn can scarcely rise faster than the economy, as that would mean shareholders winning consistently at the expense of someone else. Investment in high-growth non-OECD countries thus promises higher returns than it does for slow-growth OECD countries as long as the market is less than perfectly efficient at arbitraging away such differences. Pension funds are long-term contractual savings institutions, unlike investment funds which need to stand ready to meet at short notice requests for reimbursements. The portfolio choice of pension funds will thus not only be guided by optimizing risk–return tradeoffs, but will have to be aligned to the structure of their liabilities. The definition of retiree benefits (nominal vs real, and defined-contribution vs defined-benefit schemes), the maturity structure of receipts, and expenses will feature prominently among the determinants of portfolio investment.

In most OECD countries, quantitative limits to international investment still constrain the portfolio management of pension funds (see next section). How do pension funds invest when such limits are absent? Coote (1993) has recently looked at this question by examining *in-house investment guidelines* of life insurance and pension institutions in Australia, the Netherlands, Switzerland and the United Kingdom. The investment behaviour of these largely unconstrained institutions may be indicative of the future for those countries that decide to relax their official restrictions on international investment. Here is a short summary of Coote's findings:

1) Pension funds take a *conservative* approach to international investment, which is motivated more by risk-reducing portfolio diversification than by expectations of superior long-term returns. The emphasis on diversification benefits is reflected in the fact that in-house guidelines specify both *minimum and maximum* limits to foreign investment; it is considered just as imprudent not to have a minimum foreign exposure as to hold too many foreign assets (see Table 2.2).

Table 2.2 Maximum guideline limits for foreign investment of pension funds and life insurance companies (percentage distribution)

Class intervals	All sample pension funds	Australia	Netherlands	Switzerland	UK
<10	15	10	33	40	9
11–20	33	30	13	27	36
21–30	30	20	27	27	18
>30	22	40	27	7	36

Source: Coote (1993).

2) Investment guidelines usually specify benchmarks for the purpose of defining a neutral long-term investment position, with a breakdown for the three major international asset classes, namely equities, fixed-interest instruments, and real estate. Limits to foreign equity holdings are usually the highest, those for foreign property holdings the lowest among the three asset classes. The preference for equities reflects the advantage to participants in defined-contribution pension funds of acquiring assets of long duration with high yields and an expectation that their price movements will broadly offset inflation, a role for which equities are ideally suited. Bonds are suitable as a core holding for defined-benefit pension funds with liabilities defined in nominal terms.

3) Regional specifications cover in most guidelines minimum and maximum investment limits in three major regions – Europe, North America, and Asia Pacific. The benchmark here is often a commonly reported index such as the Morgan Stanley Market Capitalisation Weighted Accumulation Index.[8] The share of countries in this benchmark depends on the capitalization value of their respective stock markets; countries may not be overweight or underweight by more than 5 per cent of their share in the benchmark. (Note that neither Latin America nor Africa were mentioned by Coote.) The development of forward currency markets has now led most pension funds to recognize that investment in a foreign asset and investment in a foreign currency involve two separate investment decisions.

4) Pension fund portfolios nonetheless often continue to display a home bias. Goldstein and Mussa (1993, p. 24) list the possible explanations as 'transactions costs, externally-imposed prudential limits on foreign assets, uncertainties about expected returns, higher (than warranted) risk

perceptions about foreign assets due to relative unfamiliarity with those markets and institutions', and express their own belief that the latter factor is the most important. Moreover, currency matching requirements sometimes obligate the holding of excess reserves when the currency composition of assets and liabilities is mismatched; such requirements make foreign investment less attractive.[9] Another factor, which militates particularly against pension fund investment into emerging markets, is liquidity risk (Davis, 1991). Yet a further frequent explanation is the role of employee representatives, who typically favour investment at home because of a protectionist assumption that home investment promotes social welfare. In some countries, like Germany, the track record of (positive) inflation-adjusted returns on domestic government bonds and the strength of the domestic currency have also made foreign investment look less compelling. However, while pension funds have not so far pursued diversification into foreign assets to the extent predicted by modern portfolio theory, namely to the global portfolio, there is currently a clear trend to reduce the home bias of pension fund investment, so that those funds with low foreign exposure are now rapidly investing abroad, foremost in equities.

5) There is a strong tendency for portfolio behaviour to conform to industry norms, a result of the principal-agent problem. For a pension fund manager, a strategy of low personal risk is to do what the others are doing. If they are all wrong in their choices, the manager will not be held *personally* accountable. But for the principal, the sponsoring companies and the pension beneficiaries, the damage will be done.

It should be noted that future investment behaviour may be less conservative than that described by the Coote report. An increasing number of US and UK companies are turning away from traditional defined-benefit retirement plans, which guarantee employees a specific pension by investing their cash in a company-wide fund, towards defined-contribution pensions, which give employees the chance to choose from a variety of investment options, most of which are mutual funds. In the future, therefore, pension funds are likely to stress return objectives more than in the past, especially while risk-free assets (such as deposits) yield returns as low as currently in the United States.

There is currently widespread enthusiasm about the long-run prospects for portfolio flows into emerging markets based on the calculation of risk–return tradeoffs. Yet, the enthusiasm may easily be overdone. It seems obvious that in a large, well-diversified economy such as the United States there should be enough opportunities to find poorly correlated equity returns

and hence more potential for *domestic* diversification benefits than in a small, mono-structured economy. To compare standard deviations of monthly returns of a joint US index (such as the SP 500) and their correlation with smaller counterparts is thus to exaggerate the benefits of foreign diversification, because one US index would hide the domestic diversification potential for the US investor. Diversification benefits can also be overstated by the common use of monthly returns, since the correlation of stock returns falls with the frequency of observation. Since performance checks for pension funds occur often on a quarterly basis, an efficient frontier based on quarterly or longer observations (not readily available from IFC) is likely to provide a more realistic and lower estimate of the risk reduction implied by foreign investment. Standard deviations of monthly returns may also be a poor risk guide to the extent that *event risk* becomes more important (Howell *et al.*, 1992). Diversification will not eliminate systemic risks such as the 1987 crash when all markets are likely to be correlated. Finally, the low correlation of stock returns between mature and emerging markets which is currently observed cannot persist with heavy flows between these markets. The flows will help break down the historically low correlations between OECD and non-OECD stocks, just as happened with intra-OECD correlations, which strengthened during the 1980s (Mullin, 1993).

To the extent that economic development requires a long period of permanent (as opposed to temporary) capital inflows, this survey of investment strategies reveals pension funds as a particularly suitable vehicle for such inflows. In contrast to managed funds (country and mutual funds) and private domestic and foreign investors who switch assets rapidly in the search for short-term returns (Gooptu, 1993), pension funds (like life insurance companies) can be taken as a risk-averse group interested in participating in long-term investment. Pension funds are usually not forced to withdraw their assets suddenly due to a short-term demand for funds. Moreover, unlike money market funds and bond houses, pension funds are primarily interested in foreign equity investment. Pension funds in OECD countries are huge potential sources of financing for developing countries. Yet, as will be shown in the next section, regulations in many OECD countries still constitute a barrier to releasing that flow.

RESTRICTIONS ON FOREIGN INVESTMENT

Many OECD countries still retain restrictions on international investment by pension funds (Table 2.3). While most capital-account items have been brought within the full discipline of the OECD Code of Liberalisation of

Table 2.3 Regulatory constraints on foreign investment by pension funds in selected OECD countries

Country	Regulation	Source
Australia	No governmental limits to foreign investment	Coote, 1993
Austria	No more than **20** per cent of assets in bonds, domestic bank deposits and cash reserves denominated in foreign currencies. No more than **10** per cent of employed funds in foreign real estate.	Gusen, 1993
Canada	The ceiling (formerly 10 per cent) is progressively raised to reach **20** per cent for 1995 and thereafter. A tax of 1 per cent per month is levied on excess foreign property holdings.	Gusen, 1993
Denmark	Must hold at least 60 per cent of assets in domestic debt instruments (real estate, investment trusts and shares limited to 40 per cent). Only **'small proportion'** can be invested internationally.	Davis, 1992
Germany	**4** per cent limit on foreign asset holdings. **5** per cent of assets can be invested in foreign bonds.	Gusen, 1993 World Bank, 1994
Japan	Nonbinding at **30** per cent of assets in the general account.	World Bank, 1994
Netherlands	No more than **5** per cent of the General Civil Service Pension Fund. 'Prudent man' rule for private funds.	Gusen, 1993 Davis, 1992
Norway	Foreign investment prohibited.	Gusen, 1993
Portugal	No more than **20** per cent of the EC listed securities	Gusen, 1993
Switzerland	**25** per cent limit on equity holdings of foreign-based companies; **20** per cent limit on foreign currency cash or bonds. Total foreign investment limit **30** per cent.	Coote, 1993
United Kingdom	No ceiling; 'prudent man' concept.	Davis, 1992
United States	No ceiling; 'prudent man' concept.	Davis, 1992

Capital Movements[10] and have been effectively liberalized during the 1980s, investment abroad by pension funds still remains outside the scope of the Code. Restrictions are not only incorporated in exchange controls, but also in tax laws and in legislation covering financial institutions. These restrictions can be classified by the type of investment instrument (limits on foreign real estate, bonds, shares), by issuer (government vs private), by country of origin of the issuer, by whether the instruments are traded on recognized exchanges, and by the currency in which the instrument is

denominated. Restrictions can take the form of outright prohibitions, limits for particular categories of investment, or incentives offered for particular investments.

For pension funds (and other institutional investors, such as life insurance companies or mutual funds), the distinction between capital controls and restrictions is to a certain extent muted. Prudential concern is often cited as a major motive for imposing government restrictions on investment by pension funds, both at home and abroad. Authorities feel a duty to protect the financial interest of individuals who have entrusted their savings to funds. Foreign investments come under particular scrutiny in some countries, because of deficiencies in information about local business and financial conditions, including regulatory standards for the issuance of securities, settlement risk, transfer risk, and sovereign (default) risk. But these are risks which can be dealt with by the market; and other motivations for government restrictions on foreign investment closely resemble those for the more 'classical' capital controls, such as the retention of domestic savings and of monetary autonomy (see Gusen, 1993, pp. 18–20).

Restrictions on foreign investment by pension funds are often motivated by the desire to retain domestic savings for investment at home. True, it is sometimes argued that capital controls are so porous that their removal would do little to increase the export of capital. However, the mere fact that it is always possible for owners of wealth to place their funds abroad retail, at a premium, through a parallel market does not imply that controls that prevent institutions from exporting capital wholesale, at the official rate, have no effect in limiting the export of capital. Capital controls can prevent the placement abroad of long-term institutional savings. Tight restrictions, such as found in Germany, are mirrored by a low proportion of foreign assets in the portfolio of pension funds. The same observation holds for a number of other OECD countries, such as Denmark, France, Norway, Sweden, and, with regard to public pension funds, the Netherlands.

The ceilings on the share of foreign assets imposed by other OECD countries where pension funds are of any significance are generally considered to be non-binding. Examples are Japan and Switzerland, where such ceilings have been set at 30 per cent. Australian, Canadian, UK and US pension funds are subject to the 'prudent man rule'. That rule gives pension funds considerable latitude with their portfolio investments provided they can demonstrate to authorities that their investment behaviour as a whole is 'prudent'. A prudent approach to investment is interpreted to imply avoidance of excessive concentration and self-investment, as well as speculative investments.

When pension funds are free to invest abroad, they tend to extend the foreign asset share up to around 20 to 30 per cent, as seen with private

Dutch and UK funds.[11] Most empirical work on efficient frontiers displays minimum risk (for given return) in precisely the range chosen by unconstrained pension funds, i.e. at a foreign assets share which is located between 20 and 30 per cent (e.g. Greenwood, 1993). While UK and private Dutch funds have already arrived at that level, pension funds in most of the other OECD countries have only started their portfolio diversification towards optimal risk–return trade-offs. The process of portfolio adjustment does not occur overnight but stretches out over a decade or so.

In Europe, the drive towards foreign investment by pension funds could be threatened by EC regulation (see *The Guardian*, 5 Oct. 1993). A draft directive, originally proposed by Sir Leon Brittan as a measure to liberalize capital markets and create a level playing field for financial institutions, runs the risk of emerging as a protectionist measure: a majority of EU governments are now pushing for a limit of 20 per cent on the proportion of assets which may be invested abroad,[12] where 'abroad' is interpreted to include the rest of the European Union. The proposed directive would establish a European norm which could encourage or even oblige future governments to order the repatriation of foreign investments where they exceed the 20 per cent limit (as is already the case in the UK, Belgium, and Ireland).

ABOLITION OF CAPITAL CONTROLS: THE UK EXPERIENCE

In the United Kingdom pension funds already accounted for an important proportion of personal savings and of GDP (around 20 per cent) when capital controls were dismantled in October 1979. The UK experience may thus provide some insights relevant to countries considering dismantling capital controls in the presence of domestic institutional investors.

On theoretical grounds, it is usually expected that liberalizing capital inflows, and even outflows, will produce a net capital inflow, a positive wealth effect and an appreciation of the real value of the domestic currency (Fischer and Reisen, 1993). Kenen (1993) shows that, in a two-period model, the liberalization of outflow controls may lead to the repatriation of domestic assets – a net capital inflow – because controls on outflows 'tax' the option of re-exporting capital later, and so reduce the incentive to repatriate capital now. Similarly, Labán and Larraín (1993) show that a liberalization of outflows – specifically, a reduction in the minimum capital repatriation period for foreign investment – reduces the irreversibility of inward investment and therefore the option value of waiting before moving funds in, thus potentially increasing net inward investment. Realignment of

portfolio structures and the once-and-for-all attempt by foreign and domestic investors to increase their claims on a newly liberalized economy has sometimes created a spending boom, caused by the wealth effect due to the (at times euphoric) revaluation of domestic assets. All these forces will lead to a real appreciation of the domestic currency, in particular when liberalization is followed (rather than preceded) by a stabilization policy which drives real interest rates up.

In contrast to these hypotheses, the abolition of UK capital controls in the presence of important domestic institutional investors (notably pension funds) generated a wealth loss due to the disappearance of the 'investment currency' premium and heavy net outward portfolio flows, with new foreign demand for sterling assets significantly lower than the demand by UK residents for overseas assets. The net effect of portfolio flows was to raise interest rates and to depreciate sterling, even though the currency appreciated heavily in real terms due to other factors. (Although a definite decomposition of sterling's appreciation during 1979–82 has never been achieved,[13] with the development of North Sea oil, the second oil price shock, and sweeping policy changes under Margaret Thatcher coinciding with the abolition of capital controls, the fact that net portfolio flows became strongly negative implies that the abolition of capital controls limited rather than intensified the appreciation.)

The Bank of England (1981) argued that a net outflow was to be expected in the British context, given the importance of the investment currency premium over the long period when capital controls had been in place. With respect to portfolio investment, the UK controls had limited residents' purchase of foreign exchange for the purpose of investment overseas to the proceeds from the sale of existing foreign securities or from foreign currency borrowing. This constituted the 'investment currency' market, in which there was a premium over the official exchange rate, which was mostly in the range of 30 to 50 per cent, or on occasion even higher (Artis and Taylor, 1989). The size of the premium demonstrates the effectiveness of capital controls in locking in domestic savings.

The Bank of England (1981) argued that their removal triggered portfolio adjustment through four channels. First, the loss of the 'investment currency' premium constituted a *reduction in the wealth* of investors who had previously been holding overseas securities, and a disruption to their previous portfolio balance. Attempts to restore the pre-abolition share of foreign assets in portfolios would give rise to capital outflows. Second, the abolition of the premium directly reduced the *sterling price* of foreign securities, which would induce investors to raise the desired portfolio share of foreign assets beyond pre-abolition levels, as long as foreign currency yields and risks remained unchanged. Third, some *refinancing in sterling* of

investment originally financed with foreign currency borrowing was to be expected. Fourth, on top of the three stock-adjustment effects, a continuing *flow effect* was required to maintain portfolio balance as wealth increased.

Once controls were abolished, UK pension funds became the driving force for important net capital outflows. Net outward portfolio flows, which had been virtually nil when controls were still in place, cumulated to £36 billion during 1980–85. As shown in Table 2.4, the net overseas share of the assets of nonbank financial institutions rose from 5.9 per cent in 1979 (equivalent to £8.9 billion) to 14.3 per cent in 1985 (£67.6 billion). Pension funds invested almost exclusively in foreign equities, withdrawing funds from illiquid property and low-return government bonds. The foreign asset share of pension funds rose to 15 per cent in 1985, up from 7 per cent in 1979, and rose further to around 30 per cent by 1993. The switch in portfolio flows and the rise of foreign asset shares in portfolios can be put down as the 'effect' of abolishing capital controls (Artis and Taylor, 1989) – implying that controls had been very effective in preventing global diversification of UK portfolios as long as they existed. The OECD (1990) noted a further stimulus to outward portfolio investment from 1988 on, when the government started retiring debt, creating a lack of suitable domestic investment assets.

Table 2.4   UK: pension funds and portfolio flows, 1979 and after

	1979	1985
Portfolio of pension funds		
– foreign assets, %	7	15
– gov't bonds, %	22	18
– property, %	18	10
Portfolio of nonbank financial institutions		
– gross overseas, %	7.3	16.4
– net overseas, %	5.9	14.3
	1975–79	1980–85
Portfolio flows, net outward, £ bn. p.a.	−0.3	6.0

Sources: Davis (1992); Artis and Taylor (1989).

Measures of financial market integration usually focus on interest rate parity conditions. Such a focus is justified by the concern that high capital mobility erodes the effectiveness of monetary policy as an instrument to manage the domestic economy under a regime of fixed (or managed) exchange rates. UK capital controls had indeed inhibited full interest arbitrage (a further indication of their effectiveness); their removal

subsequently had a dramatic effect in eliminating deviations from covered interest parity (Artis and Taylor, 1989).[14] But it is unlikely that pension funds contributed in any great measure to short-term interest arbitrage, since their post-abolition portfolio shifts mainly involved replacing property and government bonds by foreign equity purchases.

Pension funds, as the driving force of post-abolition portfolio outflows, could nevertheless be held responsible for changes in the sterling exchange rate and interest rate *levels*. The Bank of England (1981) concluded that capital controls had contained the demand for foreign currency, and that removing them depreciated the pound and increased interest rates. Evidence in favour of this position can be found in the behaviour of onshore/offshore interest differentials: pre-abolition differentials in favour of offshore rates fell after abolition (Artis and Taylor, 1989).

The global integration of the UK stock market has undoubtedly been fostered primarily through pension funds after capital controls were dismantled. While no significant increase in the correlation of *short-run* stock market returns could be detected, the UK stock exchange became cointegrated with Continental Europe and Japan, although not with the US (Taylor and Tonks, 1989). The cointegration of different sets of stock market returns suggests that in the long run these returns are highly correlated, with the implication that the benefits from international diversification will be reduced. It is revealing for the importance of UK pension funds in fostering stock market integration to compare Taylor's and Tonk's findings with the development of the asset mix of UK pension funds over the 1980s (Davis, 1991). While the share of US paper in UK pension assets (for which no rise in integration was detected) fell from 56 to 30 per cent, the share of Japanese and European paper rose from some 30 per cent to 59 per cent.

CAPITAL MOBILITY AND MACROECONOMIC MANAGEMENT

The evidence thus indicates that the global diversification of pension fund assets fosters stock-market integration rather than interest rate linkages. This justifies the above attempt to analyse the implications of equity-capital mobility: while pension funds will doubtless undertake marginal investments in fixed-interest assets, they are primarily equity investors and their main impact on monetary autonomy will come as a result of arbitrage between the stock and bond markets. Since that arbitrage is very imperfect, stock-market integration does little to curb short-term monetary autonomy. The fear that allowing pension funds to place their assets abroad would

further limit the ability of the central bank to conduct an autonomous monetary and exchange-rate policy is thus misplaced.

Are the other arguments in favour of limiting capital mobility more persuasive when applied to the specific case of pension funds? The most important of these arguments relates to the desire to keep funds at home, in order to finance the domestic investment that is needed to promote growth. This can be a legitimate consideration at an early stage of the development process, or under conditions of great political uncertainty, since foreign investors cannot be expected to place even a small part of their portfolio in local assets in return for a modest premium on their expected rate of return if the economic risks of investing in the local economy are supplemented by political risks specific to foreign investors. In the absence of offsetting inward investment, a liberalization of outflows does indeed imply a net loss of savings to finance local investment. In contrast, once a country has got to the stage of being able to reassure foreign investors that they face no additional risks simply on account of being foreign, the potential exists for mutual gain through two-way investment that diversifies the portfolios of both parties, with local investors gaining greater security for a modest cost in lower expected yields, and the foreign investors gaining a greater expected yield for a modest cost in terms of less security. Indeed, a developing country can expect net inward investment, simply because the capital–labour ratio is relatively low and hence profit opportunities are likely to be relatively high.

Reasonable assumptions suggest, for example, that Chile could expect to have a net balance of inward investment under a scenario of full liberalization. In the not too distant future, OECD pension funds could hold 20 per cent of their assets abroad (as described above, this is the ceiling now being discussed at the European Union, a compromise found in OECD discussions, and a number close to the mean and mode of in-house investment guidelines). Respecting market weights (percentage share of world stock market capitalization) within that 20 per cent limit, $79 billion would have been invested in emerging markets and $3.2 billion of it in Chile, on the basis of 1992 assets. If OECD pension funds held a global portfolio as suggested by modern portfolio theory, they would hold $16 billion in Chile and almost $400 billion in all twenty emerging markets.

Table 2.5 compares the preceding estimates for pension-related inflows with the outflows likely after further liberalization. Currently, net foreign assets related to pension funds are negative (a net inflow), since Chile's pension funds are only starting to invest abroad. Even if the current 3 per cent limit for outward investment was fully exploited, this would mean only $375 million held abroad, still short of the $500 million estimated to be currently invested in Chile. If Chile's pension system was allowed to invest

20 per cent instead of 3 per cent abroad, and OECD pension schemes behaved likewise, nothing much would change in *net* flow terms compared with the current situation. Under the unrealistic assumption that both Chile's and the OECD's pension funds would end up with a global portfolio, Chile would enjoy net pension-related inward investment of $3.6 billion. All these numbers apply to estimated end-1992 assets, and extrapolation assumes implicitly that Chile's pension fund assets do not grow at a faster rate than do those of OECD pension funds. Chile's net foreign asset position would, of course, be raised by faster relative growth of its pension assets and reduced by relatively faster growth of its stock market capitalization.

Table 2.5   Chile: pension-related asset position

	Inward	Outward	Net foreign assets
End 1992	0.5	0.0	−0.5
Assuming 20% ceiling on foreign assets for both OECD and Chile's pension funds	3.2	2.5	−0.7
Assuming investment along world stock market capitalization	16.0	12.4	−3.6

Note:
Applies to estimated pension fund assets end 1992, when Chile's pension funds held assets of $12.5 billion.

Sources: Banco Central de Chile, *Boletin Mensual;* IFC, *Emerging Stock Markets Factbook,* 1993.

It has been argued that it would be a mistake to vary capital controls with a view to trying to fine tune the flow of capital, because of the possible perverse effect whereby a liberalization of outflow controls could stimulate a net inflow (Williamson, 1993). Our analysis above also pointed to this possibility. However, one context in which this analysis seems of questionable relevance concerns outward investment by domestically-based pension funds (as opposed to the right of foreign funds to repatriate their holdings at will). Specifically, it is difficult to see any reason why legalizing foreign investment by pension funds should encourage inward investment (except insofar as it reduces domestic asset prices and thus increases the incentive to buy domestic assets). Thus liberalization of outward investment by pension funds would seem a rather sensible response to embarrassingly large capital inflows that threaten the ability to maintain a competitive exchange rate.

Another problem with liberalizing capital outflows is that this may erode the tax base, but this also hardly seems a relevant consideration with regard to foreign investment by pension funds.

We therefore conclude that foreign investment by pension funds, both inward and outward, should be one of the first components of the capital account to be liberalized. The fact that a number of OECD countries still maintain regulations that limit outward investment by their pension funds is both anomalous and harmful to the interests of developing countries, and the discussion within the European Union of changes that would roll back past liberalization is even more regrettable. In addition, once a developing country has got to the point of appearing sufficiently reassuring to foreign investors that they perceive no risk of being treated less favourably simply because they are foreign, there is no reason for the country to fear a net loss of savings as a result of liberalizing investment by pension funds. In particular, we have argued that at that point the desirability of maintaining a degree of monetary autonomy and a competitive exchange rate do not imply any need to prohibit foreign investment by pension funds.

It is often suggested that an important reason for delaying the liberalization of outward investment by pension funds is the positive externalities that these funds provide for the widening and deepening of capital markets. For example, Vittas (1992) suggests that contractual savings institutions, essentially pension funds and life insurance companies, play a crucial role in mobilizing long-term financial resources and developing equity and bond markets (government, corporate, and mortgage). They thus fill the gap in the supply of long-term finance that exists in most developing countries, as well as facilitating the privatization of state-owned enterprises and promoting greater dispersion of corporate ownership. We would regard this argument as reinforcing the caveat expressed in the preceding paragraph, that liberalization should not be undertaken prior to a situation where foreign investors can be expected to replace any outward flow of savings by domestic pension funds.

TECHNIQUES FOR REGULATING FOREIGN INVESTMENT BY PENSION FUNDS

For completeness, we add a brief discussion of various techniques by which the foreign investment of pension funds could be regulated, were our main recommendation regarding the inadvisability of such regulation to be rejected.

1) One possible technique would be to limit domestic pension funds to portfolio swaps with foreign pension funds.[15] If the exchange control regulations prohibited reinvestment of dividends, then the only impact of the pension funds on the foreign exchange market would be the difference between the realized returns on inward versus outward investment over the period in question.

Unlike many proposals for capital controls, this one appears to be administratively feasible. Pension funds are well-defined legal entities that are in any event regulated, and it would not seem difficult to ensure that they undertook all foreign investments through a swap market.

This proposal would achieve complete insulation of the domestic economy from changes in the portfolio preferences of foreign investors. Consider, for example, the sort of shock which we established was capable of destabilizing the domestic economy, namely a downward revision of expectations for domestic earnings that was not shared by local investors. Under this scenario foreign pension funds would start to sell shares, but in order to get their funds out they would have to find a national pension fund that was willing to liquidate some of its foreign holdings and repatriate its funds. Since the national pension fund would invest its earnings in the domestic stock market, there would be no reason for any major change in the price of domestic equities; the price that would adjust to reequilibrate the market would be the premium/discount on the foreign exchange rate at which pension-fund swaps were undertaken. Some spillover on domestic markets could still occur, but only to the extent that the foreign pension funds decided to invest in other assets like bonds, and even then a move that would depress stock prices would tend to increase bond prices so that there would be no first-order effects on aggregate demand. Hence this proposal would provide an effective solution, though one to a problem that we argued to be nonexistent.

The big disadvantage of the proposal is that it would preclude developing countries financing a net resource transfer from investment by pension funds. Of course, there are times when inward investment is excessive and hence a mechanism that repels an inflow of reserves can be helpful. But if one believes that long-term investments on an equity basis provide a superior form in which to tap foreign capital, then forgoing net pension fund inflows is a high price to pay for solving a non-existent long-run problem even if there may sometimes be an incidental short-run benefit in limiting unwanted inflows as well, especially when one recognizes that it is equally likely that the inflows may at other times be very much wanted on short-run grounds.

2) Another idea is to create a special foreign exchange market for capital movements by pension funds, with its own freely floating exchange rate. Except for legal form, this proposal appears to be identical to the preceding one; in both cases an investment by a pension fund would have to be matched by an equal investment in the opposite direction, at an exchange rate determined by supply and demand of pension funds alone. Hence it too would be administratively feasible, conjuncturally pointless, and developmentally damaging.

3) It has also been suggested that it might be advisable to subject pension funds to capital controls during a transitional period when such funds were growing particularly rapidly. Presumably the fear is that there is a danger that without such controls pension funds will be net outward investors during this transitional period.

This fear does not seem very likely to be justified. Pension funds in many OECD countries have already reached maturity, so that their investments in a newly-liberalizing developing country are likely to build up much more quickly than the foreign investments of that country's pension funds. We would not object strenuously if a country decided that it wished to liberalize gradually, as many of the OECD countries have done, from time to time raising the ceiling for the proportion of assets that a pension fund was entitled to hold abroad. On the other hand, we are doubtful whether such gradualism is likely to have much impact on behaviour, given the evidence that pension funds themselves tend to respond to newfound freedom to invest abroad rather cautiously.

NOTES

1. An earlier version of this paper was presented to a conference on pensions privatization held at PUC-Santiago on 26–27 January 1994.
2. Macroeconomic models that include a stock market are Blanchard (1985), Buiter (1987), and several papers of Michael Gavin (1989, 1991a, 1991b).
3. If bonds are perfect substitutes and there are no effective controls on the movement of bond capital, then we know that the country has no monetary independence whether or not the movement of equity capital is restricted. If bonds are imperfect substitutes, then it will have a degree of monetary independence whether or not the movement of equity capital is restricted. Hence the interesting case is the one discussed in the text.
4. Note that liberalizing only the inflow of equity capital would have the same qualitative effects as are identified here, while liberalizing only the outflow would have a converse set of consequences. (The effects of liberalizing outflows when inflows are already liberalized are more debatable, as discussed subsequently.)
5. This case is analysed in Corbo and Hernández (1993, p. 6), although without recognizing the crucial importance of the implicit assumption that it is only foreigners who make a pessimistic reevaluation of the country's prospects.

6. The CAPM claims that the world market portfolio must be on the *efficient frontier* and that it is thus impossible to beat the market, whence the idea of a passive index fund approach. Such a portfolio strategy can be self-destroying when markets are not efficient. A case in point is the Japanese stock market bubble when in late 1989 the Tokyo market was worth 45 per cent of world market capitalization. For those investors following the index approach, this meant an extreme degree of concentration, not risk-reducing diversification, and subsequent tears.

7. Roll (1992) finds that different stock market returns among OECD markets are due to differences in the countries' industrial structure and the behaviour of exchange rates.

8. This finding contradicts an earlier study by Davis (1991) based on interviews with UK pension fund managers who mostly appeared unwilling to use global indexation even as a benchmark.

9. Solnik (1988) categorizes the concern as a 'misconception'. Pension funds need to worry about the real purchasing power of their assets, and long-term deviations from purchasing power parity have been widely observed. But currency risk gets partly diversified away in a well-diversified portfolio, or it can be hedged. Furthermore, foreign-currency assets can protect the real purchasing power of pension assets since foreign goods represent a sizeable part of any consumption basket, as well as reducing domestic monetary risk.

10. The Codes commit OECD Member countries to eliminate any restrictions on capital movements between one another on operations listed in the Codes. Not listed so far, and thus not under a general liberalization commitment, are mortgage and consumer credits and investment abroad by institutional investors, such as life insurance companies and pension funds.

11. As discussed earlier, the higher potential for diversification within large economies such as the United States and Japan will result in a smaller share of foreign assets held by pension funds domiciled there.

12. As a compromise between the differing attitudes among OECD countries, OECD's CMIT/CMF Joint Working Group recently recommended allowing institutional investors to place at least 20 per cent of their assets abroad, and to match liabilities in foreign currencies with foreign-currency assets up to at least equal value.

13. Despite the efforts of Bean (1988) and Buiter (1988).

14. Liberalization also reduced sharply the elasticity of long-term rates in response to short-term rates within the United Kingdom, while the correlation with foreign long rates increased (Blundell-Wignall and Browne, 1991). The weakened liquidity effect implied a further loss of power for monetary policy to influence private spending.

15. This possibility was first suggested by Alan Gelb of the World Bank.

REFERENCES

Artis, M.J. and Mark P. Taylor (1989), 'Abolishing Exchange Control: The UK Experience', *CEPR Discussion Paper*, No. 294, London.

Bank of England (1981), 'The Effects of Exchange Control Abolition on Capital Flows', *Quarterly Bulletin*, September, pp. 369–373.

Bean, Charles R. (1988), 'Sterling Misalignment and British Trade Performance', in R.C. Marston (ed.), *Misalignment of Exchange Rates: Effects on Industry and Trade*, University of Chicago Press, Chicago, pp. 39–69.

Blanchard, Olivier (1985), 'Debt, Deficits, and Finite Horizons', *Journal of Political Economy*, 93, April, pp. 223–247.

Blundell-Wignall, Adrian and Frank Browne (1991), 'Macroeconomic Consequences of Financial Liberalisation: A Summary Report', *OECD ESD Working Papers*, No. 98, Paris.

Buiter, Willem H. (1987), 'Fiscal Policies in Open Interdependent Economies', in A. Razin and E. Sadka (eds), *Economic Policy in Theory and Practice*, Macmillan, London, pp. 101–144.

Buiter, Willem H. (1988), Comment (on Bean), in R.C. Marston (ed.), op. cit., pp. 69–75.

Coote, Robin (1993), 'Self-Regulation of Foreign Investment by Institutional Investors', OECD/DAFFE/INV(93)18, mimeo.

Corbo, Vittorio and Leonardo Hernández (1993), 'Macroeconomic Adjustment to Capital Inflows: Rationale and Some Recent Experiences', paper presented to a World Bank Symposium on Portfolio Investment in Developing Countries, Washington, DC, 9–10 September.

Davanzo, Lawrence, and Leslie B. Kautz (1992), 'Toward a Global Pension Market', *The Journal of Portfolio Management*, Summer 1992, pp. 77–85.

Davis, E. Phil (1991), International Diversification of Institutional Investors', Bank of England, Discussion Papers (Technical Series) No. 44.

Davis, E. Phil (1992), 'The Structure, Regulation and Performance of Pension Funds in Nine Industrial Countries', Bank of England, mimeo.

Fischer, Bernhard, and Helmut Reisen (1993), *Liberalising Capital Flows in Developing Countries: Pitfalls, Prerequisites and Perspectives*, OECD Development Centre Studies, Paris.

Gavin, Michael (1989), 'The Stock Market and Exchange Rate Dynamics', *Journal of International Money and Finance*, 8, pp. 181–200.

Gavin, Michael (1991a), 'Animal Spirits, Terms of Trade and the Current Account', mimeo, Columbia University.

Gavin, Michael (1991b), 'Equity Markets in the World Economy: Capital Flows, Asset Prices, and the Transfer Problem', mimeo, Columbia University.

Goldstein, Michael, and Michael Mussa (1993), 'The Integration of World Capital Markets', paper presented to the Conference on 'Changing Capital Markets: Implications for Monetary Policy', sponsored by the Federal Reserve Bank of Kansas City at Jackson Hole, Wyoming, 19–21 August.

Gooptu, Sudarshan (1993), 'Portfolio Investment Flows to Emerging Markets', *WPS* 1117, The World Bank, Washington, DC.

Greenwood, John G. (1993), 'Portfolio Investment in Asian and Pacific Economies: Trends and Prospects', *Asian Development Review*, Vol. 11.1, pp. 120–150.

The Guardian (1993), *EC Set to Put Ceiling on Pension Funds' Foreign Holdings*, 5 October.

Gusen, Peter (1993), 'Investment Abroad by Institutional Investors', OECD/DAFFE/INV(83)14, mimeo.

Howell, Michael, Angela Cozzini, and Luci Greenwood (1992), *Cross Border Capital Flows: A Study of Foreign Equity Investment*, 1991/92 Review, Baring Securities, London.

Kenen, Peter (1993), 'Financial Opening and the Exchange Rate Regime', in H. Reisen and B. Fischer (eds), *Financial Opening: Policy Issues and Experiences in Developing Countries*, OECD, Paris, pp. 237–261.

Labán, Raúl and Felipe Larraín (1993), 'Can A Liberalization of Capital Outflows Increase Net Capital Inflows?', PUC-Santiago, Documento de Trabajo no. 155.

Mullin, John (1993), 'Emerging Equity Markets in the Global Economy', *Federal Reserve Bank of New York Quarterly Review*, Vol. 18.2, pp. 54–83.

Mundell, Robert A. (1968), *International Economics*, Macmillan, London.

OECD (1990), *OECD Economic Surveys: United Kingdom*, Paris.

OECD (1993), *Economic Outlook*, No. 53, Paris.

Roll, Richard (1992), 'Industrial Structure and the Comparative Behaviour of International Stock Market Indexes,' *Journal of Finance*, Vol. 42.1, pp. 3–42.

Solnik, Bruno (1968), *International Investments*, Addison-Wesley, Reading, MA.

Solnik, Bruno and Bernard Noetzlin (1982), 'Optimal International Asset Allocation', *Journal of Portfolio Management*, Fall, pp. 11–21.

Taylor, Mark and Ian Tonks (1989), 'The Internationalisation of Stock Markets and the Abolition of U.K. Exchange Control', *The Review of Economics and Statistics*, Vol. 71.2, pp. 332–336.

Vittas, Dimitri (1992), 'Contractual Savings and Emerging Securities Markets', World Bank Research Paper Working Paper WPS 858.

Williamson, John (1993), 'A Cost–Benefit Analysis of Capital Account Liberalisation', in H. Reisen and B. Fischer (eds), *Financial Opening*, op. cit., pp. 25–34.

World Bank (1994), *Averting the Old Age Crisis*, Oxford University Press, New York.

3. Liberalizing Foreign Investments by Pension Funds: Positive and Normative Aspects[*]

INTRODUCTION

Whether and when to free international investment by fully-funded pension schemes is urgently debated by governments in industrial and developing countries alike. This paper is written with several developing countries in mind (notably in Latin America) where public provision of unfunded, earnings-related pay-as-you-go (PAYG) pensions is being or has been replaced by a new system of privately-managed, fully-funded and defined-contribution pension schemes. The question is: How should these countries regulate the permissible share of foreign assets to be held by the new pension funds?

In the developing-country context, the nascent literature has given strikingly divergent answers to that question. Pointing to Chile's experience, where foreign investment of pension funds was gradually permitted only ten years after their creation, Fontaine (1996) and Vittas (1995) favour an initial full localization requirement. The major reason for the initial outflow controls that these authors advance is (a) that pension funds help to develop domestic capital markets, and (b) that they help ease the fiscal cost of moving from a PAYG to a fully-funded system. By contrast, in view of Bolivia's recent social security reform, Kotlikoff (1994) recommends establishing a single Bolivian pension fund whose managers would be instructed simply to hold the world portfolio. Apart from several other considerations (to save administrative costs, to signal openness), Kotlikoff's suggestion seems largely inspired by the theory of portfolio choice.

The paper will focus on these propositions; two companion papers that discuss the pros and cons of liberalizing foreign investment from the perspective of ageing OECD countries as well as of macroeconomic stability are Fischer and Reisen (1994) and Reisen and Williamson (1994).

[*] Originally published as OECD Development Centre Technical Paper No. 120, Paris, 1997, and in *World Development*, Vol. 25.7, July 1997, pp. 1173–1182.

First, the paper argues that high volatility of developing-country asset returns combined with low risk tolerance of pensioners with low lifetime incomes would suggest that the benefits of global portfolio diversification advanced by the theory of portfolio choice apply particularly to developing-country pension assets. However, pension funds worldwide display a strong preference for domestic assets (a so-called 'home bias') which can be rationalized (but not easily quantified) with a multitude of factors that the paper will discuss. The following section examines some positive externalities that have been suggested for the impact of domestically-held pension assets on developing-country capital markets. The section places doubt on the proposition that these externalities justify outflow controls. There are essentially two reasons for this. Cross-country evidence shows little support for the claim that the accumulation of pension assets would provide strong external benefits for financial development. Second, those benefits that pension funds do provide for the development of domestic capital markets can also be realized under a liberal 'prudent man' rule such as in Britain, given the 'natural' home-asset preferences of pension funds. The final section, however, concurs with Fontaine (1996) that the fiscal cost of transition from PAYG to fully-funded pension systems provides a case for initial outflow restrictions when fiscal illusion and domestic tax collection costs are important. The major reason is that the straightforward way to finance social-security reform is to replace the implicit social-security debt of the PAYG system by issuing explicit government debt. Such explicit build-up of government debt is usually massive; if it is not invested into the new fully-funded pension scheme, it will lead to high tax collection costs, a strong rise in domestic interest rates and a crowding-out of private investment.

GLOBAL DIVERSIFICATION BENEFITS AND HOME-ASSET PREFERENCES

The potential for risk reduction seems particularly high for Latin America and Africa, regions which have been more volatile than any other region in the world, due to policy and to external shocks (see Table 3.1). Risk reduction via international diversification will thus clearly protect developing-country pensioners (in the case of defined-contribution funds) or offer pension sponsors such as private companies a hedge against shortfall risk for defined-benefit funds.

Modern portfolio theory (see, for example, Solnik, 1988) and its major tool, the capital asset pricing model (CAPM), hold that the world market portfolio is the optimal portfolio in a fully efficient and integrated capital

Table 3.1 Volatility indicators (standard deviation of annual observations, 1970–92)

	Industrial countries	Latin America	East Asian Miracle	South Asia	Sub-Saharan Africa
Private consumption growth	2.1	5.6	4.1	5.4	10.3
Fiscal deficit (% of GDP)	2.4	4.7	2.4	4.2	3.7
Narrow money (% of GDP)	2.4	5.5	1.9	1.4	3.8
Terms of trade (growth rate)	8.9	15.1	8.0	7.9	22.1
Int'l capital flows (% of GDP)	1.7	2.8	1.5	1.1	6.1

Source: Hausmann and Gavin (1996).

market. For any portfolio underinvested in foreign assets (as a percentage of world market capitalization) there is the prospect of a 'free lunch': international diversification can lower risk by eliminating nonsystemic volatility without sacrificing expected return.[1] Alternatively, global diversification will raise the expected return for a given level of risk. The diversification benefits consist of reduced risk, usually measured by the annualized standard deviation of monthly returns, by investing in markets which are relatively uncorrelated (or even negatively correlated) with the investor's domestic market. International diversification reduces risk faster than domestic diversification because domestic securities exhibit stronger correlation as a result of their joint exposure to country-specific shocks.

The benefits of global diversification, however, look very different from the developing-country perspective compared to the industrial-country perspective. While the OECD-based investor who starts to diversify into emerging markets can enjoy a 'free lunch' of simultaneously raising mean returns *and* reducing the overall risk of his portfolio (up to around a 20 percentage point share of emerging-market stocks), the Latin American investor will have to buy lower overall risk by lowering the mean return on his portfolio when he starts to diversify into the global portfolio. Table 3.2 exemplifies the point.

While the high mean return yielded in Latin America's stock markets in the first half of the 1990s is unlikely to be sustained, Table 3.2 nevertheless reveals the strong risk–return trade-off that Latin America's pension funds face in view of global diversification. Under Kotlikoff's instruction rule, Peru's pension funds could only hold 0.07 per cent of their assets in domestic equities. To exclude pension funds from the domestic stock market by instructing them to hold the global portfolio implies denying to the holders of pension rights the strong capital gains that are likely to arise in the early stages of pension reform. On the other hand, if the high return

obtainable in domestic equity markets induces pension funds to hold largely home assets, pension benefits (in defined-contribution schemes) and thus private consumption will remain largely correlated to idiosyncratic shocks.[2] The optimal portfolio of pension assets will depend on pensioners' degree of risk aversion; from the developing-country perspective, a higher risk aversion will imply a higher share of foreign assets. Note that the degree of risk aversion is negatively correlated with the per capita level of income and pension benefits.

Table 3.2 Total stock market return indexes (US$; Dec. 1990 – Dec. 1995)

	Annualized mean return, %	Annualized standard deviation	Correlation with S&P 500	Domestic market weight in global capitalization, %, end 1995
Latin America	26.52	27.12	0.38	
. Argentina	48.84	61.14	0.31	0.21
. Chile	34.32	28.13	0.26	0.42
. Peru	35.88	39.56	0.19	0.07
US, S&P 500	15.96	10.15	1.00	
FT Euro Pac	10.20	15.97	0.38	

Source: IFC, *Emerging Stock Markets Factbook 1996.*

Pension and other institutional assets in OECD countries have displayed a strong 'home bias', a lack of foreign diversification compared to what standard models of global portfolio choice would predict. The growing literature on that international diversification puzzle (summarized, e.g., by Lewis, 1994) generally agrees that capital controls and other official impediments to foreign investment cannot fully explain the home bias in institutional assets. As far as pension funds are concerned, several explanations (apart from localization requirements) have been advanced:

– Pension funds not only seek to maximize return: they also worry about the real purchasing power of their assets. In fact, there have been long-term deviations from purchasing power parity (PPP) due mainly to currency fluctuations. To the extent that pensioners consume non-traded, rather than traded goods, pension assets will be biased towards home securities. Pension funds may therefore seek a currency exposure comparable to the traded-goods proportion of the basket of goods consumed by the typical pensioner. Investors in small countries should thus hold a higher share of foreign assets than investors in large, more self-sufficient countries (which moreover provide more potential for

domestic diversification benefits than do small mono-structured economies). However, the argument ignores the fact that currency risk gets partly diversified away in a well-built portfolio, or can be hedged.

−　Second, the observation that pension funds and life insurance companies display a stronger home-asset preference than do mutual funds in industrial countries has been interpreted as a sign of low-risk tolerance of pension fund trustees (Folkerts-Landau and Ito, 1995). The latter's contracts or jobs are fully exposed to shortfall risk. If pension fund managers bear more downside risk than the pension beneficiaries, but do not fully capture the upside potential of their investment decisions, unlike the mutual fund managers who are typically compensated as a proportion of net asset value, they will tend to allocate pension assets in safe, domestic assets.

−　Third, unlike mutual funds which are by definition fully funded, pension funds have to align the mix of their asset holdings to the structure of their liabilities. The definition of retiree benefits (nominal vs real, defined-contribution vs defined benefit) and the maturity structure of receipts thus feature prominently among the determinants of portfolio investment. Mature pension funds, particularly if they are at risk of actuarial insolvency, will shy away from instruments that entail currency risk and potential capital loss, and instead will prefer domestic bonds. A conservative asset allocation, however, is induced in several OECD countries by accounting rules that impose penalties for temporary deficits and by restrictions on overall equity holdings (Davis, 1995).

−　Fourth, a track record of high real returns on domestic bonds and loans, such as observed in Germany and the Netherlands, may seem to justify a conservative asset allocation in favour of domestic bonds. The growing integration of capital markets, however, makes superior inflation-adjusted bond returns increasingly unlikely, raising the shadow costs of regulation that locks pension funds into domestic fixed-income instruments.

While these factors may explain the observed home-asset preference of pension funds in the OECD countries, they may well operate quite differently in the developing-country context. First, with developing-country assets yielding a higher return at the cost of higher volatility than industrial-country assets, the risk–return trade-off would suggest a negative rather than a positive association between the degree of home-asset

preference and of low-risk tolerance. Second, most pension funds, notably in Latin America, are in an early maturity phase and are defined-contribution funds; they can therefore tolerate currency risk and potential capital loss better than mature funds, favouring equity exposure and thus foreign investment. Third, except perhaps in Chile, there is no long-term track record of higher real returns on domestic bonds that would justify a heavy exposure in domestic paper as it did in Germany and the Netherlands. Finally, the lack of suitable domestic investment assets and the illiquidity in domestic securities markets might also militate for a 'foreign-asset preference' of developing-country pension funds. Note, however, that Chile's pension funds did not generally invest abroad even after localization requirements were gradually relaxed in 1991.

PENSION FUNDS AND CAPITAL MARKETS

Fully-funded pension systems do not provide benefits to the pensioners alone, but they may also exert strong externalities that may benefit the overall economy. The most widely-acclaimed externality that fully-funded pension schemes are held to generate is their stimulus for financial development. It is often claimed, for example, by Davis (1995) or Vittas (1995), that fully-funded pension systems help (a) raise the supply of long-term funds, (b) strengthen the efficiency of fund allocation, and (c) stimulate the financial infrastructure of a country. Moreover, it is often asserted that a funded pension system would also help stimulate the level of national savings. Fontaine (1996) has argued that 'until 1989 [regulations] banned any international portfolio diversification of pension funds. This was probably the most crucial restriction in explaining why the Chilean domestic capital market grew in size and depth, ... despite an internal climate of debt crisis and great uncertainty.'

Before we can concur with Fontaine, though, several points have to be settled. First, how important is financial development for economic growth? Second, how firm is the evidence that funded pensions contribute to financial development and to higher domestic savings? Third, are localization requirements necessary in a developing-country context to capture the externalities? Only if all three questions can be firmly answered in a positive way, can a solid case be made that (initial) localization requirements should be imposed on the new pension system.

To consider the first question, the literature on the relationship between financial development and economic growth, recently reviewed by De Gregorio and Guidotti (1995), suggests indeed that some proxies of financial development are strongly associated with real per capita GDP

growth in a large cross-country sample. To be sure, empirical studies have been hampered so far by the lack of a sufficiently rich variety of reliable indicators of financial intermediation which could have been observed for a longer period on a large cross-country basis. It has been nonetheless shown that (a) the level of development of the banking system (proxied by the ratio of the total claims of deposit money banks to GDP), (b) the fraction of domestic credit allocated to the private sector (again, in relation to GDP), and (c) an index of overall stock market development that averages the means-removed values of market capitalization, total value traded and turnover ratios to GDP, are strongly correlated with subsequent long-run growth of real per capita GDP (King and Levine, 1992, 1993; De Gregorio and Guidotti, 1995; Levine and Zervos, 1996).

The indicators, unlike many other proxies of financial development (such as the size of the financial sector or the level of interest rate spreads for borrowing minus lending), have displayed a strongly positive and significant correlation with real per capita GDP growth after controlling for initial core conditions (such as the initial GDP per capita level) and measures of monetary, fiscal and trade performance.[3] Moreover, each of the three proxies of financial development has a distinct theoretical background. The proxy for banking development reflects the fact that capital markets cannot develop without a reliable banking system, because securities dealers operate by borrowing short-term funds from the banking system and because institutional investors, such as pension funds, have to develop faith into the short-term segment of the financial system before they invest into long-term securities (Rojas-Suarez and Weisbrod, 1996). The proxy that measures asset distribution (to the private sector) reflects the presumption that a financial system that simply allocates credit to the public sector may not provide as many screening services as financial systems that primarily fund private firms. Finally, the stock market indicators stand for the hypothesis that thick and liquid equity markets increase risk-sharing benefits and facilitate longer-run higher-return projects (Demirgüç-Kunt and Levine, 1996). The main channel of transmission from financial development to growth appears to be the efficiency, rather than the volume of investment (De Gregorio and Guidotti, 1995).

It is hard to provide sufficient empirical content, for various reasons, to answer the second question. Time-series analysis, for example in the Chilean context, is hampered by strong structural breaks that have characterized the economy since the pension reform in 1981, resulting in non-stationary behaviour of ratio variables. Cross-country studies are complicated by country-specific differences in pension fund regulation (such as the restrictiveness of investment regulations) and by limited data comparability, for example on pension assets. Table 3.3 seeks to establish

whether there is at least a positive association between the importance of private pension and insurance assets, relative to GDP, and the proxies of financial development that have been identified to be strongly associated with growth. The table, adding data for Chile to the sample based on Demirgüç-Kunt and Levine (1996), shows the annual averages from 1986 through 1993 of total private pension and insurance fund assets as a fraction of GDP, plus the three proxies for financial development that have been discussed above to be strongly associated with subsequent real per capita GDP growth. These are the claims of deposit banks to GDP, domestic credit to the private sector and the annual growth rate of a stock market development index that averages market capitalization, total value traded and turnover as a fraction of GDP.

Table 3.3 shows how the development of the pension and insurance assets is linked to indicators of financial development that have been identified to have a strong predictive power for GDP growth for 23 countries (of which 13 belonged to the OECD during the observation period). The correlation between pension and banking development is positive, but fairly weak; the correlation coefficient is 0.37. The correlation between pension assets and the share of domestic credit allocated to the private sector is somewhat stronger, with a coefficient of 0.50. By contrast, there is weak negative correlation between pension and stock market development. The correlation coefficients are all significant at the 0.01 level.

The negative association between pension assets and stock market development could be due to several factors. First, the observation period 1986–93 has seen deep structural reform and renewed access to private foreign capital flows in some of the non-OECD sample countries, with a corresponding effect on asset-price inflation which in turn has inflated the growth rate of the stock market development index in these countries. Second, pension funds are often not only heavily regulated with respect to localization requirements, but also through ceilings and accounting rules which limit the permitted share of equity stocks in their asset portfolios (Reisen, 1994). Third, even in the absence of any regulative limits on their equity exposure, pension funds tend to follow a 'buy and hold' strategy in their equity acquisitions and thus may have little effect on stock market liquidity. These factors, and the cross-country evidence produced here, would thus suggest that the development of a fully-funded pension system is unlikely to develop local stock markets per se.

By contrast, the positive if weak association between pension assets and banking development reported here is also in line with Chile's experience. Rojas-Suarez and Weisbrod (1996) point out that Chile's pension funds first largely invested in short-term bank deposits; subsequently, pension funds'

Table 3.3   Pension assets and indicators of financial development, 1986–93
*   (annual average)*

Country	Assets of private pension and insurance funds to GDP		Claims of deposit banks to GDP		Domestic credit to private sector to GDP		Growth rate of stock market development index	
	Rank	Value	Rank	Value	Rank	Value	Rank	Value
Australia	8	0.35	14	1.19	12	1.07	18	0.05
Canada	6	0.48	18	0.93	18	0.86	20	0.02
Chile	11	0.24	19	0.90	17	0.93	13	0.14
Colombia	19	0.03		..	23	0.25	7	0.31
Denmark	5	0.54	13	1.20	16	0.98	6	0.33
Finland	9	0.33	9	1.60	6	1.60	13	0.14
France	12	0.20	3	2.00	4	1.77	16	0.07
Germany (West)	10	0.33	2	2.16	3	1.80	12	0.17
Italy	17	0.06	15	1.01	19	0.71	22	−0.03
Japan	7	0.43	1	2.58	1	2.27	23	−0.07
Jordan	18	0.07	10	1.52	11	1.24	8	0.31
Korea, Rep. of	13	0.14	16	1.00	14	1.33	10	0.23
Malaysia	15	0.10	8	1.61	9	0.29	1	0.68
Mexico	20	0.02	21	0.48	22	1.53	4	0.37
Netherlands	1	1.08	4	1.97	7	0.55	2	0.51
Pakistan	23	0.00	20	0.70	20	0.34	11	0.20
Philippines	21	0.01	22	0.48	21	1.64	5	0.37
Singapore	14	0.11	7	1.87	5	1.31	9	0.27
Spain	16	0.08	6	1.89	10	0.98	17	0.06
Sweden	4	0.56	11	1.41	15	0.99	21	0.01
Thailand	22	0.01	12	1.23	13	0.99	3	0.46
United Kingdom	2	0.92	4	1.97	2	1.97	15	0.11
United States	3	0.67	17	0.99	8	1.42	19	0.03
Average		0.30		1.40		1.17		0.18
Correlation coefficient				0.37		0.50		−0.17
(*t*-value)				(5.89)		(4.20)		(−2.67)
Number of observations	23			22				23

Note:
See text for the definition of financial indicators.

Sources: Demirgüç-Kunt and Levine (1996); Superintendencia de AFPs de Chile.

willingness to invest in long-term central bank liabilities exposed them to bank risk; from the early 1990s when Chile's pension funds increasingly invested in corporate bonds, liquid bank deposits still remained a safe haven for the pension system to be used when conditions in the corporate bond market were not favourable for investing. The development of faith in the short-term segment of the banking system could well be a requirement for the stable accumulation of pension (and insurance) assets.

Chile stands out in Latin America as the only country that has durably raised its saving rate. The boost in the Chilean saving rate has come in the period when Chile's funded pension system has flourished. Pension reform can raise private savings in different ways. A tax-financed transition from PAYG may reduce consumption of the current work force; higher rates of return on pension assets may stimulate savings, if the intertemporal substitution effect of interest rates outweighs its income effect; a reform-induced higher growth rate may raise savings under consumption habit persistence; as a result of growing pension assets on individual accounts, the awareness of the need to save for the future may be strengthened (Corsetti and Schmidt-Hebbel, 1996).

Table 3.4 collects data on private pension and insurance assets and on private saving rates for those 20 OECD and non-OECD countries for which reliable information is available. The correlation coefficient between private pension assets and private saving rates, both as a fraction of GDP, is not significantly different from zero. While the correlation does not build on any structural identification of saving determinants, there are several reasons why the growth of fully funded pension systems might also depress the private saving rate.

First, in defined-contribution schemes high real returns on pension assets require a lower rate of saving from achieving a targeted pension level and may encourage an early retirement. Second, the rise of pension assets usually goes along with a higher supply of loanable funds that may stimulate household access to consumer and mortgage credits. Third, funded pensions may imply greater credibility of future pension benefits than in unfunded systems, reducing the need for precautionary savings (Vittas, 1995). The World Bank (1994) asserts that pension reform will produce a higher national saving rate under a mandatory fully-funded scheme than under a mandatory PAYG system. But there is an obvious lack of convincing evidence on the issue.

Though the cross-country evidence shows little support for the claim that the accumulation of pension assets would provide strong external benefits for financial development, that evidence is limited to those variables that are quantifiable in a large cross-country sample. Diamond and Valdés-Prieto (1994), for example, point out that Chile's pension funds have helped to

create a corporate bond market and to develop the financial infrastructure of the country. In a regime that allows free portfolio choice, pension reform can foster the development of local securities markets by substituting the intergenerational contract implicit in unfunded pay-as-you-go systems by an explicit demand for long-term securities. For example, most of the demand in Chile's long-term corporate bond market comes from pension funds and life insurance companies. Chile's authorities are also reported to have been stimulated to ensure transparency of their local capital market as pension assets have been rising.

Table 3.4 Pension assets and savings performance, 1986–93 (annual averages)

Country	Assets of private pension and insurance funds to GDP	Private saving rate (to GDP)
Australia	0.35	0.19
Canada	0.48	0.22
Chile	0.24	0.15
Colombia	0.03	0.18
Denmark	0.54	0.16
Finland	0.33	0.20
France	0.20	0.19
Germany (West)	0.33	0.22
Italy	0.06	0.26
Japan	0.43	0.25
Korea, Rep. of	0.14	0.32
Malaysia	0.10	0.20
Mexico	0.02	0.10
Netherlands	1.08	0.25
Philippines	0.01	0.11
Spain	0.08	0.21
Sweden	0.56	0.15
Thailand	0.01	0.24
United Kingdom	0.92	0.15
United States	0.67	0.16
Average	0.30	0.20
Correlation coefficient		0.00
(*t*-value)		(0.05)
Number of observations	20	20

Sources: Demirgüç-Kunt and Levine (1996); IMF data base.

The third question is, do the reported effects of pension reform on capital markets and saving provide a sufficient rationale to impose restrictions on foreign investment by the new pension funds? Hardly. To begin with, the home-asset preference that has been observed with OECD pension funds would suggest that those externalities that fully-funded pensions do generate for domestic capital markets can also be captured under a liberal 'prudent man' rule as in Great Britain. This proposition should even hold under the qualification that the 'home bias' in developing-country assets will be less pronounced under a free regime than in OECD countries. Then, even if we accept the proposition that pension reform does raise savings, outflow restrictions on the new pension funds do not seem justified. The old two-gap literature has suggested that growth in developing countries can be savings-constrained, and in the absence of offsetting inward investment, a liberalization of outflows does indeed imply a net loss of savings to finance local investment. In contrast, with the possibility of offsetting inward investment, the potential exists for mutual gain through two-way investment that diversifies pension portfolios at home and abroad. Controls on capital outflows reduce the incentive for inward investment by 'taxing' the option of re-exporting capital later (Kenen, 1993).

PENSION REFORM AND THE GOVERNMENT BUDGET

Any country that undertakes a reform from an unfunded PAYG system to a fully-funded pension system will face major fiscal implications. The implicit social security debt is the net present value of pledged state pension benefits minus future state pension contributions; the calculation of the implicit PAYG debt is therefore heavily sensitive to assumptions about the discount rate and future wage and productivity trends. Pension reform will redefine pledged state pension benefits as well as future state pension contributions: The PAYG debt will now only include pensions for those who have already retired, pensions for those who will stay in the old system (minimum pensions for the poor, for example), and accumulated pension entitlements under the old system for those who switch to the new fully-funded system; and pension contributions (taxes) of the latter group that have financed the old pension system will now be diverted into the new pension system (World Bank, 1994). With respect to flows in public finance, government revenues will fall sharply as contributions are diverted to the new system while the call on government pension expenditures will only gradually decline.

There are essentially two ways to finance the transition from PAYG to a fully-funded pension system. First, paying off the implicit PAYG debt by

issuing the equivalent amount of government debt or by selling state assets (as in Bolivia); debt financing the PAYG deficit avoids a double burden on the current labour force and is fair in intergenerational terms. Second, the transition can be financed by generating an equivalent non-pension budget surplus through higher tax receipts or lower public spending; a tax-financed transition – as any restrictive fiscal policy which pays off government debt through taxes and hence shifts resources from current to future generations – encourages higher savings, probably higher investment and output levels in the future (Schmidt-Hebbel, 1995).

The implicit PAYG debt is usually massive; in Chile, for example, its present value has been estimated at 80 per cent of GDP (Arrau, 1992). It is therefore unrealistic to assume that debt financing of at least an important share of the implicit PAYG debt can be avoided; a lack of marketable public enterprises will usually preclude financing PAYG debt totally through privatization; tax finance would generate short-term deadweight cost and easily run into political opposition from the affected cohorts of the population. The transition will hence usually involve a combination of debt and other ways of financing.

To the extent that the pension reform is debt financed, it leaves the net wealth position of the public sector unchanged although the budget deficit is increased by the amount of the pension deficit. If the private sector equates the old implicit pension debt with the new explicit public debt, there is no fiscal illusion. Abstracting from second-order effects that arise from the distortion costs of taxation, efficiency gains of privatization, etc., the absence of fiscal illusion would imply that debt financing the pension reform will not generate first-order effects on interest rates on government debt. However, some degree of fiscal illusion cannot be ruled out. The fact that the Chilean pension reform did not affect interest rates much, although it was partly debt financed, does not imply the absence of fiscal illusion in Chile, since the localization requirements imposed on the pension funds were very tight.

In the presence of fiscal illusion, a fiscally weak government will want to restrict the investment of pension funds outside government debt in order to enhance the funding available for the transition deficit. To see why, we have to consider the distortions and collection costs that will arise from future taxation to service the domestic debt build-up, in conjunction with the government's need to recycle its domestic debt at market terms. These elements feature prominently in the two-period model developed by Aizenman and Guidotti (1994).[4] The model is useful to arrive at a normative statement on whether the fiscal costs of pension reform can justify the imposition of localization requirements for second-best welfare maximization. Aizenman and Guidotti model capital controls as a tax on

foreign-interest income that introduces a wedge between the international and the domestic real interest rate in much the same way as a localization requirement would; this proposition has strong empirical support (see, e.g., Dooley, 1995). While the wedge driven between domestic and foreign interest rates represents a welfare-reducing distortion to the private consumption–savings choice, it mitigates the welfare loss associated with tax collection. The net welfare enhancement depends directly on both the marginal tax collection costs and the level of private financial asset holdings. Capital controls reduce the domestic interest rate on government debt. The 'effective' tax base, therefore, is not only the private holdings of foreign assets, but in addition the domestic public debt. Moreover, by lowering the interest bill on its domestic debt, the government obtains revenue that is not subject to collection costs.[5] Aizenman and Guidotti also show that a tax on foreign interest income is welfare-superior to a quota, since the latter reduces the revenue collected by the government and thus implies higher tax collection costs.

Table 3.5, based on numerical simulations by Aizenman and Guidotti (1994), offers a rough idea of the orders of magnitude involved for the optimal tax on foreign interest income. The simulation assumes constant real income (endowment) levels in the two periods considered, an international interest rate of 10 per cent and quadratic tax collection costs with a constant parameter αT^2, as it is assumed that tax collection costs rise exponentially with the level of tax burden. The table is set up in a way which shows that both the efficiency of tax administration as well as the level of domestic public debt exert a strong incentive on the government to impose a tax on foreign interest income or, alternatively, localization requirements on pension funds. The initial debt stock determines the amount of debt that has to be recycled which, in turn, determines the optimal tax on foreign interest income. As the initial public debt stock grows from 25 to 75 per cent of GDP, the optimal tax on foreign interest income rises from 6.6 to 60 per cent, inducing a fall in the domestic interest rate differential from −0.7 to −6.2 percentage points. Likewise, as the tax collection cost parameter is raised from 0 to 0.2 – for an initial stock of domestic debt of 50 per cent of GDP – the optimal tax on foreign interest income increases from zero to 52 per cent.

As a result of controls on capital outflows, the private assets held abroad are implied to fall accordingly, from zero to 2.6 per cent of GDP. A new pension system can be expected to accumulate 2 per cent of GDP annually (Vittas, 1995), so that after the first ten years (before pension benefits will start to grow and affect the level of pension assets) the new scheme will have accumulated 20 per cent of GDP. If we assume that pension funds would invest 30 per cent of these assets abroad (6 per cent of GDP) if they

were totally unrestricted in the investment choice, we can carry the numerical simulations a bit further. Table 3.5 shows that the restrictions on foreign pension fund investment to achieve the necessary demand for the recycling of domestic debt would vary from none (complete freedom to invest abroad) down to 14 per cent of pension assets as a result of the various configurations of initial debt levels and tax collection costs.

Table 3.5 Public debt, tax collection costs and capital controls: numerical simulations

Public debt, % of GDP recycled in		Tax collection cost parameter	Optimal tax on foreign investment income, %	Implied real interest diff., % p.a.	Implied change in foreign assets, % of GDP	Implied restriction on foreign asset share[a]
Period 0	Period 1					
25.0	11.6	0.1	6.6	−0.7	−0.3	28.5
50.0	23.8	0.0	0.0	0.0	0.0	None
50.0	23.1	0.1	26.3	−2.8	−1.2	24.0
50.0	22.2	0.2	52.5	−5.5	−2.4	18.0
75.0	34.8	0.1	60.0	−6.2	−2.6	14.0

Notes:
a. Assumes pension assets of 20 per cent of GDP, of which 30 per cent would be invested abroad in the absence of any restrictions, implying a foreign asset share of 6 per cent of GDP. The implied restrictions of foreign asset shares are calculated to achieve the implied change in foreign assets.

Source: Aizenman and Guidotti (1994); own calculations.

If the new pension funds are not willing to hold the massive explicit debt build-up connected with pension reform, interest rates would be driven up which, in turn, would worsen government finances and crowd out private investment (Corsetti and Schmidt-Hebbel, 1996). This effect will be even more pronounced with a fragile domestic banking system which alternatively could, in principle, intermediate the funds between the new pension funds and the government. To reduce the temptation for the government to force pension funds to hold government paper at less than market-clearing interest rate levels, however, the Chilean approach seems very helpful. The government never forced pension funds to hold a given proportion of their assets in public debt (on the contrary, limits were placed on their maximum holdings), but by reducing the menu of available investment options – including outflow restrictions – pension funds were indirectly induced to seek government debt. Consequently, Chile managed to finance its transition deficit without interest rate repercussions. Fontaine (1996) also points to a long-run advantage of pension investment in government bonds to cope with the external transfer problem. In the 1980s,

when capital markets required many Latin American countries to generate a net external transfer, this could be financed by tapping pension funds without the interest-rate hikes observed elsewhere in Latin America. Conversely, when the heavy net capital inflows in the early 1990s required massive sterilized intervention[6] in the foreign exchange markets, the corresponding sale of sterilization bonds did not generate an upward pressure on domestic interest rates because pension funds were willing to hold these bonds.

NOTES

1. The CAPM claims that the world market portfolio must be on the efficient frontier and that it is thus possible to beat the market, whence the idea of a passive index fund approach. Such a portfolio strategy can be self-destructive when markets are not efficient. A case in point is the Japanese stock market bubble when in late 1989 the Tokyo market was worth 45 per cent of world market capitalization. For those investors following the index approach, this meant an extreme degree of concentration, not risk-reducing diversification, and subsequent tears.

2. This lesson was taken in 1995 by Chile's pension funds which despite a gradual relaxation of localization requirements had invested virtually all assets at home. After 13 years of high returns – 13.3 per cent on average – the funds' 1995 results plummeted to −3.7 per cent through end October, due to heavy exposure to domestic electric and telecommunications companies (Jackson, 1995).

3. De Gregorio and Guidotti (1995) show, however, that the ratio between domestic credit to the private sector and GDP is negative in a panel data for Latin America, presumably as a result of financial liberalization in a poor regulatory environment.

4. A limitation of the Aizenman–Guidotti model is its two-period framework: whatever happens in period one, both the behaviour of market participants and macroeconomic results will be heavily influenced by the proximity of the second period.

5. To be sure, tax collection costs also arise with the various forms of taxation on capital flows, if evasion is important. The taxation of institutional investors, such as pension funds, is less likely to be evaded than the tax on foreign-interest income imposed on the individual investor, however (Williamson, 1993).

6. Intervention in the foreign exchange market to prevent a nominal currency appreciation requires an equivalent reduction in domestic credit, in order to keep money supply unchanged.

REFERENCES

Aizenman, J. and P.E. Guidotti (1994), 'Capital Controls, Collection Costs and Domestic Public Debt', *Journal of International Money and Finance*, Vol. 13.1.

Arrau, P. (1992), 'El Nuevo Regimen Previsional Chilena y su Financimento Durante la Transicion', Coleccion *Estudios CIEPLAN*, Vol. 32.

Corsetti, G. and K. Schmidt-Hebbel (1996), 'Pension Reform and Growth', in S. Valdés-Prieto, *Pensions: Funding, Privatization and Macroeconomic Policy*, Cambridge University Press, Cambridge.

Davis, P. (1995), *Pension Funds: Retirement-Income Security and Capital Markets. An International Perspective*, Clarendon Press, Oxford.

Demirgüç-Kunt, A. and R. Levine (1996), 'Stock Market Development and Financial Intermediaries: Stylized Facts', *The World Bank Economic Review*, Vol. 10, No. 2.

Diamond, P. and S. Valdés-Prieto (1994), 'Social Security Reform', in B. Bosworth, R. Dornbusch and R. Labán (eds), *The Chilean Economy: Policy Lessons and Challenges*, The Brookings Institution, Washington, DC.

Dooley, M. (1995), 'A Survey of Academic Literature on Controls Over International Capital Transactions', *NBER Working Paper,* No. 5352.

Fischer, B. and H. Reisen (1994), *Pension Fund Investment: From Ageing to Emerging Markets,* Policy Brief No. 9, OECD Development Centre, Paris.

Folkerts-Landau, D. and T. Ito (1995), *International Capital Markets: Developments, Prospects and Policy Issues,* International Monetary Fund, Washington, DC.

Fontaine, J.A. (1996), 'External Investments by Pension Funds: Consequences for Macroeconomic Policy', in S. Valdés-Prieto (ed.) (1996), op. cit.

De Gregorio, J. and P.E. Guidotti (1995), 'Financial Development and Economic Growth', *World Development,* Vol. 23, No. 3.

Hausmann, R. and M. Gavin (1996), 'Stability and Growth in a Shock-Prone Region', in R. Hausmann and H. Reisen (eds), *Securing Stability and Growth in Latin America,* OECD Development Centre, Paris.

Jackson, S. (1995), 'Chile's Vaunted Private Pension System Has Big Problems', *Business Week,* 18 December.

Kenen, P. (1993), 'Financial Opening and the Exchange Rate Regime', in H. Reisen and B. Fischer (eds), *Financial Opening: Policy Issues and Experiences in Developing Countries,* OECD Development Centre, Paris.

King, R.G. and R. Levine (1992), 'Financial Indicators and Growth in a Cross Section of Countries', *Policy Research Working Papers,* WPS 819, The World Bank, Washington, DC.

King, R.G. and R. Levine (1993), 'Finance and Growth: Schumpeter Might Be Right', *Quarterly Journal of Economics,* Vol. 108, No. 3.

Kotlikoff, L.J. (1994), 'A Critical Review of Social Insurance Analysis by Multilateral Lending Institutions', *Revista de Analysis Economico,* Vol. 9, No. 1.

Levine, R. and S. Zervos (1996), 'Stock Market Development and Long-Run Growth', *The World Bank Economic Review,* Vol. 10, No. 2.

Lewis, K.K. (1994), 'Puzzles in International Financial Markets', *NBER Working Paper,* No. 4951, National Bureau of Economic Research, Cambridge, MA.

Reisen, H. (1994), 'On the Wealth of Nations and Retirees', in R. O'Brien (ed.), *Finance and the International Economy,* 8, The Amex Bank Review Prize Essays, Oxford University Press, Oxford.

Reisen, H. and J. Williamson (1994), *Pension Funds, Capital Controls and Macroeconomic Stability,* Technical Paper No. 98, OECD Development Centre, Paris, reprinted in S. Valdés-Prieto (1996), *Pensions,* op. cit.

Rojas-Suarez, L. and S. Weisbrod (1996), 'Building Stability in Latin American Financial Markets', in R. Hausmann and H. Reisen (eds), op. cit.

Schmidt-Hebbel, K. (1995), 'Colombia's Pension Reform: Fiscal and Macroeconomic Effects', *World Bank Discussion Papers,* 314, The World Bank, Washington, DC.

Solnik, B. (1988), *International Investments,* Addison-Wesley, Reading, MA.

Vittas, D. (1995), *Pension Funds and Capital Markets,* mimeo, The World Bank, Washington, DC.

Williamson, J. (1993), 'A Cost-Benefit Analysis of Capital Account Liberalization', in H. Reisen and B. Fischer (eds), op. cit.

World Bank (1994), *Averting the Old Age Crisis,* Oxford University Press for the World Bank, Oxford.

4. The Economics of Global Pension Flows[*]

DEMOGRAPHIC TRENDS INSIDE AND OUTSIDE THE AGEING OECD AREA

Despite some uncertainties in forecasting demographic trends over the next 50 or so years, uncertainties which are mostly due to assumed changes in fertility rates, some demographic trends can be predicted with a high degree of confidence. Three salient aspects deserve to be highlighted, because of their great importance for the future economic interdependence between the ageing OECD[1] and the non-OECD area:

- While population ageing is a global phenomenon, OECD populations are ageing from the 'middle' of the age pyramid, in contrast to non-OECD which is ageing from the 'bottom'. In other words, the prospective demographic changes imply divergent trends across the two regions. Labour force growth rates will strongly decline in the ageing OECD area and turn negative after 2010. In strong contrast, ageing is increasing the labour force in the non-OECD area; the proportion of the working-age group in total non-OECD population will roughly remain constant (see Figure 4.1).

- Ageing from the 'middle', the ageing OECD area will face a strong drop in the ratio of workers to retirees, in particular after 2010. Likewise, the support ratio will start to fall in the non-OECD area, but from much higher levels than in the OECD area (Figure 4.2).

- A much-neglected aspect of prospective demographic changes is that it will shift the balance between the age groups that may be characterized as net borrowers and net savers. Changes in the age composition of the

---

[*] Originally published as 'Warning: Past Pension Fund Performance is No Guarantee for Future Performance' in OECD, *Institutional Investors in the New Financial Landscape*, Paris, 1998, pp. 333–348.

Figure 4.1　Relative change of labour force (= age group 15–60)
　　　　　　　OECD and NMEs, 1951–2050

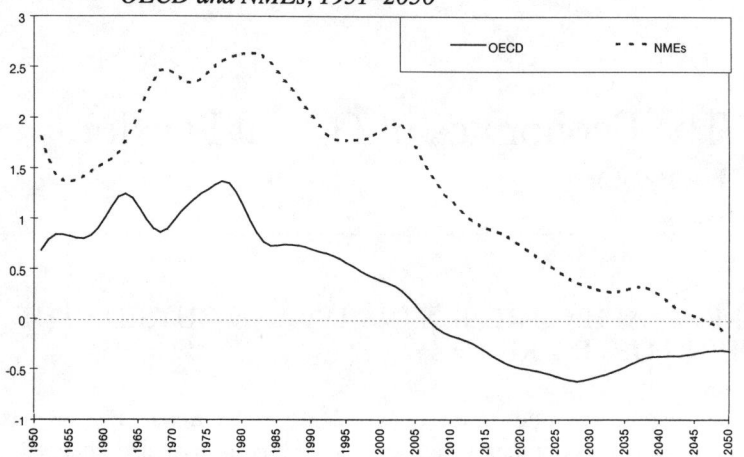

Figure 4.2　Support ratio = age group (15–60)/age group 60 ++
　　　　　　　OECD and NMEs, 1050–2050

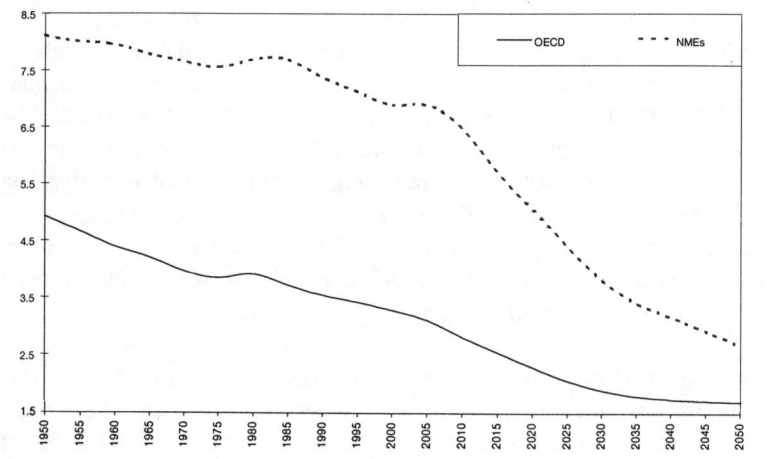

population will have consequences for the rate of net financial asset
accumulation and on the rate of return of financial assets. The United
States shows relatively high household savings in the high-income age
cohorts (40–60), whereas net savings in the other age cohorts is low or

negative (Attanasio, 1994). As the 'baby boom' generation filters through its peak asset accumulation years, the ratio of prime savers to the working age population will rise until the year 2007 and then decline. For the entire ageing OECD, the prime savers ratio will peak somewhat later (2015), before it starts to drop. By contrast, the rise of the prime savers ratio in the rest of the world, which started around 1990, will not halt before the year 2050 (Figure 4.3).

Figure 4.3   Prime savers ratio = age group (40–60)/age group (15–60)
OECD and NMEs, 1950–2050

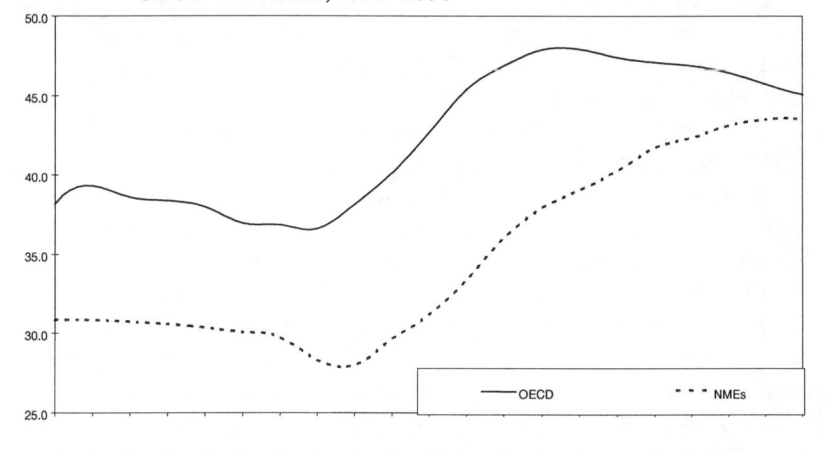

To see how the ageing OECD can benefit from the delayed ageing process in the non-OECD area, the above three demographic aspects will be analysed for their implications as suggested by neoclassical growth theory, prospective asset developments and modern portfolio theory.

THE DEMOGRAPHIC IMPACT ON CAPITAL RETURNS IN A NEOCLASSICAL GROWTH MODEL

The arithmetic of unfunded, earnings-related pensions is largely governed by changes in the support ratio and by real wage growth (which in turn depends on labour productivity in the long run). These pension arrangements are essentially locked into the ageing economy, unable to escape the prospective demographic pressures resulting from the expected drop in support ratios.

It is little understood, however, that even fully funded pension schemes will not escape demographic pressures in the absence of considerable capital flows (retirement-related or other) between the ageing OECD and the younger part of the world. First, higher life expectancy will put pressure on the arithmetic of funded pensions. Second, the demographic changes highlighted above may well add to that pressure by driving down the rate of return on pension investments.

The autarkic response to higher age dependency in the OECD area is to lower output per capita relative to the case of no ageing and, with a lag, consumption per capita. Slower and negative labour force growth will reduce investment requirements, because it lowers the capital-widening investment demand per worker. With a fixed saving rate, lower labour force growth promotes capital deepening, that is a rise in the capital–labour ratio. That, in turn, will lower the marginal productivity of capital, relative both to the rate of time preference and to the marginal productivity of labour. The drop in capital productivity will be exacerbated by diminishing returns to scale. Lower capital productivity results in lower returns on savings, both in absolute terms and relative to real wages.

Table 4.1 reports some selected results from simulating age-structure effects and two scenarios on future financial integration between the OECD and the non-OECD area. The results are based on MacKellar and Reisen (1998) who use a neoclassical economic-demographic accounting model in which age-specific saving and labour force participation rates are held constant. In the baseline scenario, which in view of assumed growth differentials in favour of the South corresponds roughly to a situation of autarky, OECD investors – including pension funds – allocate 10 per cent of their annual investment expenditure to the non-OECD. In the alternative scenario, designed to illustrate the impact of financial globalization, this share is increased to reflect the growing share of non-OECD in global stock market capitalization and in global output.

With financial autarky, the drop in the Northern labour force will lead to higher capital–labour ratios in the OECD, resulting in a drop to capital returns by 150 basis points in the OECD area. Lower capital returns in turn drive net savings lower, from 6.9 per cent of GDP in 1995 to 2.7 per cent in 2050. But even under the autarky scenario, net pension flows from the OECD to the non-OECD will strongly rise by the year 2020 and rise further (albeit more slowly) for the rest of the century. These trends result from growth differentials that favour the non-OECD area, reinvested pension returns and higher OECD pension assets. Other capital flows to the non-OECD will even rise more strongly, as high capital returns are reinvested (by half of earnings). This will result in a higher non-OECD share of OECD pension assets until 2050, before the run-down of pension assets invested

abroad and more favourable demographic trends in the OECD area will lead to reversals in these trends.

Table 4.1   Summary results of the MacKellar/Reisen simulation

	1995	2020	2050
Rate of return to capital, OECD (%)			
Autarky scenario	8.0	7.1	6.5
Globalization scenario	8.0	7.3	6.9
Difference	-	0.2	0.4
Net saving rate, OECD (% of GDP)			
Autarky scenario	6.9	5.0	2.7
Globalization scenario	6.9	5.4	3.4
Difference	-	0.4	0.7
Non-OECD share of OECD pension assets (%)			
Autarky scenario	0.9	6.4	7.5
Globalization scenario	0.9	14.1	22.0
Difference	-	7.7	14.5
Net foreign assets, OECD (% of GDP)			
Autarky scenario	2.6	9.3	10.3
Globalization scenario	2.6	24.3	54.9
Difference	-	15.0	44.6
Income at retirement age, OECD			
(1995 US dollars per person aged over 60)			
Autarky scenario	16 830	17 947	19 005
Globalization scenario	16 830	18 092	19 754
Difference (per cent)	-	0.8	3.9

Source: MacKellar and Reisen (1998), *A Simulation Model of Global Pension Fund Investment'*, OECD Development Centre Technical Paper No. 137.

Financial globalization can only attenuate, not compensate the demographic impact on capital returns and net savings in the neoclassical simulation model. Globalization leads to a partial convergence of capital returns between the two regions, reducing the ageing-induced drop in the North by 40 basis points by 2050. Globalization is estimated to slow the drop in the net saving rate in the OECD countries by one half of one percentage point over the next half-century. Analysis of the components of saving reveals that this increase in aggregate savings is entirely attributable to increased corporate savings. Higher capital returns on domestic capital and a higher share of foreign investment abroad where capital returns are higher account for this result. By contrast, globalization depresses household savings below their already sluggish level in the baseline

scenario, as OECD labour is equipped with relatively less capital and thus earns lower wages.

The distributional effects of globalization are much discussed, but the generational dimension is underappreciated. Improved performance of retirement saving portfolios in the globalization scenario raises the income of the OECD retirees significantly, by roughly 3 per cent in 2020–30, when retirement of the baby boom generation will peak. Lower availability of capital in the OECD, on the other hand, slightly hurts the income of workers. In other words: financial globalization may hurt OECD retirees as long as a large share of their pensions is pegged to wages through the PAYG system; it only will benefit retirees with funded pensions.

Finally, net foreign asset positions and net capital flows grow so important in terms of OECD output under the globalization scenario that they will become clearly vulnerable to sovereign risk and changes in investor sentiment (witness Asia's crisis in 1997–98). As the MacKellar/Reisen simulation suggests only modest benefits for capital returns and savings from financial globalization which in turn implies massive exposure of OECD pension assets to sovereign risk, it is suggested that global diversification will not be able to 'beat demography'.

THE DEMOGRAPHIC IMPACT ON PENSION FUND PERFORMANCE

The rate of return is proxied in the neoclassical growth model by the rate of return to physical capital, but institutional pension assets tend to be held in equities, bonds and real estate. The ageing process can be expected to affect the return on these broad asset classes; research on this is virtually non-existent. It can be hypothesized, however, that real estate prices should be negatively affected by a shrinking population (Mankiw and Weil, 1989); bond yields by the decline in investment needs as analysed in the growth models, and by higher relative bond demand as pension funds mature; and equity prices as lower growth will translate into lower corporate profits (Bakshi and Chen, 1994; Yoo, 1994). While financial markets are usually assumed to be efficient, no arbitrage opportunities exist to exploit the price trends predicted above if demographics affect the demand for assets in a similar way.

This section will focus on the life cycle and cohort effects that the transgression of the US 'baby-boom' generation is expected to exert on financial asset accumulation and then decumulation (McKinsey Global Institute, 1994; Attanasio, 1994). The strong baby-boomer cohort (those

born between 1950 and 1967) is now between 47 and 30 years old. These large cohorts have now entered the period in their life cycle (40–60 years) when their liabilities are decreasing on average, and they are saving at higher rates from an increasing income. While it seems that the United States is the only major OECD country that fits the hump-shaped life-cycle saving profile postulated by standard economic theory (Börsch-Supan, 1996), the US case will be of major importance for financial-asset developments and returns. First, in 1992, US citizens held more than 40 per cent of the financial stock in the OECD area. Second, financial market returns in OECD countries (except Japan) are highly correlated with and governed by the US financial markets.

Figure 4.4   Prime savers ratio = age group (40–60)/age group (15–60)
           United States, 1950–2050

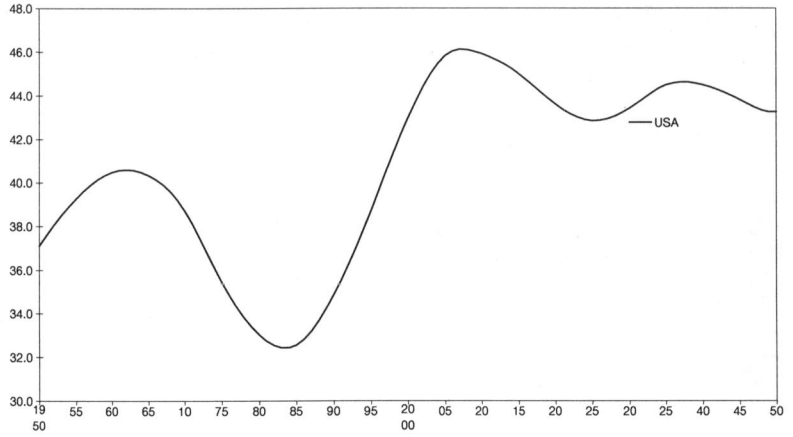

Figure 4.4 shows a strong increase in the ratio of prime-saving cohorts relative to the working-age population for the United States, up to the year 2007. While the ratio peaked first around 1960 at 40 per cent, it fell continuously until 1984 (to 32 per cent). Since then, the ratio has steadily risen and will continue to rise until 2007, when it will peak at 46 per cent. From then on, the prime savers ratio is prospected to decline gently. As the baby boom generation enters its peak asset accumulation years, a strong increase in the rate of net financial asset accumulation can be expected (McKinsey Global Institute, 1994). Allowing for cohort effects should reinforce the result because the large baby boom cohorts are saving at higher rates at every age than earlier cohorts and they are saving from higher income levels (Attanasio, 1994). Likewise, the combination of life cycle effects and cohort effects implies that the rapid phase of financial

asset accumulation relative to earlier levels will, ten years from now, give way to financial asset stagnation or even decumulation. Then, not only will the prime savers ratio decline, but the large baby boom cohort will start to retire and to draw on the accumulated pension assets, while the subsequent prime savers cohorts will be much smaller. The support ratio in the United States will soon start a strong decline, as can be seen from Figure 4.5.

Multiplying the prime savers ratio (40–60 years old/15–60 years old) with the support ratio (15–60 years old/60+) yields another ratio that relates the prime savers cohort in the United States with the age cohort of people 60 years and older. This demographic variable, which corresponds to the peak asset accumulation relative to the peak asset decumulation cohorts according to the life cycle hypothesis, can be expected to drive financial asset accumulation and stock market valuations, at least in the United States. Indeed, it does.

Figure 4.5   Support ratio = age group (15–60)/age group 60++ United States, 1950–2050

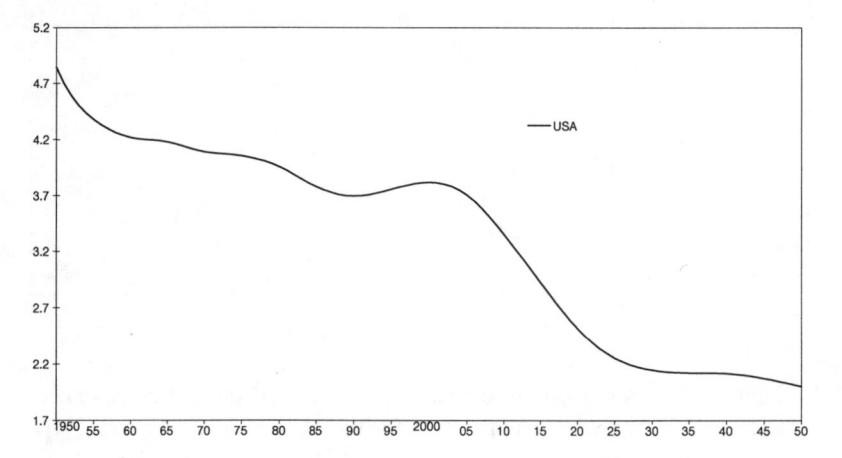

Table 4.2 presents regression analysis for the determinants of Standard and Poor's 500 annual average price-earning ratio for the observation period 1977–96, based on 20 annual observations. The SP 500 P/E ratio is determined within a standard stock market valuation model, with the demographic variable (40–60 years old/60 years+), the (inverse of the) US Federal Reserve discount rate and the annual change in average hourly wages as explanatory variables. All these variables enter the regression with the expected sign and are significant at the 1 per cent level. The adjusted R^2 indicates model completeness, and the Durbin-Watson coefficient close to 2 indicates the absence of autocorrelation.[2]

Table 4.2   The S+P 500 price/earning ratio and demography (st. error in brackets)

Dependent variable	Explanatory variables		
SP 500 P/E ratio	Prime savers (40–60) as % of 60 years +	FRBNY discount rate (inverse)	Change of hourly wages
	0.09***	46.1***	−1.5***
	(0.02)	(7.7)	(0.45)

Number of observations: 20
Period: 1977–96
Adjusted R^2: 0.88
Durbin-Watson: 1.98
*** = significant at the 0.01 level

Sources: Own calculations based on data provided by Dresdner Bank (SP 500 P/E); UN Population data file; IMF, *International Financial Statistics* (items 60 and 65ey).

Despite the importance of US interest rates in determining the price–earning ratio, the regression shows that US stock market valuations have been significantly supported by the rise in the prime savers ratio (since 1983), while the support ratio has remained fairly stable. That favourable demographic support for valuations will not last for much longer, as around the year 2000 the support ratio is prospected to start a 30-year long decline, to be reinforced by the prospected decline of the prime savers ratio from the year 2007. Figure 4.6 provides an out-of-sample forecast, assuming interest rates staying at the 1996 level and hourly wage rises along the pace experienced over 1986–96. The out-of-sample scenario, which is fully driven by the ratio of prime savers to people older than 60, tells us that the US stock market valuations will peak at a price–earning ratio of 20 and then start a long decline, before P/E ratios will stabilize at a level of around 14 at around 2030. The prospective drop in the SP 500 P/E ratio would represent a decline of 30 per cent, on account of deteriorating demographic fundamentals.

While all this is highly speculative, it confirms earlier concerns (Schieber and Shoven, 1994) that, as US funded pensions cease to be a source of net savings, asset prices will be negatively affected.[3] This can reinforce the maturity-induced shift of pension portfolios from equities and long-term bonds into short-term securities or cash, as Schieber and Shoven suggest, but it can also lead to a shift of equity portfolios into the younger economies where the prime savers ratio will continue to rise well into the year 2050.

Figure 4.6 S&P 500 price/earning ratio: fitted values and projection

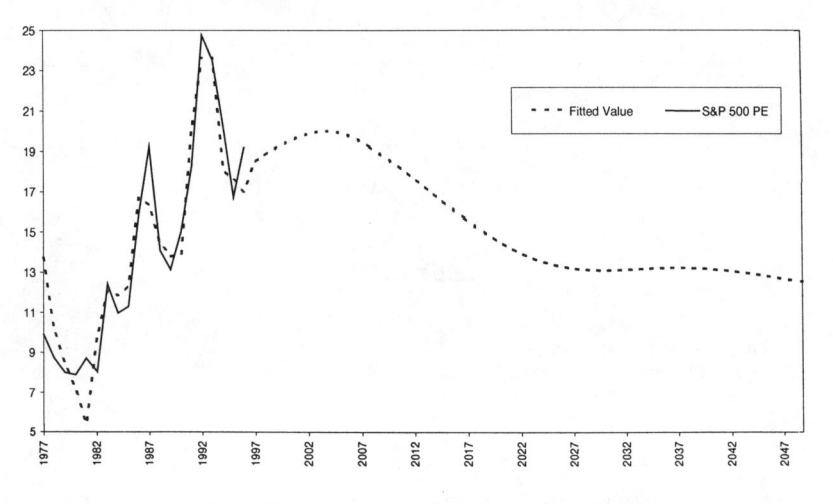

EMERGING MARKETS AND GLOBAL DIVERSIFICATION BENEFITS

In principle, the case for mutual benefits arising from the global diversification of portfolios is nowhere stronger than for funded retirement savings (Reisen, 1994). While unfunded (pay-as-you-go) pension schemes are locked into the ageing economy, fully funded pension schemes would not escape demographic pressures if their assets were to remain invested in ageing countries alone. Indeed, when the baby boom generation starts to draw on the funded pension schemes, the impact of that decumulation on local asset prices and thus on pension benefits might be negative. The diversification of OECD pension assets into the non-OECD stock markets provides the prospect of higher expected return for a given level of risk or, put alternatively, lower risk by eliminating non-systemic volatility without sacrificing expected return. It is less the superior growth performance of the non-OECD area than the low correlation of returns generated by the emerging stock markets with those of the OECD stock markets that governs this expectation. The correlation between returns on OECD and emerging stock markets will remain low even when diversification gains are seriously exploited. Differences between the two areas with respect to the exposure to country-specific shocks, the stage of economic and demographic maturity and the (lack of) harmonization of economic policies suggest that the diversification gains for OECD pension assets will not disappear quickly.

The benefits of global portfolio diversification also apply to emerging country pension assets as they could diversify away some of the risks stemming from high exposure to shocks in their own countries by investing a portion of their pension assets in OECD countries (Reisen, 1997).

Figure 4.7   Risk vs return: emerging market and US stocks, 1985–96

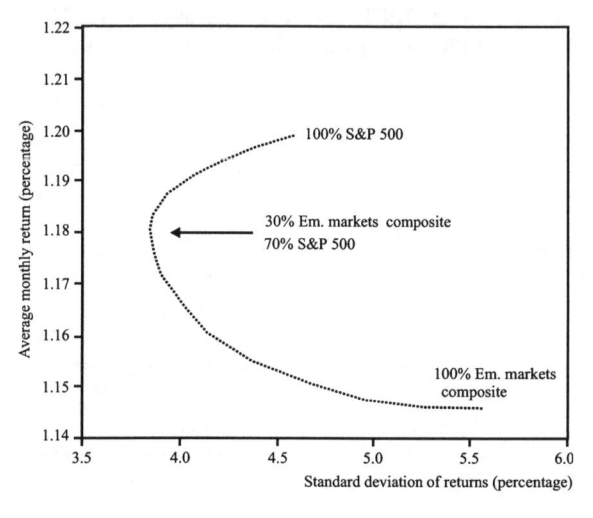

Source: Goldman Sachs Global Research.

The evidence, as seen from the efficiency frontier depicted in Figure 4.7, has not been kind to the reasoning outlined above. Two distinct regional currency crises, the 1994–95 tequila crisis in Latin America and the 1997–98 Asian crisis, have tarnished the reputation of emerging stock markets to provide superior returns to OECD-based investors. While the emerging economies have grown more quickly than the OECD countries, this has not translated into higher earnings per share growth in the emerging markets. Earnings per share growth has averaged only some 0.95 that of underlying corporate revenue growth. By contrast, earnings per share growth has been almost 1.20 that of revenue growth in the US (King Street Advisors, see *EMI* December 1997). The emerging markets have to increase corporate profitability if they are to attract a growing share of OECD pension assets.

Moreover, both the Tequila and the Asian crisis have triggered strong contagion effects. Contagion of currency crises leads to higher correlation of stock market returns among the emerging markets, taking away their potential diversification benefits. Contagion leads to shrinking benefits of

international portfolio diversification as returns to emerging stock markets are driven by systemic factors external to these markets themselves. Global diversification can reduce only non-systemic risk. Finally, currency crises will introduce frictions into world trade as they risk re-igniting protectionism in the OECD to ward off imports from super-competitive emerging markets whose real exchange rates become grossly undervalued.

Therefore, emerging markets will only then be able to improve OECD pension returns if they catch up with OECD levels of corporate profitability and if they reduce their vulnerability to the currency crises witnessed in the 1990s.

NOTES

1. Some OECD member countries, notably Korea, Mexico and Turkey, are excluded from the definition of 'ageing OECD' since they tend to share the demographic features of the non-OECD world.
2. Since SP 500 price–earning ratios were only available from the year 1977 onwards, a similar regression for the consumer price index adjusted SP 500 index was performed for the period 1950–1996. After correcting for autocorrelation, the regression test statistics were very similar to the ones reported here, with a high adjusted R^2, a Durbin-Watson coefficient close to 2, and with all three explanatory variables highly significant.
3. While Schieber and Shoven's (1994) pension saving model predicts that pension benefits will first exceed contributions in 2006, they expect net asset decumulation at around 2030, thanks to annual investment income on accumulated pension assets.

REFERENCES

Attanasio, O. (1994), 'Household Saving in the US', in J. Poterba (ed.), *International Comparisons of Household Savings*, University of Chicago Press, Chicago.
Bakshi, G.S. and Z. Chen (1994), 'Baby Boom, Population Ageing, and Capital Markets', *Journal of Business*, Vol. 67.2.
Börsch-Supan, A. (1996), 'The Impact of Population Ageing on Savings, Investment and Growth in the OECD Area', in OECD (ed.), *Future Global Capital Shortages: Real Threat or Pure Fiction?*, OECD, Paris.
MacKellar, L. and H. Reisen (1998), *A Simulation Model of Global Pension Fund Investment*, Technical Paper No. 137, OECD Development Centre, Paris.
Mankiw, N.G. and D.N. Weil (1989), 'The Baby Boom, the Baby Bust, and the Housing Market', *Regional Science and Urban Economics*, Vol. 19.
McKinsey Global Institute (1994), *The Global Capital Market: Supply, Demand, Pricing and Allocation*, Washington, DC.
Reisen, H. (1994), 'On the Wealth of Nations and Retirees', in R. O'Brien (ed.), *Finance and the International Economy*, 8, The Amex Bank Review Prize Essays, Oxford University Press, Oxford.
Reisen, H. (1997), 'Liberalizing Foreign Investments by Pension Funds: Positive and Normative Aspects', *World Development*, July 1997.
Schieber, S. and J. Shoven (1994), 'The Consequences of Population Ageing on Private Pension Fund Saving and Asset Markets', *NBER Working Paper*, No. 4665.
Yoo, P. (1994), 'Age Distributions and Returns of Financial Assets', Federal Reserve Bank of St. Louis, Research Division Working Papers 94-002 B.

Part 2

Savings

Savings

One of the few undisputed observations in economics is the strong association between domestic saving rates and long-run growth performance. While the interpretation and policy implications of the relationship between saving and growth remain controversial, the link nevertheless suggests the existence of poverty traps through undersaving or, alternatively, the existence of virtuous circles of saving and prosperity. Development economists have generally maintained that the causation runs from savings to growth, to the extent that saving translates into productive capital accumulation. However, new empirical evidence in the wake of a seminal paper by Chris Carroll and David Weil (1993: NBER Working Paper, No. 4470) has stressed the reverse causation from growth to saving, where sustained growth fuels corporate and household saving rates. This new evidence underlies very much the three following essays which form the second part of the present collection.

The next essay was written for an OECD book *Future Global Capital Shortages: Real Threat or Pure Fiction?*, published early 1996. The essay addresses the fear that, with the collapse of communism and the rapid spread of free-market policies, more than half of the world's population has joined the international competition for capital. Since the ageing populations in the rich countries will soon be making increased demands on the public purse and pushing down saving rates, a world capital shortage could loom by perhaps 2005 or 2010. The resulting rise in world interest rates might well hurt the OECD area disproportionately, by choking off investment, lowering productivity and putting pressure on wages and jobs. For the threat of a developing-country driven capital shortage, however, my essay comes up with a reassuring analysis. The evidence which the essay collects on saving determinants, on the likely changes of these determinants through to the year 2015, and on the limits to sustained net cross-border capital flows, support an optimistic assessment. Most fears about a developing-country driven capital shortage originate in the superior growth performance of these countries, and (to a lesser extent) their increased financial openness. The essay calms these fears by pointing to the various channels and magnitudes by which higher growth will raise developing-country savings.

The second essay of this part of the book is the summary of the conference volume *Promoting Savings in Latin America* (1997) that I have edited, jointly with Ricardo Hausmann (the Chief Economist of the Inter-American Development Bank), with whom the OECD Development Centre has been organizing the annual International Forum on Latin American Perspectives since November 1995. The observation that saving rates usually increase only after a sustained period of high growth let the IDB economists doubt whether savings should be an intermediate target for economic policy. The conference brought into focus the possible trade-offs involved for economic policy: promoting growth, although that has often implied a transitory decline in savings, or targeting higher saving rates, even if this implies a slower pace of economic reform. The essay ignores that possible trade-off and identifies appropriate policies for the promotion of savings through domestic financial reform, fiscal policies, and tax incentives.

Although it is often assumed that the growth in funded pension assets represents a net increase in savings, such asset growth may simply reflect a shift in the form of saving, with pension funds displacing other savings. The third essay is the first to have produced significant international evidence in support of the premise that the development of funded pensions does, indeed, contribute to higher savings. The biggest impact on savings can be expected from funded pension schemes that are mandatory and that discourage borrowing against accumulated mandatory pension assets.

The final essay in Part 2 was originally presented at the conference 'Managing Capital Flows and Exchange Rates: Lessons from the Pacific Basin', which Reuven Glick organized at the Center for Pacific Basin Monetary and Economic Studies of the Federal Reserve Bank of San Francisco in September 1996. The essay first surveys several theoretical strands in the economic literature and finds, perhaps surprisingly, that the benefits of large foreign savings are actually fairly small. It then defines the size of current account deficits that should be sustainable in the long run. The essay recommends resisting some debt-augmenting capital inflows when they are seen to coincide with unsustainable currency appreciation, excessive risk-taking in the banking system and a sharp drop in private savings.

5. Developing-country Savings and the Global Capital Shortage[*]

THE GLOBAL SETTING

Recent economic reform and the financial opening of many developing countries, covering more than half of the world's population, have raised new fears about developing-country growth – fears that focus not only on trade and jobs but also on capital flows. Fast-growing developing economies are thirsty for capital to finance the business investment and public infrastructure needed to sustain rapid growth. To the extent that the developing-country demand for capital is not financed by developing-country savings, such demand could drain the private and public savings of OECD countries. The resulting global capital 'shortage' would then raise real interest rates, which in turn would choke off some investment – probably disproportionately in OECD economies where the productivity of capital falls short of the levels prevailing in capital-poor countries. The North-to-South investment flow would imply that OECD-area productivity and wages (or jobs, in rigid labour markets) would suffer, since OECD-area labour would be equipped with relatively less capital and would thus be less productive. Such fears have been fuelled by the emerging-markets boom of the 1990s, which witnessed considerable portfolio and foreign direct investment flows from OECD countries to Asia and Latin America.

How large has the capital drain been in practice? Table 5.1 gives the answer for three distinct periods. During the late 1970s and early 1980s, many commercial banks in the Member countries lent large sums of money to the developing world, in particular to Latin America. Considerable capital flows resumed in the 1990s, with net capital flows to developing countries averaging more than $120 billion.

The recent episode of heavy net capital flows to the developing world peaked in 1993, at an amount of $159.2 billion; the combined deficit on current account (the savings 'shortfall'), however, was much smaller at

[*] Originally published in OECD, *Future Global Capital Shortages: Real Threat or Pure Fiction?*, Paris, 1996, pp. 143–160.

$98.3 billion for that year, with the residual essentially feeding developing-country reserves. While such numbers may sound impressive enough to keep concerns about a global capital shortage alive, the 1993 flows to the developing countries need to be put into perspective.

Table 5.1   Developing countries: net capital inflows (annual averages in $ bn)

	1977–82	1983–89	1990–94
Developing countries: total	30.5	8.8	123.9
Africa	9.0	−0.1	5.0
Latin America	26.3	−16.6	37.1
Asia	15.8	16.7	52.3
Middle East and Europe	−20.9	8.7	29.3

Source: IMF, *World Economic Outlook*, various issues.

Table 5.2 shows that the considerable amount of net capital flows to developing countries over the peak year 1993 was a mere 0.8 per cent of the combined (at current exchange rates) GDP of all member countries, which totalled almost $20 trillion. Incidentally, this is close to the 0.7 per cent pledged (but rarely delivered) as aid to developing countries by the DAC members. Moreover, the 0.8 per cent of their income which the OECD countries transferred to the developing world is smaller than the statistical discrepancy for net world savings (an '*ex-post* world savings gap') arising from a world investment ratio of 23.0 per cent financed by a world savings ratio of 21.9 per cent (IMF, 1995). Even in 1993, net flows to developing countries did not reach a fifth of the combined budget deficits of member country governments, the most important absorber of private savings in the OECD area. The combined investment (gross capital formation) of all OECD countries was almost $4 trillion in 1993; their combined capital stock has been estimated at $60 trillion (Krugman, 1994). The 1993 flows thus diverted 4 per cent of OECD investment from domestic use and reduced the growth in the capital stock by merely one-quarter of 1 per cent. These numbers, then, give little support to the concern that the developing countries contribute significantly to a global capital shortage.

Table 5.2   The emerging-markets boom in perspective

Net capital flows to developing countries, 1993	$159.2 bn
As a percentage of:	
OECD GDP	0.8
OECD gross capital formation	4.0
OECD government financial deficits	17.8

Source: OECD, *National Accounts*, 1995; own calculations.

Speculations that the developing countries will tap rich-country savings on a much larger scale are at times nourished by the pre-1914 experience (Krugman, 1993; Woodall, 1994). At that time, a surge in investment into the developing countries of the day – America, Argentina, Australia and Canada – was generously financed by large current account surpluses in the United Kingdom and some other European countries. That period, however, was characterized by at least three elements that are unlikely to be repeated in the foreseeable future. First, the pre-World War I flows happened under colonial order, when default risk was reduced by a much larger ability to enforce creditor claims. Second, the government budgets in the capital-source countries were largely balanced while the absence of public pension schemes stimulated precautionary private savings; the result was ample excess savings looking for high returns elsewhere. Third, very little of the pre-1914 flows reflected a transfer from rich to poor, from capital-abundant to labour-abundant countries. European investors then supplied capital to a very selective group of newly settled high-income regions, not to low-wage economies such as India. These regions did not have large indigenous populations; most of the savings to finance their investment had to come from abroad. By contrast, today (and tomorrow) the bulk of developing-country investment is (and will be) financed by domestic savings.

The Mexican *tesobono* crisis of late 1994 has reminded us that even under exceptionally favourable circumstances, countries cannot rely for too long on considerable foreign savings to finance domestic investment. This evidence is in contrast with the literature estimating the financing 'needs' of developing countries, a literature which is based on the long-rejected two-gap theory by Chenery and Bruno (1962). The theory held that developing-country growth was limited not only by the country's domestic savings ratio, but also by the foreign exchange constraint, since with limited export earnings, too rapid a

growth of the economy would cause a balance-of-payments crisis as a result of high imports of capital goods. Whatever a country's capital 'needs', there is now abundant empirical evidence suggesting that changes in domestic investment, on average and over longer periods of time, respond to changes in domestic savings (Feldstein and Horioka, 1980). That finding, often challenged in the literature but never seriously rejected (Coakley, Kulasi and Smith, 1995), holds also when the developing countries are included in the sample. The only exceptions are the countries dependent on aid to sustain their current account deficits (Dooley, Frankel and Mathieson, 1987). Considerations about the contribution of developing countries to a global capital 'shortage' will thus have to focus on their savings performance, not on their financing needs.

Table 5.3   Feldstein–Horioka in developing countries (percentage of GDP)

	1973–80	1981–89	1990–94
Africa			
Saving	26.5	18.5	16.9
Investment	31.7	22.9	21.6
Net lending	−5.2	−3.4	−4.8
Asia			
Saving	25.5	28.1	31.4
Investment	26.0	28.6	31.9
Net lending	−0.5	−0.5	−0.5
Latin America			
Saving	20.5	19.4	18.3
Investment	23.8	20.5	20.4
Net lending	−3.3	−1.1	−2.1
Middle East and Europe			
Saving	34.5	21.1	19.4
Investment	24.4	23.1	23.0
Net lending	10.1	−2.0	−3.6
Developing countries: total			
Saving	25.7	23.1	25.6
Investment	25.7	24.6	27.2
Net lending	-	−1.5	−1.6

Source: IMF, *World Economic Outlook*, May 1995.

Table 5.3 confirms the close match between developing-country savings and investment, with the exception of aid-dependent Africa (a region that hardly gives rise to concerns about a global capital shortage). The developing world as a whole (even during the emerging-markets boom of the 1990s) has relied on foreign savings at a very small fraction of their GDP, about 1.5 per cent – that is, only 6 per cent of developing-country investment has been financed by the rich countries. Asia, the most important source for concern due to its high level of capital accumulation, its vibrant growth and its big population, has constantly relied on foreign savings during the past two decades, but the amount has been modest in relation to its combined domestic product (0.5 per cent). Asia is the only continent which has seen rising savings and investment ratios over the past twenty years.[1] All other regions have experienced declining savings and investment ratios; their growth performance has consequently been mixed. This indicates that whenever high investment and growth rates are observed in the developing world, they will not drain the global supply of capital for long; growth will not be sustained unless it is backed by domestic savings.

Indeed, it is a likely scenario that further developing-country growth and falling dependency ratios, particularly in Asia, will help boost the world saving rate over the next decades. To see why, it is necessary to take a closer look at the determinants of private and public saving rates in the developing world.

DETERMINANTS OF DEVELOPING-COUNTRY SAVING RATES

How will developing-country savings evolve over the next two or three decades? Any answer to that question has first to explain past savings behaviour across countries or over time. Unfortunately, broad comparative analyses of developing-country savings have been hampered by unreliable data, by measurement problems and by ill-determined causality of savings and other variables. Yet, the growing number of national account observations and the important cross-country variability in developing-country saving performance now enable developing-country saving rates to be determined with a reasonable degree of confidence.

Thanks to Asia, the developing world saves a higher proportion of its (smaller) income than do the OECD countries. In fact, with an average saving rate of more than 30 per cent over the 1990s, Asia saves a much larger share of its income than does the rest of the world. That result is heavily influenced by the East Asian 'supersavers': Singapore saves around 40 per cent, Korea 35 per cent, China 37 per cent and Chinese Taipei 29 per cent of their income

(1990–93). By contrast, saving rates in South Asia (and in the Philippines) are around 20 per cent. The developing world also incorporates the world's lowest-saving countries, most of them in Africa, where the saving rate averaged 17 per cent over the 1990s. Latin America's saving performance has been equally weak, due to very low private saving rates (Edwards, 1995). Only Chile managed to raise its saving rate durably in recent years, due to a radical shift from pay-as-you-go pensions to a flourishing funded pension system, a shift that was financed by a restrictive fiscal stance. With high compulsory contributions, the fully funded pension schemes in Singapore and Malaysia had already since the 1970s helped boost the national saving rate.

Table 5.4   Government savings, 1983–92 (as a percentage of national savings)

Africa	5.4
Asia	15.9
Latin America	14.4
Industrialized countries	−3.9

Source: Edwards (1995); own calculations.

Some of Asia's superior saving performance is due to important government savings (the consolidated public-sector budget surplus). Table 5.4 indicates that Asia's government sector contributed around 15 per cent to national savings during 1983–92, in striking contrast to Africa (and to the OECD countries). In Latin America too, government budgets have contributed a sizeable amount to (comparatively low) national savings, thanks to significantly improved public finances in the post-debt crisis period. Most saving studies have treated government savings as exogenously given, but Edwards (1995) has recently found that they respond to economic and political (strategic) determinants. Growth of GDP per capita is the most important variable in explaining cross-country differences in government savings (as a fraction of GDP); this implies, *ceteris paribus*, that high growth in developing countries will help boost government and thus national savings, if the developing world is not suitably Ricardian (see below). Edwards identified political instability, defined as the frequency of transfer of political power, as the second most important determinant of government savings. This finding is backed by recent literature on the political economy of macroeconomic policy, which has postulated a low level of government savings when governments often alternate, since the rewards of savings

(investment and growth) then come with a lag too long to be exploited by the incumbent government. A further significant determinant of government savings has been the inflow of foreign savings; these reduce government savings, with an offset coefficient of around 0.5. This finding gives some support for the presumption that aid and private capital flows to developing countries may undermine their fiscal discipline.

The determinants of *private* developing-country savings, both household and corporate, have been subject to much theoretical debate, but have only recently been analysed empirically in a comprehensive framework. The rest of this section will borrow heavily from two recent studies, by Edwards (1995) and by Masson, Bayoumi and Samiei (1995). Table 5.5 displays their most important results for a sample of 24 (Edwards), and 40 (Masson *et al.*) developing countries.[2] The dependent variable is the ratio of private national savings to GDP, obtained from the IMF data set. The independent variables reflect various theoretical debates, and were defined as follows:

GDP Growth

Does saving cause growth or does growth cause saving? Theoretically, the link from savings to growth may be more straightforward, since higher savings raise the growth rate of output by increasing capital accumulation (Mankiw *et al.*, 1992). Recent causality tests, however, have emphasized the link from growth to saving (Carroll and Weil, 1993); that causation is in line with East Asia's experience where increases in saving rates have tended to lag a few years behind increases in GDP growth rates. That evidence is backed in theory by the life-cycle model hypothesis, because a growing economy raises the income of the saving working population relative to the dissaving retirees; the evidence is also in line with simple habit persistence. A recent theory, backed with evidence from Chinese Taipei, has stressed the importance of investment-motivated saving in high-growth countries where imperfect domestic capital markets induce agents to save more in order to undertake lumpy physical investment in the future (Liu and Woo, 1994).

Table 5.5 confirms the growth–saving link for the cross-country estimates: a (sustained) rise in per capita income growth of 1 per cent raises the country's private saving rate by half a percentage point. The computation of standardized beta coefficients indicates that GDP growth is the most important variable for explaining cross-country differences in private savings (Edwards, 1995). The time series regression (third column) indicates, however, that savings are less sensitive to short-term differences in output growth; the latter have a high cyclical component that should affect savings much less than long-term differences in output growth.

Table 5.5   Determinants of private savings in developing countries (t-statistics in parentheses)

	Cross-country estimates		Time series
GDP growth[a]	0.52	1.73	0.16
	(2.8)	(3.1)	(4.0)
Relative GDP[b]	0.00	0.72	0.87
	(2.2)	(2.1)	(4.0)
Gov't savings/GDP[c]	−0.36	−0.61	−0.66
	(−3.5)	(−2.0)	(−17.4)
Gov't capital expenditure/GDP	–	–	−0.30
			(−3.9)
Social security[d]	−0.12	–	–
	(−1.5)		
Age dependency ratio[e]	−0.06	−0.05	−0.18
	(−1.2)	(−1.0)	(−6.0)
Urban concentration[f]	−0.12	–	–
	(−3.2)		
Money/GDP[g]	0.29	–	–
	(3.9)		
Real interest rate[h]	−0.04	–	–
	(−1.1)		
Current account surplus/GDP	0.63	–	0.47
	(2.8)		(11.4)
Number of observations	100	40	480
Adjusted R[2]	0.61	0.37	0.30
Observation period	1970–92	1983–92	1982–93
Source	Edwards (1995)	Masson *et al.* (1995)	Masson *et al.* (1995)

Notes:
a. real, per capita in Edwards (1995), real total in Masson *et al.* (1995).
b. PPP-adjusted GDP per capita in Edwards (1995), PPP-adjusted GDP per capital relative to the US in Masson *et al.* (1995).
c. not specified in Edwards (1995), otherwise central gov't budget surplus/GDP.
d. ratio of public expenditure on social security and welfare to total public expenditures.
e. population younger than 15 years old plus population over 65 years old, as a percentage of working-age population.
f. proportion of urban to total population.
g. ratio of 1970 stocks of M_1 and M_2 to GDP.
h. ex-post real deposit interest rate.

Relative GDP Level

Rich countries should be able to save more than poor countries. Consumption smoothing – whether over several years or over the life cycle – is restricted in poor countries by the high share of subsistence consumption and by imperfect financial markets that offer limited saving vehicles. Thus, a country's private saving rate should rise with its relative income level.

Table 5.5 bears out that expectation. Both Edwards (1995) and Masson *et al.* (1995) find that catching up to the PPP-adjusted US income level will raise a country's saving rate. Other research has found that the relationship between the level of income and the saving rate is nonlinear. The largest increases in the saving rates occur in the transition from low- to lower middle-income (Ogaki *et al.*, 1995), above a per capita GDP of $695 (World Bank definition).

Government Savings

The Ricardian equivalence theory suggests that government deficits (or dissaving) should be fully offset by an increase in private savings that allows for future taxes. While the theory has generally been rejected by the data for OECD countries, the existence of liquidity constraints and of widespread tax evasion should militate for an even lower offset in developing countries.

The offset coefficients given in Table 5.5, ranging from –0.36 to –0.66, confirm earlier studies that have found that changes in government saving offset private savings by roughly 50 per cent. Although higher government savings crowd out some private savings, they will not do it one-to-one. This is important, because it means that fiscal restraint can improve a country's saving rate. Edwards (1995), moreover, has identified government savings as the second most important variable (after GDP growth) in determining the private saving rate.

Government Capital Spending

Ricardian equivalence may also suggest that public investment, to the extent that it is viewed as productive, will not be expected to require future taxes, and hence should generate a smaller private saving response than a government deficit. Table 5.5 confirms: when the fiscal deficit rises as a result of higher government investment rather than of lower taxes, the offset on private saving is only half as large.

Social Security

The life-cycle hypothesis implies a negative relationship between the extent and coverage of public pensions and the amount of private savings by the active population. The coefficient in Table 5.5 is indeed negative, but quite low. To raise the private saving rate by one percentage point would require an 8 per cent drop in the ratio of public welfare spending to total public expenditures.

Age Dependency Ratio

A central implication of the life cycle hypothesis is that a country with a high dependency ratio – a large number of inactive young and old people relative to the (saving) active working population – will show a lower private saving rate. The extensive literature attempting to link a country's age profile and its saving performance, however, has not always been conclusive.

The results given in Table 5.5 support the view that demographics matter for developing-country savings. A falling dependency of the young and old non-earners on the working-age population will significantly raise private savings; just by how much is not easy to determine, since cross-country estimates produce much lower coefficients than the time series regression. Note that separate estimates for the elderly versus youth dependency ratios did not produce significantly different results; the overall dependency ratio should thus serve as a reliable parameter for out-of-sample simulations.

Urban Concentration

The precautionary motive for savings may be particularly important for poor countries since a volatile income will at times mean a painfully low level of consumption. Saving rates can thus be expected to be higher in countries where income is more volatile in order to smooth consumption levels; this applies often to countries with a high share of agriculture and a low degree of urban concentration. As seen in Table 5.5, Edwards (1995) identifies a significant negative relationship between the proportion of urban-to-total population and a country's private saving rate.

Money/GDP

The McKinnon–Shaw hypothesis of financial repression in developing countries holds that negative real deposit rates, high reserve requirements and public credit allocation would depress financial and private savings (and the productivity of investment). The ratio of M_2 to GDP is generally taken as a

proxy for the depth and sophistication of the financial system, with the hypothesis that a higher degree of financial intermediation will stimulate private savings. However, that ratio can also be seen as a proxy for the borrowing constraint; a binding borrowing constraint makes it difficult to advance consumption and thus may raise private savings. While Masson *et al.* (1995) find that the money/GDP variable is insignificant, Edwards' (1995) result does confirm the McKinnon–Shaw hypothesis.

Real Interest Rate

Another implication of the McKinnon–Shaw hypothesis, namely that allowing real interest rates to rise to market levels would encourage aggregate savings, has generally not been confirmed. Higher interest rates entail a positive inter-temporal substitution effect, emphasized by McKinnon and Shaw, and a negative income effect on private saving. The income effect is enhanced by defined-benefit pension schemes that translate higher interest returns into higher income available for pensions and hence allow lower contributions, i.e. savings.[3] As seen in Table 5.5, the real interest rate is never a significant determinant of private savings in these studies, in line with both earlier empirical analyses and with the ambiguous theoretical hypotheses.

Current Account Surplus

In open economies, foreign borrowing can be used to smooth consumption through time. Foreign savings will thus substitute for domestic savings. This is also in line with the Harberger–Laursen–Metzler effect which postulates a positive relationship between a country's terms of trade, its saving rate and its trade balance. The hypothesis is confirmed by both studies reviewed in Table 5.5: foreign savings offset private domestic savings by about one-half.

It is important to note that the results discussed above seem to be quite robust across regions. (It is often speculated that Asia has a higher inclination to save than other regions in the developing world, in spite of the fact that Asia's saving rates were still quite low in the 1950s and 1960s.) Edwards (1995) finds that the coefficients of the policy variables and of growth are not significantly different across regions. While the same equation can thus describe private savings across regions, the values of the significant saving determinants differ. This means that the results presented in Table 5.5 can usefully serve for some out-of-sample forecasts to inform the debate on future global capital shortages. It should be borne in mind, however, that institutional measures that have succeeded in raising private savings – such as the introduction of pension reform or the encouragement of postal savings –

are generally unreported in cross-country empirical work because of the unavailability of appropriate indicators.

PROSPECTIVE CHANGES IN DEVELOPING-COUNTRY SAVINGS

One message to emerge clearly from this somewhat speculative section is that if rapid developing-country growth is what feeds concerns about a future global capital shortage, then these concerns are most likely to be misplaced. Rapid growth in poor countries will boost their domestic savings, through improved government budgets, higher private savings and a positive income-level effect. Moreover, a declining dependency ratio should add to future developing-country savings. Other saving determinants, such as the degree of financial intermediation or political instability, might lower or raise developing-country savings, but are difficult to predict and probably less important on a global scale.

Table 5.6   Growth of real per capita GDP, average per annum

	1974–94	1995–2004
Asia	4.5	5.6
China	7.4	–
India	2.4	–
Latin America	0.7	1.9
Africa & Middle East	−1.9	0.6
Sub-Saharan Africa	−0.9	0.9
Developing countries including the former Soviet Union and other ex-communist countries	1.1	3.3
Developed countries	2.0	2.4

Source: World Bank, *Global Economic Prospects and the Developing Countries*, 1995; own calculations.

Growth of real per capita GDP in the developing world might materialize at lower values than those predicted in Table 5.6; however, that downside possibility should not cause concern here, because low developing-country growth would remove the major cause of a developing-country-driven capital shortage. In any case, the World Bank estimates presented in Table 5.6 are anything but rosy. Only Asia's per capita growth is predicted to exceed the 2.4 projected for high-income (mostly OECD) countries over the next decade. Due to the large and growing weight (on a PPP-adjusted GDP basis) of the Asian region, developing-country growth per capita is expected to outpace industrial-country growth, with an average of 3.3 per cent per year. Ignoring population growth, the World Bank forecasts the developing world to grow by an annual 4.9 per cent, versus 2.8 per cent for the high-income countries.

Table 5.7   Catching up to the United States

	1993 real per capita GDP, US $		PPP estimates of GNP per capita (US = 100)	
	at current prices and exchange rates	PPP-adjusted	1993	2015[a]
United States	24 740	24 740	100.0	100.0
China	490	2 330	9.4	24.3
India	300	1 220	4.9	6.6
Indonesia	740	3 150	12.7	32.8
Brazil	2 930	5 370	21.7	19.8
Nigeria	300	1 400	5.7	4.1
Developing countries	–	2 598	10.5	12.9

Notes:
a. The projection is based on the sub-regional GDP per capita growth projections for 1995–2004 given in *Global Economic Prospects*; the average annual percentages are: United States = 2.3, China and Indonesia = 6.6, India = 3.6, Brazil = 1.9 and Nigeria = 0.9.

Sources: World Bank, *World Development Report 1995*; World Bank, *Global Economic Prospects 1995*; IMF, *World Economic Outlook*, May 1995; own calculations.

If it is assumed that the World Bank projections on growth hold for the next 20 years (instead of only 10), how might the developing countries then

catch up to the per capita income level of the United States? Table 5.7 offers some illustrations. Applying the respective sub-regional growth projections (for want of country-specific projections) to the very big emerging economies, China and Indonesia make considerable progress, up to a level now reached by Thailand, Malaysia or Mexico. India, by contrast, moves up only a little, while Brazil and Nigeria fall back relative to US per capita income.

PPP estimates are country-specific (because they are based on country-specific price relationships), so it is tricky to calculate the projected catch-up for the whole developing world. According to the IMF (1995), the developing-country share of total world GDP was 40.1 per cent in 1994, based on PPP valuation of country GDPs; the respective share of the United States was 21.2 per cent. Dividing the GDP shares through the respective population numbers – 4.69 billion in the developing world vs 256 million in the United States – showed that the average developing-country income per head was at 10.5 per cent of the respective US level in 1993. By the year 2015, assuming the projected per capita GDP growth of 2.3 per cent per year in the United States and 3.3 per cent in the developing world, the latter will have caught up on US levels by 2.4 percentage points, up to 12.9 per cent.

Table 5.8 displays projections for another important saving determinant, the age dependency ratio. Up to the year 2015, the proportion of the young and old to the working-age population will significantly decline in the developing countries. With falling fertility rates, the poor countries will have to feed a relatively lower number of persons aged under fifteen. By contrast, the dependency ratio of the rich countries is expected to rise due to its increasingly greying populations, in particular after the year 2015. Rising prosperity in Asia will mean a higher life expectancy. After 2015, the dependency ratio in Asia, in particular in China, will thus significantly rise again, due to higher old-age dependency. India, by contrast – predicted to be the world's most populous country some 40 years from now – will see its dependency ratio largely unchanged between 2015 and 2035, paralleling the average for the developing world.

Another significant determinant for both government and private savings has been the current account balance as a percentage of GDP. Higher growth rates in the years ahead would enable developing countries to operate under looser current account constraints, without fuelling debt/GDP ratios. The World Bank prediction that real GDP growth in the developing countries will be 4.9 per cent per year rather than the 3 per cent experienced over the period 1974–94 should imply that developing countries can raise their *sustainable current account deficit* (with effective interest rates unchanged) by 1.9 percentage points of GDP. (The growth prediction, however, does not

imply that the poor countries will in practice raise their current account deficits.)

Table 5.8   Projected dependency ratios

	1995	2015	2035	Population projection for 2015 (billions)
Africa	89.6	73.8	55.7	1.18
Asia	59.9	48.6	52.3	4.43
China	48.4	41.4	57.3	1.39
India	66.5	49.2	49.2	1.24
Latin America	63.4	47.9	51.1	0.62
Developing countries	64.8	52.6	52.7	6.01
< 15 years	56.9	43.4	36.8	
> 65 years	7.9	9.2	15.9	
Developed countries	50.8	53.4	67.6	1.34
< 15 years	31.1	27.7	29.7	
> 65 years	19.7	25.7	37.9	

Source: World Bank, *World Population Projections 1994–95*.

Table 5.9 selects the significant coefficients of the (vaguely) predictable saving parameters. The government saving function is based on Edwards (1995). By his estimates, a country's GDP growth and its current account surplus/GDP determine the saving rate with a coefficient of 1.80 and 0.82, respectively.[4]

The private saving function is based on Masson *et al.* (1995), since in the 1980s – their time reference – saving estimates were produced with a greater reliability than in the 1970s. Importantly also, the GDP growth estimate is more in line with prior empirical evidence than Edwards' results. A sustained rise in the real GDP growth rate of one percentage point will raise the private saving rate by 1.73 percentage points. Growth will have a further impact on private savings through the income-level effect: catching up to the US level of income per capita (=100) by one percentage point will boost the private saving rate by 0.72 percentage points. A fall in the age dependency ratio – the

proportion of young and old persons to the working-age population – will also stimulate private savings. A fall of 20 percentage points will translate into a 1 per cent gain of the private saving rate.[5] A rise of the sustainable current account deficit in the order of 1 per cent of GDP will lower the private saving rate by 0.63 percentage points. Finally, any improvement in government savings will offset the private saving effort by 61 per cent.

Table 5.9   Preferred saving coefficients, from cross-country estimates (t-statistics in parentheses)

	Government saving	Private saving
Real GDP growth[a]	1.8 (3.3)	1.73 (3.1)
GDP per capita, PPP-adjusted	not significant	0.72 (2.1)
Age dependency ratio	not significant	−0.05 (−1.0)
Current account/GDP	0.82 (2.5)	0.63 (2.8)
Government saving	–	−0.61 (−2.0)

Note:
a. per capita for the growth determinant of government savings.

Sources: Edwards (1995) for government saving; Masson *et al.* (1995) for private saving.

To develop a scenario for the prospective changes in developing-country savings 20 years from now, Table 5.10 multiplies the preferred saving coefficients by the predicted changes in the significant saving variables as discussed in this section. Government savings are predicted to rise by 1.1 per cent of GDP, as a result of higher growth which is partly counteracted by a higher sustainable current account deficit. Private savings will rise by 2.8 per cent, positively stimulated by higher growth, a positive income-level effect and a falling dependency ratio, and negatively affected by a higher sustainable

current account deficit as well as some Ricardian offset of higher government savings. The total change of the developing-country national saving rate is expected to be nearly four percentage points of their GDP. Given that developing countries represent 40 per cent of world GDP on a PPP basis now (and 50 per cent by the year 2015), the prospective increase in developing-country savings should roughly offset a saving decline of 3 per cent of GDP in the industrial countries.

Table 5.10   Prospective changes in developing-country savings by the year 2015 (in percentage of GDP)

Determinant	Predicted change of determinant	Government saving	Private saving	National saving
GDP growth	From 3% p.a. in 1974–94 to 4.9% p.a. over 1995–2015	3.9	3.3	7.2
Per capita GDP relative to US (=100)	From 10.5% in 1993 to 12.9% in 2015	–	1.7	1.7
Age dependency ratio	From 64.8% in 1995 to 52.6% in 2015	–	0.6	0.6
Sustainable current account/GDP	From a 1.5% deficit in the 1980s to a 3.4% deficit over 1995–2015	–2.8	–2.1	–4.9
Government savings	–	–	–0.7	–0.7
Total change	–	1.1	2.8	3.9

Source: Own calculation, see Table 5.9 and text.

THE LIMITS OF INTERNATIONAL CAPITAL MOBILITY

No matter how large the future developing-country savings, the supply may still fall short of domestic investment demand in what had been called the 'Third World'. In terms of a future global capital shortage, what matters is not just the quantity of savings, but also its ability to move across borders. Some observers misinterpret the tremendous rise in international securities transactions and in global foreign exchange trading since the 1980s as an indicator that international capital mobility has become virtually unlimited.

But the integration of wholesale markets of highly liquid and largely default-free financial assets should not be confounded with the integration of asset markets for the broader categories of world saving and wealth (IMF, 1995), which is limited. The Feldstein–Horioka finding of a close association between national saving and national investment, implying a small volume of sustained net international capital flows, has remained a robust empirical regularity.

The limited ability of savings to move across borders is reflected in the 'home bias' of investment portfolios and in the limited positions of net foreign liabilities in domestic markets. Available data on international portfolio positions suggest that the OECD countries are not diversified nearly to the extent that the modern portfolio theory predicts for investors who want to maximize risk-adjusted returns (on the subject of OECD pension funds see, for example, Fischer and Reisen, 1995). This non-diversification puzzle is not yet convincingly explained; the reasons often put forward include prudential limits on foreign assets, exchange rate-induced deviations from purchasing power parity, internationally asymmetric information, tax laws, and default risk.

During the 1990s, however, OECD institutional investors have started to diversify globally their portfolios, a diversification that includes a larger presence on the emerging stock and bond markets. Should this recent trend continue, and should investors in the OECD area target a neutral weighting (along country shares in world stock market capitalization), the result will almost certainly be a transitional period of high (gross, not necessarily net) capital flows to the emerging markets. Fischer and Reisen (1995) have recently estimated that such diversification of OECD pension assets could mean a flow of $40 billion annually to the emerging markets.

Since sovereign claims are basically unenforceable, however, foreign investors do not tolerate a rising foreign debt/GDP ratio for too long. Unfortunately, only very rough rules of thumb are available to set a prudent limit on the size of capital flows that can be sustained (Reisen, 1995). While in 1994 many observers began to realize that Mexico's current account deficit was reaching a level that would be unsustainable (8 per cent of GDP), there was no theory behind such observation. In practice, the inter-temporal budget constraint does not help, because many poor countries have been allowed to run deficits for an almost unlimited period. Some capital flows, such as foreign direct investment inflows, are less vulnerable to withdrawal and are not debt-creating – but they cannot be fully ignored either, since they also generate a need for foreign exchange earnings to service remittances. Therefore, when asked to assess prudent limits for current account deficits, economists tend to fall back on a debt-dynamics equation:

$$d_t = d_{t-1} \, (i^* - n) + c_t \qquad (5.1)$$

where the debt/GDP ratio rises when the interest rate on existing debt, i^*, exceeds GDP growth, n, or by the amount of the current account deficit as a fraction of GDP, c_t. The relevant interest rate here is the effective rate, which is the weighted average across all kinds of debt, creditors and currency denominations. Equity-related inflows can be incorporated in principle, by giving them lower weight in the effective interest rate.

A prudent limit for sustainable current account deficits can then be derived. It is obvious that the size of the sustainable deficit depends very much on the effective interest rate and on the country's growth rate. With more concessional flows or equity-related inflows, a bigger deficit ratio can be sustained; the same holds for a high-growth country. An often-quoted rule of thumb for the external debt/GDP ratio is that it should not exceed 40 per cent. Once the country has reached that level, the current account as a fraction of GDP should prudently not (at least for long) exceed the difference between its growth rate and the effective interest rate if the debt/GDP ratio is to be stabilized, so that

$$c_t = n - I^* \qquad (5.2)$$

Since the effective interest rate on external debt for market borrowers, corrected for US inflation, fluctuates around 3.5 per cent per annum, GDP growth rates above that level determine the sustainable current account deficit/GDP. For the developing world as a whole, this would imply that, with projected GDP growth of nearly 5 per cent, a combined deficit on the current account of 1.5 per cent of GDP would be sustainable. To the extent that capital flows are not debt-creating, the combined sustainable deficit could be double that level, i.e. 3 per cent of GDP. High-growth countries such as Thailand (unlike Mexico) may sustain a current account deficit that is correspondingly higher. The mega-countries – such as China – may, by contrast, never have that option: a high current account deficit would in their case rapidly skew the country diversification of investors' assets and probably induce an earlier rationing of capital flows than for relatively small countries.

CONCLUSIONS

This paper has evaluated fears about a developing-country-driven future capital shortage. It has argued that such an evaluation should not be based on speculation about the capital needs of the developing world, but rather should focus on future developing-country savings and on the ability of savings to

move across borders. The evidence which the paper collects on saving determinants, on the likely changes of these determinants through to the year 2015 and on the limits to sustained net cross-border capital flows support an optimistic assessment. Most fears about a developing-country-driven capital shortage originate in the superior growth performance of those countries and (to a lesser extent) their increased financial openness. This paper rejects these fears by pointing to the various channels and magnitudes by which higher growth will raise developing-country savings; moreover, the widespread dismantling of capital controls in the OECD area and elsewhere has not resulted in a markedly looser association of national savings and national investment over longer periods.

Any positive assessment, however, bears a downside risk. The biggest risk in this context is that the growth–savings nexus is not as solid as implied by recent econometric evidence, or that it will break down in the future. For example, it is perfectly envisageable that the importance of investment-motivated saving in high-growth countries such as China will decline because a deepened domestic capital market will relieve borrowing constraints for investment and consumption purposes. Another risk is that the income elasticity of savings will decline once the fast-growing countries have reached a certain level of per capita income. The world's two very big countries, China and India, will need close scrutiny because a rise in, say, political instability or divorce rates will inevitably translate into lower national savings than predicted by econometric cross-country evidence of past saving behaviour. With ongoing growth and high investment demand in these two countries, the result could be an important drain on world savings. Unlike Indonesia, Brazil and many other big emerging economies, neither China nor India have yet reached a considerable foreign debt/GDP ratio of 40 per cent; consequently, the steady-state assumptions underlying the size of the sustainable deficit on current account may well not apply to these countries in the foreseeable future. Finally, the theoretical complexity of the saving process (certainly not emphasized in this paper), the poor quality of savings statistics, and the host of simultaneity and causality problems connected with saving determination should all serve to warn against arriving at any firm conclusions. But when all is said and done, the answer to the conference question, from the developing-country perspective, would be 'Future Global Capital Shortages: Fiction, rather than Fact'.

NOTES

1.   In fact, it is domestically financed capital accumulation – not productivity – that mostly explains (East) Asia's superior growth performance over that period (Young, 1994).

2. Both studies estimate private savings equations using instrumental variables on panel data to deal with simultaneity and causality problems.
3. Ogaki *et al.* (1995) have recently found that the interest elasticity of private savings rises with the transition from low-income to middle-income levels once subsistence plays a smaller role in the expenditure patterns of most households. That result is confirmed neither by Edwards (1995) nor by Masson *et al.* (1995) – even when breaking the data set down into different income groups (not reported in Table 5.5).
4. It should be noted, however, that his sample for the government saving function included both industrialized and developing countries; isolated estimates for the latter group are not available. Another significant determinant of government savings, the frequency of government changes, is impossible to predict.
5. Importantly, however, the confidence level of the respective coefficient could only be estimated at around 85 per cent (a *t*-value of 1.0 with 35 degrees of freedom).

REFERENCES

Carroll, C. and D. Weil (1993), 'Savings and Growth: A Reinterpretation', *NBER Working Paper*, No. 4470.

Chenery, H. and M. Bruno (1962), 'Development Alternatives in an Open Economy: The Case of Israel', *Economic Journal*, 57, pp. 79–103.

Coakley, J., F. Kulasi and R. Smith (1995), 'The Feldstein–Horioka Puzzle and Capital Mobility', *Birkbeck College Discussion Papers in Economics*, 6/95.

Dooley, M., J. Frankel and D. Mathieson (1987), 'International Capital Mobility: What Do Saving–Investment Correlations Tell Us?', *IMF Staff Papers*, 34, pp. 503–529.

Edwards, S. (1995), 'Why Are Saving Rates So Different Across Countries?: An International Comparative Analysis', *NBER Working Paper*, No. 5097.

Feldstein, M. and C. Horioka (1980), 'Domestic Saving and International Investment', *Economic Journal*, 90, pp. 314–329.

Fischer, B. and H. Reisen (1995), *Pension Fund Investment: From Ageing to Emerging Markets*, Policy Brief No. 9, OECD Development Centre, Paris.

Krugman, P. (1993), 'International Finance and Economic Development', in A. Giovannini (ed.), *Finance and Development*, Cambridge University Press, pp. 11–30.

Krugman, P. (1994), 'Does Third World Growth Hurt First World Prosperity?', *Harvard Business Review*, July–August, pp. 113–121.

Liu, L. and W.T. Woo (1994), 'Saving Behaviour under Imperfect Financial Markets and the Current Account Consequences', *Economic Journal*, 104, pp. 512–527.

International Monetary Fund (1995), *World Economic Outlook*, May.

Mankiw, N.G., D. Romer, and D. Weil (1994), 'A Contribution to the Empirics of Economic Growth', *Quarterly Journal of Economics*, 107, pp. 407–437.

Masson, P.R., T. Bayoumi and H. Samiei (1995), 'International Evidence on the Determinants of Private Savings', *IMF Working Paper*, 95/91.

Ogaki, M., J.D. Ostry and C.M. Reinhart (1995), 'Saving Behaviour in Low- and Middle-Income Countries: A Comparison', *IMF Working Paper*, 95/3.

Reisen, H. (1995), 'Managing Temporary Capital Inflows: Lessons from Asia and Latin America', *Pakistan Economic Review*.

Woodall, P. (1994), 'War of the Worlds (A Survey of the Global Economy)', *The Economist*, 1 October.

World Bank (1995), *Global Economic Prospects*.

Young, A. (1994), 'The Tyranny of Numbers: Confronting the Statistical Evidence of the East Asian Growth Experience', *NBER Working Paper*, No. 4680.

6. Promoting Savings in Latin America: Some Insights[*]

The Seventh International Forum on Latin American Perspectives not only debated whether to promote savings in Latin America, it also succeeded in designing savings-enhancing policies. Very much as an investor – who cannot predict the rate of return on a specific asset – diversifies his investments, the policy-maker who observes the lack of consensus among economists about the growth–savings nexus, who knows that eastern Asia did not wait for growth to stimulate savings but that it actively promoted it, or who simply wants to sustain high growth through high investment rates but shies away from the risks implied by foreign savings to finance investment, will want to diversify his policy instruments by targeting higher growth and higher savings simultaneously. East Asia did not experience a temporary drop in savings as a result of structural reform: consequently, a trade-off between targeting savings and targeting growth did not materialize there.

PRICE STABILIZATION

It is often held that Latin America's record of high inflation explains the region's low level of savings (and investment), because wealth risks being confiscated in a bout of unexpectedly high inflation. However, while substantial progress has been made in Latin America in bringing inflation down, the process of price stabilization has depressed savings even further unless it was money-based. Exchange rate-based stabilization plans have often been accompanied by a boom in bank lending, which in turn has fuelled a boom in consumption spending. Unlike under money-based stabilization, disinflation produces a rise in real-money balances, as a result of central bank intervention to peg the currency and of higher money demand after disinflation sets in. The unsterilized intervention on the foreign exchange market is fully intermediated into the banking system.

[*] Originally published in R. Hausmann and H. Reisen (eds), *Promoting Savings in Latin America*, Inter-American Development Bank and OECD Development Centre, Paris, 1997, pp. 273–276.

This allows a boom in credit to agents who have been rationed previously as a result of inflation and financial regression. Inflation inertia leads to an overvalued exchange rate which further depresses savings as residents intertemporally substitute present for future consumption.

Monetary policy in Latin America can thus promote savings by opting for money-based rather than exchange rate-based stabilization, which implies a higher degree of nominal exchange rate flexibility than has been observed in many countries of the region. However, a restrictive monetary policy under floating exchange rates does not only imply the control of domestic monetary aggregates, but it also operates through an exchange rate appreciation. The problem of monetary policy in Latin America is thus the optimal rate of inflation and the optimal speed of disinflation towards such rate. Under almost unrestricted capital mobility, a savings-enhancing policy is wise not to be overambitious and single-minded with inflation targets in the low-level single-digit rate.

FINANCIAL-SECTOR REFORM

In the past, Latin American financial systems could be characterized as bank-dominated, low-confidence systems with high corporate-to-household liquidity ratios and low savings rates. Recent reform, however, has increased confidence in the domestic financial system which has been reflected in a large rise of financial savings placed in Latin America. Notwithstanding earlier theories that predicted a positive savings response to deregulated (typically higher) interest rates and financial deepening, financial reform in Latin America has, as in many OECD countries, resulted in a drop of private savings rates.

We have learned, meanwhile, that savings-enhancing financial reform has to avoid the uprise of excessive risk-taking in the banking system, to slow the removal of liquidity constraints and to reduce the transaction costs for low-income savers to access profitable savings instruments. The pace of financial reform should therefore not exceed a country's capacity to build appropriate institutions that monitor and supervise credit risk within a newly established framework of prudential regulation. Comprehensive monitoring of consumer lending, tight credit lines for mortgage lending, the credible removal of bank deposit insurance and the enforcement of bankruptcy claims against ailing debtors should help avoid any substantial expansion in consumption, mortgage and high-risk corporate lending. In order to tilt the balance of financial reform further towards raising the national savings rate, a dense network of accessible financial institutions, such as the postal savings banks common to many East Asian countries or public savings

institutions as in Continental Europe should be seriously considered. Such institutions will help to raise the confidence of low-income savers that they can expect reliable and decent returns for thrift.

While pension reform (from pay-as-you-go to fully-funded schemes) is justified on many grounds other than savings, some governments aim to raise their country's savings rate with such reform. However, the hope for pension reform to enhance savings is at times based on a misreading of Chile's experience where the reform per se did not contribute much to the impressive rise of the country's savings rate; the transition from an unfunded to a funded system of old-age security was more tax-financed than seems possible in the rest of Latin America, and it was the growth- and incentive-induced rise in corporate savings that explains most of Chile's higher savings. Moreover, cross-country evidence does suggest that the importance of funded pension assets (as a fraction of GDP) and a country's savings rate is not significantly different from zero. Several explanations can be advanced for the lack of pension reform to stimulate savings: high returns on pension assets require a lower rate of savings for achieving a targeted pension level (inducing early retirement); the rise of pension assets stimulates the supply of loanable funds, facilitating household access to consumer and mortgage lending credits; funded pensions, implying greater credibility of future pension benefits than in unfunded systems, reduce the need for precautionary savings. Consequently, for pension reform to result in high savings it must be heavily tax financed, mandatory with high contribution rates, and be accompanied by liquidity constraints in the rest of the financial sector. Singapore and Switzerland, where these requirements have been met, have indeed combined a high importance of pension assets with a high national savings rate in contrast to most Anglo-Saxon countries.

PUBLIC SAVINGS

While public savings have increased significantly in most of Latin America, the corresponding decline in private savings has denied many countries in the region a rise in total domestic savings. Most estimates of the Ricardian offset coefficient put it at 50 per cent for Latin America, meaning that private savings tend to decline by 50 cents for every dollar by which public savings increase. An important finding, however, is that the average Ricardian offset coefficient conceals two very different saving responses to fiscal policy for normal times, and for crisis periods, respectively. Unlike in OECD countries, fiscal policy behaves very procyclically in Latin America, largely due to financial distress during crisis periods. This implies a

Ricardian offset coefficient much higher than average during bad times, and much lower during good times.

In the absence of any crisis, raising national savings by one percentage point would require an increase in fiscal surplus of a full five percentage points. Raising tax rates further to achieve a national savings target would intensify economic distortions, possibly up to a point where it would be counterproductive even from the perspective of raising the domestic savings rate.

The appropriate way out is to strengthen budgetary institutions in order to increase the public sector's creditworthiness by making better use of surpluses in good times and reassuring investors in bad times. This must be complemented by effective bank regulation and supervision, for any major bank crisis will usually involve extremely high fiscal spending on bank crisis resolution. This strategy does not exclude the need to raise public savings in good times, if the destabilizing mix of procyclical fiscal policies and low offset coefficients is to be avoided during recessions. The way to do it, more in Latin America than anywhere else, is not to raise taxes, but to combine lower taxes with a strict enforcement of tax base broadening. The removal of tax exemptions and tax holidays is certain to meet opposition from forceful interest groups, but the economic reward of ignoring such opposition will be very high.

TAX INCENTIVES

A government seeking to encourage savings can in principle choose between global tax incentives and targeted incentives. In practice, a comprehensive income tax treatment or an expenditure tax treatment will be difficult to implement in Latin America because of shortcomings in income accounting and tax administration. Moreover, the comprehensive income tax – very much like flat rate taxes on investment income – raises the problem of taxing unrealized capital gains. The expenditure tax – like the tax-free savings account – is regressive. On the other hand, a flat rate tax on investment income allows capital taxes to be levied at source through withholding, which combats tax evasion – notorious in Latin America and increasingly facilitated by the globalization of international capital flows. Source-based income taxation should be coupled with residence-based consumption taxes, in order to minimize overall tax distortions and to make the tax system less vulnerable to administrative problems. In order to avoid incentives to employ transfer prices and other financial constructions by multinational corporations, some co-ordination between Latin American countries is needed in selecting the best mix between source- and residence-

based taxation. Likewise, co-ordination with the OECD countries is needed in this area.

Targeted incentives on specific savings instruments, such as for vehicles of retirement savings, will not have a great impact on Latin America's savings rates. Such incentives do have an important impact on household portfolio composition and they do change the real return on savings. However, the induced change in the asset mix does not raise the overall level of savings, nor will a rise in the real rate of return to savings achieve higher savings as negative income effects outweigh positive substitution effects. This at least is what OECD evidence suggests.

7. Do Funded Pensions Contribute to Higher Aggregate Savings? A Cross-country Analysis[*]

INTRODUCTION

Although quite diverse in scope and nature, pension reforms world-wide share a common aim in that the majority of them strive to move towards a system that would rely more heavily on funded pensions.[1] An important motivation underlying this policy objective is the notion that the accumulation of pension assets contributes to stimulating aggregate savings. In industrialized countries, the recognition that population ageing requires increased savings for retirement is the main factor driving policy-makers to promote higher saving rates. In emerging markets, on the other hand, the desire to raise savings is motivated by the belief that higher levels of domestic savings are necessary in order to finance higher levels of investment, which – together with the externalities on productivity that they entail – are thought to be central to the growth process.[2]

Empirical support for the premise that an increase in funded pensions would positively impact savings is largely based on the results of household-level studies that have been conducted for a few industrialized countries.[3] Although informative in assessing how a household's savings will be affected by an increase in its pension wealth, this body of empirical work can not directly address the issue of how *aggregate savings* will behave in response to a national build-up of pension assets. A few studies – based on the experiences of Chile, Malaysia and Singapore – have examined this question from an aggregate perspective but have failed to produce conclusive evidence.[4]

In addition to yielding mixed outcomes, these aggregate-level studies also suffer from an important shortcoming in that their econometric analysis is based on a relatively small number of degrees of freedom. Indeed, the time series employed are relatively short because annual figures related to

[*] Originally published as OECD Development Centre Technical Paper No. 130, December 1997 and in *Weltwirtschaftliches Archiv*, Vol. 134.4, 1998, pp. 692–711.

funded pensions are, in general, not available for a very long time period. One way to overcome this problem would be to pool data across a group of countries. To the best of our knowledge, no existing study has empirically investigated the role of funded pension wealth in the determination of aggregate savings in a cross-country context.

The purpose of our paper is to test the hypothesis that increases in funded pension wealth contribute to higher aggregate savings by employing a panel data set of ten countries (both industrialized and emerging-market) over the 1982–1993 period. In doing so, we are able to draw on a variety of country experiences and hence to utilize a richer set of information in estimating the impact of increases in funded pension wealth on aggregate savings than would be available with any individual country. We develop a proxy for changes in funded pension wealth for this sample of countries based on pension fund asset data. Using this constructed measure and controlling for other determinants of savings, we estimate the relationship between aggregate saving rates and changes in funded pension wealth. Our results suggest that the build-up of pension assets does indeed exert a positive and statistically significant effect on aggregate saving rates, and that this impact differs for OECD and non-OECD countries.

FUNDED PENSIONS AND SAVINGS: THEORETICAL BACKGROUND

In this section, we review the theoretical foundations underlying the premise that an accumulation of pension assets by households leads to an increase in aggregate savings. We first examine the relationship between funded pensions and savings in the context of a simple overlapping generations (OLG) model and then we discuss some important issues that are not addressed in this simplistic framework.

The OLG model, based on the seminal papers of Samuelson (1958) and Diamond (1965), is the basic framework employed for analysing the macroeconomic effects of pensions.[5] Saving behaviour in this model is consistent with the life-cycle hypothesis – i.e. individuals save during their working lives to finance their consumption during retirement.[6] It is assumed that it is this life-cycle saving by households that generates the capital stock and therefore that changes in household savings translate into changes in aggregate savings. The analysis thus abstracts away from corporate and government savings.

We present a simple two-period, two-generation version of the Diamond– Samuelson OLG model, similar to that used in Blanchard and Fischer (1989), and then show how the establishment of a fully-funded pension scheme

affects aggregate savings. The economy consists of two overlapping generations of identical individuals. Each generation lives for two periods, works only in the first period and then retires in the second period. The capital stock is owned by the older generation which, together with the labour supplied by the young, is used to produce output in the economy. Thus, the savings of the younger generation in the first period are transformed into the capital stock when they retire in the second period.

In this set-up, an individual born at time t maximizes the following utility function:

$$u(c_{1t}) + (1+\theta)^{-1} u(c_{2t+1}) \tag{7.1}$$

subject to:

$$c_{1t} + s_t = w_t \tag{7.2}$$

$$c_{2t+1} = (1+r_{t+1})s_t \tag{7.3}$$

$$c_{1t}, c_{2t+1} \geq 0 \tag{7.4}$$

where c_{1t} is consumption while young, c_{2t+1} is consumption while old, w_t is the wage received in period t and r_{t+1} is the interest rate paid on savings held from period t to period $(t+1)$. In period one, the individual works and must decide how much of his/her wage to allocate to current consumption and how much to save for future consumption. In period two, the individual retires, consumes all his/her wealth (both interest and capital) and dies at the end of the period. The individual's inter-temporal consumption (and thus saving) behaviour is thus guided by the following first-order condition:

$$u'(c_{1t}) - (1+r_{t+1})(1+\theta)^{-1} u'(c_{2t+1}) = 0. \tag{7.5}$$

By making the appropriate substitutions for the consumption levels in the two periods, the following implicit savings function can be obtained from the first-order condition:

$$s_t = s(w_t, r_{t+1}) \tag{7.6}$$

where it is assumed that the impact of an increase in the wage on savings is positive whereas the impact of an increase in the interest rate on savings is ambiguous, depending on the relative magnitudes of the substitution and

income effects. Assuming that the population grows at rate n (so that $N_t = N_0(1+n)^t$) then aggregate savings at time t (S_t) can be obtained as follows:[7]

$$S_t = N_t s(w_t, r_{t+1}) \qquad (7.7)$$

Assuming that our representative economy is characterized by imperfect capital mobility then the capital stock at time $t+1$ (K_{t+1}) is the sum of aggregate domestic savings at time t and any net foreign assets (NFA_t):

$$K_{t+1} = N_t \, s(w_t(K_t), r_{t+1}(K_{t+1})) + NFA_t \qquad (7.8)$$

It should be noted that in the case of a semi-closed economy such as this one, the wage rate and the real interest rate are endogenously determined.

Let us now introduce a fully-funded pension system into the model. In this type of pension plan, each generation finances its own pensions. This is in contrast to a pay-as-you-go (PAYG) pension scheme where the pension benefits of the older generation are financed by taxing the younger generation. Let us assume that each individual is forced to save s^F_t in pension contributions while young and receives $(1+r_{t+1}) \, s^F_t$ in the form of a pension while old. Household savings will now have two components:

$$s_t = s^F_t + s^V_t \qquad (7.9)$$

where s^F_t are forced savings through the pension plan and s^V_t are voluntary savings.

Interestingly, instituting a fully-funded pension system into this simple framework will have no effect on aggregate savings. This is because households will simply reduce their voluntary savings (s^V_t) by the same amount as the increase in their pension contributions (s^F_t), leaving total household savings (s_t) unchanged. Even if households were forced to save more for retirement through their funded pension plan than they would have voluntarily, they could still offset this 'excessive' amount of savings by borrowing at the market rate of interest. In the latter case, s^V_t would be negative and would represent the amount that the typical household borrows in the first period to achieve its optimal level of consumption while young and then repays (with interest) in the second period.

This benchmark result can be modified by introducing a borrowing constraint into this framework. This can done by introducing the following equation:

$$s^V_t \geq -b \qquad (7.10)$$

which establishes that borrowing while young cannot exceed a certain level b. Depending on the circumstances of the individual, this constraint may or may not be binding. Assuming that our typical household born at time t is forced to save more through its pension plan than it would voluntarily *and* that the borrowing constraint in (7.10) is binding then the establishment of a funded pension scheme (or an increase in pension contributions), *ceteris paribus*, would increase household savings.

A borrowing constraint such as (7.10) can easily be justified in this type of model if we assume that collateral is required to borrow and that the pension benefits paid out to workers when they retire in the second period cannot be used as collateral for a loan in the first period. This kind of assumption seems reasonable in light of the fact that anticipated pension benefits are not, in general, accepted as collateral for loans.

In the framework we presented above, individuals are all identical. Thus to generate a positive link between aggregate savings and funded pensions, we must assume that all individuals in the economy are compelled to accumulate more than their desired level of assets through mandatory pension plans (and that they are limited in their ability to offset any excess savings by borrowing). In reality, however, economies are made up of heterogeneous agents who have different propensities to save and face varying levels of borrowing constraints. As pointed out by Munnell (1987), lower-paid workers are more likely to be forced to save more with a pension plan than they would voluntarily because they tend to have a lower propensity to save than their higher-paid counterparts and are also more likely to face binding borrowing constraints. Therefore, at the aggregate level, an increase in the level of funded pension contributions could lead to an increase in savings if even only a fraction of households in the economy are being forced to save at a higher rate.

In addition to the question of heterogeneous agents, there are several other issues that are not addressed in the simple OLG framework presented above that might influence the impact of an increase in funded pension contributions on aggregate savings. For instance, the net rate of return on pension and non-pension savings might not be the same. Indeed, pension contributions are often granted preferential tax treatment thus enabling them to earn a higher net rate of return relative to other saving instruments. A higher rate of return for pension savings will cause an income effect on the desired level of savings but no offsetting substitution effect. Desired savings for all households will thus decrease. Households who are not credit-constrained will lower their savings whereas the savings of credit-constrained households will remain unchanged. Aggregate savings will thus decrease if the rate of return on mandatory savings rises.

Also, this model does not take into account the fact that individuals may have other motivations for saving than simply providing for their retirement. For instance, households may want to prepare for unforeseen contingencies by engaging in precautionary saving. Pension assets are rather poorly suited for these purposes and therefore households might prefer not to hold all (or a large majority) of their wealth in this form (Munnell, 1987). As a result, they might choose to reduce their non-pension wealth less than one-for-one when their pension wealth increases.

Alternatively, precautionary savings may fall if workers perceive that there is an increase in the credibility of their pension program (Vittas, 1995). As pension plans have developed in many countries, governments have found it desirable to adopt appropriate regulations.[8] As a result of this increased regulation, the perceived credibility of pension schemes could be positively impacted. In such a situation, overall savings could fall if the stock of precautionary savings falls by more than the increase in pension wealth. Conversely, the fact that pensions are annuities – and thus provide insurance against uncertain lifespan – tends to reduce the total amount of savings households need for retirement.

The development of funded pension schemes might also raise awareness among the general population of the need to save for retirement. This 'recognition effect' was coined by Cagan (1965) who studied the impact of private pension plan participation on household savings rates in the United States. This type of increased awareness of the need to save for retirement might incite individuals to augment their overall savings.

And finally, the proliferation of funded pension plans is enabling many workers to retire earlier. This is due to the fact that many pension schemes have provisions that allow workers to retire earlier than they otherwise would (Munnell and Yohn, 1992). As discussed by Feldstein (1974), households that decide to retire earlier can be expected to increase their savings during their working years because they must accumulate a larger amount of assets over a shorter working life in order to finance a longer retirement. Even if each household has zero net saving over their lifetime, the net effect on aggregate savings will be positive as long as the population and/or per capita income are increasing in the economy (and thus the additional saving by workers will exceed the extra dissaving by retirees).

In summary, our theoretical discussion has enabled us to identify the circumstances under which the development of funded pensions is most likely to contribute to higher aggregate savings. Savings will tend to respond positively to an increase in funded pensions in economies where a significant proportion of workers are being forced to save at a higher rate through their pension plans than they would otherwise and are unable to offset this excess saving by borrowing. This will be the case in countries

where funded pension schemes are mandatory and cover a substantial proportion of the workforce, and where credit markets are characterized by relatively high borrowing constraints. On the other hand, a positive link between aggregate savings and funded pensions may not emerge if the growth in funded pensions is accompanied by a decrease in other forms of household savings. As discussed, this could occur because households are requiring less precautionary savings due to the insurance-like nature of pensions or as a result of the increased credibility of pension schemes.

EMPIRICAL METHODOLOGY AND DATA

In order to test the hypothesis that increases in funded pensions contribute to higher aggregate savings, we assembled a panel data set of saving rates and their determinants for a sample of ten countries over the 1982–1993 period. We selected the ten countries – listed in the appendix – for which internationally-comparable data on funded pensions were available for the time period chosen.[9] We had originally included the United States in our sample but later removed it because the data on funded pensions was not compatible with that from other countries. Indeed, the pension figures for the United States included assets from 401(k) plans which are essentially voluntary pension plans. Pension figures for all the other sample countries are for pension plans that are mandatory from the workers' perspective.

Of our ten sample countries, six were classified as industrialized (i.e. OECD member countries) over the sample period whereas the other four were categorized as being emerging-market economies. Our sample represents a wide enough variety of country experiences and pension regimes without creating a sample where the countries have such dramatically different levels of development that the assumption of common slope parameters in the econometric analysis would become unreasonable.

The following equation describes the econometric specification employed:

$$SAV_{it} = \alpha_i + \beta'x_{it} + \delta't_{it} + \varepsilon_{it} \tag{7.11}$$

where SAV_{it} is the ratio of aggregate savings to gross domestic product (GDP) for country i and time period t, α_i is a country-specific constant, x_{it} is a vector of control variables for country i and time period t (including a measure of changes in funded pension wealth), t_{it} is a country-specific time trend that varies by country i and time period t and ε_{it} is a classical disturbance term.[10] The fixed effects specification defined in equation

(7.11) is a classical regression model and can thus be estimated using ordinary least squares (OLS).

Country-specific fixed effects were included in the regression specification to capture any unobservable characteristics that vary across countries (but not over time) and that influence saving rates. In addition, we account for heterogeneity among the cross-sectional units in some of our regressions by letting the effect of pension wealth on savings differ for our two major country groupings. We allow for a differential impact by interacting the pension wealth variable with two dummy variables that identify whether or not the country was a member of the OECD during the sample period.

Both private and national savings were employed in constructing our dependent variable. Even though our theoretical discussion in the previous section and our choice of control variables both reflect motivations for saving from the household's perspective, we do not use aggregate household savings because of the difficulties involved in obtaining internationally-comparable figures for savings undertaken strictly by households. Indeed, changes in tax codes and different accounting conventions often blur the distinction between corporate and household savings. In using private or national savings as our dependent variable, we are implicitly assuming that household and corporate savings are perfect substitutes.

We use the change in assets managed by pension funds as a proportion of the working-age population (*PENSION*) as a proxy for the change in pension wealth in each country.[11,12] We express our funded pension variable in flow form as it seems to be appropriate in this context given that the dependent variable is a flow variable. The pension figures for Canada, Finland, Germany, Korea, the Netherlands, Norway, and the United Kingdom were obtained from OECD (1997b). The figures for Chile, Malaysia and Singapore were obtained from national sources (see the appendix for more details).

In addition to *PENSION*, vector **x** is comprised of seven other variables that have been identified in the literature as being important determinants of saving rates across countries.[13] They are: the dependency ratio, the growth rate of real per capita GDP, the government budget surplus, the real interest rate, domestic credit as a proportion of GDP, real per capita GDP, and real government pension spending per retired person. A description of all the variables employed in the econometric analysis is provided in the appendix. As discussed in Edwards (1995), from theory we expect the following coefficient signs on these explanatory variables:

- *Dependency ratio (DEP)*: Negative. According to the life-cycle hypothesis, a country with a relatively high proportion of dependents (i.e. inactive young and old) relative to the working – and thus saving – population will also experience relatively lower savings.

- *Growth rate of real per capita GDP (GROWTH)*: Positive. Another implication of the life-cycle hypothesis is that in a growing economy, saving by workers will increase relative to dissaving by the retired, resulting in a rise in overall savings.

- *Government budget surplus (GOV)*: Negative. Government savings are expected to crowd-out private savings.

- *Real interest rate (RINT)*: Ambiguous. Depending on the relative magnitudes of the income and substitution effects, the impact of a real interest rate increase can be either positive or negative (or null if the two effects offset one another).

- *Domestic credit as a proportion of GDP (CREDIT)*: Negative. As credit markets develop (and thus domestic credit as a proportion of GDP increases), borrowing constraints are eased which should negatively impact savings.

- *Real per capita income (INC)*: Positive. It has been suggested that high-income households save a larger proportion of their income than do their low-income counterparts. At the macro level, this would imply that richer countries should save more than poorer ones.

- *Real government pension spending per elderly person (PAYG)*: Negative. According to the life-cycle hypothesis, if individuals anticipate higher benefits from the public PAYG pension system (proxied here by spending) they will reduce their savings.

Equation (7.11) can thus be rewritten as:

$$SAV_{it} = \sum_{i=1}^{11} \alpha_i + \beta_1 DEP_{it} + \beta_2 GROWTH_{it} + \beta_3 GOV_{it} + \beta_4 RINT_{it}$$
$$+ \beta_5 CREDIT_{it} + \beta_6 \log(INC_{it}) + \beta_7 \log(PAYG_{it}) +$$
$$\beta_8 \log(PENSION_{it}) + \sum_{i=1}^{11} \delta_i t_i + \varepsilon_{it} \tag{7.12}$$

We express the three variables that are measured in real national currency units in terms of their natural logarithms. We do this for two reasons. First, the semi-log specification facilitates the interpretation of the coefficient on our pension wealth variable (*PENSION*) which is the coefficient of interest in our analysis. In this specification, β_8 thus represents the effect on the private saving ratio of an additional percentage point increase in the real flow of pension fund assets per working-age individual. And second, the use of a semi-log form together with country-specific fixed effects allow us to use the three aforementioned variables measured in national currency units instead of expressing them in a common currency, such as the dollar. This allows us to circumvent the potential problem of large variations in pension wealth occurring due to exchange rate fluctuations.

The estimation of semi-reduced equations such as (7.12) generally presents problems of endogeneity. As discussed in Carroll and Weil (1994), there are theoretical arguments to justify a two-way causality between the growth rate and savings. Such a two-way causality would result in the error term being correlated with the growth rate and the OLS estimates being biased and inconsistent. This problem is addressed by estimating (7.12) using two-stage least squares (2SLS) where population growth, the inflation rate and all the other exogenous explanatory variables are employed as instruments for the growth rate in the first stage. Given our assumption of a semi-closed economy, we also instrument for the real interest rate.

ESTIMATION RESULTS

The results of the estimation of equation (7.12) are presented in Table 7.1. The first two regressions are estimated using regular OLS whereas the latter two are estimated by instrumenting for the growth rate and the real interest rate using 2SLS. In the second and fourth equations, the impact of pension wealth on savings is allowed to differ for OECD and non-OECD countries. This is done by interacting the pension wealth variable with two different dummy variables: *OECD* (which takes on a value of 1 for OECD countries and 0 otherwise) and *Non-OECD* (which takes on a value of 1 for non-OECD countries and 0 otherwise).

We did not find any significant difference in the estimation results when we performed the regression analysis on national rather than private saving rates; we therefore only report the results of the estimations employing the private saving rate as the dependent variable. This finding suggests that government savings were not negatively affected by funded pensions in our sample in spite of the fact that the returns on pension savings were generally tax-exempt. The finding may rest on several explanations which have not

Table 7.1 Aggregate savings and funded pension wealth (panel estimates for 1982–1993 using the private savings rate as the dependent variable)

	R1	R2	R3	R4
Estimation method	OLS	OLS	2SLS	2SLS
Dependency ratio	−0.1350	−0.1134	−0.1058	−0.1004
	(0.1981)	(0.1912)	(0.2302)	(0.2239)
Growth rate of real	−0.0728	−0.0490	0.2390	0.2018
Per capita GDP	(0.1818)	(0.1686)	(0.3040)	(0.2948)
Government budget	−0.4763 ***	−0.4577 ***	−0.4620 ***	−0.4435 ***
Surplus / GDP	(0.1045)	(0.0941)	(0.1054)	(0.1028)
Real interest rate	0.0372	0.0451	0.1398	0.1425
	(0.0532)	(0.0536)	(0.0979)	(0.0957)
Domestic credit / GDP	−0.0921 ***	−0.0881 ***	−0.0760 ***	−0.0753 **
	(0.0328)	(0.0321)	(0.0386)	(0.0376)
Log (real per capita GDP)	0.0093	−0.0069	−0.0562	−0.0644
	(0.0563)	(0.0563)	(0.0799)	(0.0783)
Log (real public pension	−0.0535 *	−0.0576 *	−0.0510 **	−0.0571 **
spending / population 65+)	(0.0316)	(0.0329)	(0.0257)	(0.0250)
Log (real pension fund	0.0083 *		0.0110 **	
assets / population 19–65)	(0.0044)		(0.0054)	
OECD × Log (real pension fund		−0.0010		0.0009
assets / population 19–65)		(0.0035)		(0.0066)
Non-OECD × Log (real pension		0.0207 ***		0.0236 ***
fund assets / population 19–65)		(0.0071)		(0.0076)
Obs.	117	117	117	117
Adj. R-squared (within)	0.66	0.68	0.65	0.67
F(fixed effects)	15.37 ***	16.67 ***	14.63 ***	18.03 ***
F(time trends)	8.19 ***	6.33 ***	8.24 ***	6.24 ***

Notes:
(1) Country-specific time trends and country-specific fixed effects were included in each regression. (2) The standard errors (corrected for heteroscedasticity using White's method) are in parentheses. (3) (***), (**) and (*) indicate statistical significance at the 1%, 5% and 10% levels, respectively. (4) Population growth, the inflation rate and all the other exogenous explanatory variables were employed as instruments for the growth rate and the real interest rate in regressions R3 and R4. (5) F(fixed effects) and F(time trends) are the F-statistics used to test the joint significance of the country dummies and country time trends, respectively.

been explored here: tax-exempt pension schemes may be self-financing as they foster capital accumulation, growth and higher corporate tax receipts; or they may be financed by reduced government spending rather than by a rise in government budget deficits.

The overall fit of our regressions is quite good as suggested by the relatively high adjusted-R^2s. Indeed, the various specifications of our model explain between 65 per cent and 68 per cent of the variation in private saving rates in our sample. The measure of goodness of fit that we report is for the within-estimator and it therefore does not account for any variation explained by the country-specific fixed effects. Furthermore, we found no significant changes in the R^2s when we ran the regressions without the time trends. We can thus be reasonably confident that the determinants of savings that we selected as explanatory variables – and not the country dummies or time trends – are doing a good job in explaining the variation in our dependent variable.

Our results concerning the explanatory variables other than the funded pension wealth variable are generally consistent both with priors based on the life-cycle model and past empirical studies. The coefficients on the government savings rate and the domestic credit ratio are both negative, as expected, and statistically significant at the 1 per cent or 5 per cent levels in all the regressions. The coefficient on the real public pension spending per retired person variable is negative and statistically significant at the 5 per cent or 10 per cent levels in all the regressions. And finally, the coefficients on the dependency ratio, the growth rate of real per capita GDP, the real interest rate and real per capita GDP are not statistically significant at conventional levels.

We do find some evidence that the build-up of pension assets relative to the working-age population exerts a positive and statistically significant impact on aggregate savings rates. For example, the coefficient on our pension wealth variable for the full sample using OLS (regression R1) is 0.0083. Thus, a one percentage increase in the flow of pension assets per working-age individual would translate into a 0.008 percentage point increase in the private saving rate. This implies that for the private saving ratio to increase by one percentage point, the flow of pension assets per working-age individual would have to increase by 125 per cent.

We do, however, find conflicting evidence when we allow the impact of pension wealth on savings to differ for our two major country groupings. For the four non-OECD countries, we continue to find a statistically significant relationship between changes in pension wealth and savings and one which is larger in magnitude than in the full sample analysis. Indeed, as shown in regression R2, the coefficient on our pension wealth variable jumps to 0.02. Thus, in this case a one percentage increase in the flow of

pension assets per working-age individual would translate into a 0.02 percentage point increase in the private saving rate. This implies that for the private saving ratio to increase by one percentage point, the flow of pension assets per working-age individual would have to increase by only 50 per cent instead of 125 per cent. By contrast, we do not find a statistically significant relationship between changes in pension wealth and savings for the six OECD countries.

Our results appear to indicate that the impact of funded pensions on the private saving ratio differs in OECD and non-OECD countries. This outcome can be explained in the context of our earlier theoretical discussion. Indeed, factors that were found to be important in predicting a positive impact of funded pensions on savings were present in the four non-OECD countries over the sample period: tight borrowing constraints for most pension savers and the mandatory status of the funded pension schemes. Conversely, the six OECD sample countries could be characterized by more developed capital markets and a higher degree of voluntarity in the decision to contribute to funded pension schemes.

CONCLUDING REMARKS

Stimulating aggregate savings is an important motivation for governments who are encouraging the accumulation of funded pension assets. In OECD countries, it is the insight that population ageing requires higher savings for retirement which is largely driving such saving targets; in the slowly ageing emerging markets, such motivation stems rather from the evidence that higher domestic savings are required to durably finance investment and growth. The desire to increase aggregate savings by promoting the development of funded pensions, however, has been based on very limited empirical evidence thus far. The few aggregate-level studies on this issue have yielded mixed results and suffer from an important shortcoming in that the econometric analysis is based on too few degrees of freedom.

Based on the collection of comparable cross-country data of pension and life insurance assets for eleven countries over the 1982–93 period, this study has produced statistically significant international evidence in support of the premise that the development of funded pensions does indeed contribute to higher aggregate savings. The analysis suggests that it is crucial to stimulate a positive impact from the low-savers group and to maintain a certain degree of liquidity constraint in the economy. This would require that funded pension schemes are mandatory rather than voluntary, that the pension coverage of the working-age population is comprehensive and that it is discouraged from borrowing against accumulated (and

mandatory) pension assets. Mandatory pension schemes that effectively cover the low-savers group will not only stimulate current savings, they are also an important policy vehicle to help make retirement income levels and wealth distribution more equal between low and high savers.

NOTES

1. A funded pension plan is one in which pension obligations are covered, either partially or fully, by assets.
2. In theory, domestic investment can also be financed by external savings and hence low levels of domestic savings, *ceteris paribus*, need not necessarily lead to lower growth. In practice, however, few countries have been able to rely on substantial amounts of foreign capital to finance domestic investment over a considerable period of time (see Reisen, 1996 for more details).
3. See Gale (1995), OECD (1997a) and Schmidt-Hebbel (1997) for a discussion of these studies.
4. In their analysis of the Chilean experience, Corsetti and Schmidt-Hebbel (1996) and Morandé (1996) provide some support for the idea that the 1981 pension reform – and the subsequent growth in private pension funds – contributed to increasing private savings over the 1980s and early 1990s. Faruqee and Husain (1994) found evidence that provident fund saving had impacted the private savings rate over the 1970–92 period in Singapore but not in Malaysia. And finally, Husain (1995) found provident fund saving to be a statistically insignificant determinant of private consumption in Singapore, thus contradicting the results in Faruqee and Husain (1994).
5. Samuelson (1958) developed a general equilibrium model where interest rates are determined by consumptions loans between individuals of different ages; he thus established the basic multi-generational framework needed to study pension systems. Diamond (1965) extended Samuelson's analysis by incorporating production.
6. The life-cycle hypothesis was first developed by Modigliani and Brumberg (1954) and later generalized by Feldstein (1974).
7. It should be noted that the assumption of constant population growth is not necessary to derive equation (7).
8. For a review of recent changes in the regulation of funded pension plans in various countries, see Davis (1995) and World Bank (1994).
9. We selected the time period that maximized the total number of observations. We were constrained to start the time period in the early 1980s because pension fund data was not available for most of our countries prior to that time. We could not extend our data set beyond 1993 because the figures on public pension spending for the OECD countries for 1994 were not yet available.
10. Country-specific time trends were introduced to address the problem of autocorrelation of the residuals.
11. This data does not cover pension arrangements which do not constitute a separately organized fund or those in which the reserves of the funds are simply added to that employer's own reserves or invested in securities issued by that employer.
12. We constructed another measure of pension wealth by adding the assets of life insurance companies to those of pension funds. We thought it appropriate to consider the life insurance sector in this context given that the assets of certain pension schemes are managed by life insurance companies. As there were no significant differences in our estimation results employing both measures of pension wealth, we report only those using pension fund assets.
13. For examples of recent studies in this literature, see Edwards (1995) and Masson, Bayoumi and Samiei (1995).

APPENDIX

A. Country lists

Full Sample (10 countries): Canada, Chile, Finland, Germany, Korea, Malaysia, Netherlands, Norway, Singapore, United Kingdom

OECD Sample (6 countries): Canada, Finland, Germany, Netherlands, Norway, United Kingdom

Non-OECD Sample (4 countries): Chile, Korea, Malaysia, Singapore

B. Sources and Definitions of Variables

Dependent Variable:

1. Private savings / GDP
[calculated by adding investment (IFS line 93) to the current account (IFS line 78ald) and subtracting the budget surplus of the consolidated central government (IFS line 80) and then dividing by GDP (line 99)]

Explanatory Variables:

2. Dependency ratio – ratio of the dependent population (persons under 19 and over 65) to the working-age population (persons between 19 and 65) [calculated using the United Nation's *Population Statistics Data File*]

3. Growth rate of real per capita GDP
[calculated as the log difference of annual real per capita GDP using real GDP and population figures from IFS line 99]

4. Government budget surplus / GDP – the budget surplus of the consolidated central government as a proportion of GDP
[IFS lines 80 and 99]

5. Real interest rate – Short-term interest rate less the CPI inflation rate
[IFS lines 60 and 64]

6. Domestic credit / GDP – Domestic credit claims on the private sector as a proportion of GDP
[IFS lines 32d and 99]

7. *Real per capita GDP* – Real GDP per capita (measured in real national currency units)
[Calculated using real GDP and population figures from IFS line 99]

8. *Public pension spending / population 65+* – Government spending on public PAYG pension schemes (measured in real national currency units) as a proportion of population over 65
[The public pension figures are from: (i) OECD (1996) – for all OECD countries except Korea; (ii) the World Bank's *World Development Indicators* for Korea; (iii) Espinoza and Marcel (1997) – for Chile; (iv) Asher (1997) – for Malaysia; (v) Department of Statistics, Singapore various years) – for Singapore; and the population figures are from the United Nation's *Population Statistics Data File*]

9. *Flow of pension fund assets / population 19–65* – Change in the stock of pension fund assets (measured in real national currency units) as a proportion of the working-age population
[The pension fund assets are from: (i) OECD (1997b) – for all OECD countries; (ii) Superintendencia de Administradores de Fondos de Pensiones (1996) for Chilean pension fund assets; (iii) Bank Negara Malaysia (various years) – for Malaysia; (iv) Department of Statistics, Singapore (various years) – for Singapore; and the population figures were calculated using the UN's *Population Statistics Data File*]

Instruments:

10. *Inflation rate* – CPI inflation rate
[IFS line 64]

11. *Population growth rate*
[calculated as the log difference using population figures from IFS line 99]

C. Pension Fund Figures

This section provides a more detailed description of the pension fund figures for each country.

Canada:

The pension figures are for autonomous pension funds which are principally trusteed pension plans (non-insured plans).

Chile:

The pension figures are for the mandatory pension system where the assets are administered by private pension funds.

Finland:

The pension figures are for occupational pension schemes which are officially part of the social security sector but are run by private pension insurance companies and other pension organizations.

Germany:

The pension figures are for autonomous pension funds which include private pension funds and burial funds.

Korea:

The pension figures are for the following four large pension funds: Korea Teacher's Pension, Military Pension, Government Employees Pension Corporation and the Korean Teacher's Mutual Fund.

Malaysia:

The pension figures are for a small group of provident and pension funds, the largest being the Employees Provident Fund.

Netherlands:

The pension figures are for autonomous pension funds.

Norway:

The pension figures are for autonomous pension funds which include private and municipal pension funds.

Singapore:

The pension figures are for the compulsory Central Provident Fund.

<u>United Kingdom</u>:

The pension figures are for autonomous pension funds. These funds are generally run by boards of trustees on behalf of members.

REFERENCES

Asher, M.G. (1997), 'Social Security Arrangements in Southeast Asia', mimeo, National University of Singapore.
Bank Negara Malaysia, *Annual Report*, various years.
Blanchard, O.J. and S. Fischer (1989), *Lectures on Macroeconomics*, MIT Press, Cambridge, MA.
Cagan, P. (1965), 'The Effect of Pension Plans on Aggregate Saving: Evidence from a Sample Survey', *NBER Occasional Paper*, No. 95.
Carroll, C. and D. Weil (1994), 'Saving and Growth: A Reinterpretation', *Carnegie-Rochester Conference Series on Public Policy*, 40 (June), pp. 133–197.
Corsetti, G. and K. Schmidt-Hebbel (1996), 'Pension Reform and Growth', in S. Valdés-Prieto (ed.), *Pensions: Funding, Privatization, and Macroeconomic Policy*, Cambridge University Press, Cambridge.
Davis, E. Philip (1995), *Pension Funds. Retirement-Income Security and Capital Markets: An International Perspective*, Clarendon Press, Oxford.
Department of Statistics, Ministry of Trade and Industry, Singapore, *Yearbook of Statistics*, various years.
Diamond, P.A. (1965), 'National Debt in a Neoclassical Growth Model', *American Economic Review*, 55(5), pp. 1126–1150.
Edwards, S. (1995), 'Why are Saving Rates so Different Across Countries?: An International Comparative Analysis', *NBER Working Paper*, No. 5097.
Espinoza, J. and M. Marcel (1997), 'Descentralización Fiscal: El Caso de Chile', Serie Política Fiscal No. 57, CEPAL.
Faruqee, H. and A.M. Husain (1994), 'Determinants of Private Saving in Southeast Asia: A Cross-Country Analysis', Southeast Asia and Pacific Department, International Monetary Fund.
Feldstein, M. (1974), 'Social Security, Induced Retirement, and Aggregate Capital Accumulation', *Journal of Political Economy*, 82(5), pp. 905–926.
Gale, W. (1995), 'The Effects of Pensions on Wealth: a Re-evaluation of Theory and Evidence', mimeo, The Brookings Institution.
Husain, A. (1995), 'Determinants of Private Saving in Singapore', in K. Bercuson (ed.), *Singapore: A Case Study in Rapid Development*, International Monetary Fund Occasional Paper, No. 119.
Masson, P., T. Bayoumi and H. Samiei (1995), 'International Evidence on the Determinants of Private Saving', International Monetary Fund Working Paper, No. 95/51.
Modigliani, F. and R. Brumberg (1954), 'Utility Analysis and the Consumption Function: An Interpretation of Cross Section Data', in K. Kurihara (ed.), *Post-Keynsian Economics*, Rutgers University Press, New Brunswick, NJ.
Morandé, F. (1996), 'Savings in Chile: What Went Right?', Inter-American Development Bank Working Paper, No. 322.
Munnell, A. (1987), 'The Impact of Public and Private Pension Schemes on Saving and Capital Formation', in *Conjugating Public and Private, the Case of Pensions*, Studies and Research, 24, International Social Security Association, Geneva.
Munnell, A.H. and F.O. Yohn (1992), 'What is the Impact of Pensions on Saving?', in Z. Bodie and A.H. Munnell (eds), *Pensions and the Economy: Sources, Uses and Limitations of the Data*, Pension Research Council of the Wharton School of the University of Pennsylvania.
Organisation for Economic Co-operation and Development (OECD) (1996), *Social Expenditure Statistics of OECD Member Countries*, OECD, Paris.
Organisation for Economic Co-operation and Development (OECD) (1997a), 'The Macroeconomics of Ageing, Pensions and Savings: A Survey', ECO/CPE/WP1(97).
Organisation for Economic Co-operation and Development (OECD) (1997b), *Institutional Investors Statistical Yearbook*, OECD, Paris.

Reisen, H. (1996), 'Developing-Country Savings and the Global Capital Shortage', in *Future Global Capital Shortages: Real Threat or Pure Fiction?*, OECD, Paris.

Samuelson, P. (1958), 'An Exact Consumption–Loan Model of Interest with or without the Social Contrivance of Money', *Journal of Political Economy*, 66(6), pp. 467–482.

Schmidt-Hebbel, K. (1997), 'Does Pension Reform Really Spur Saving and Growth?', mimeo, Central Bank of Chile.

Superintendencia de Administradores de Fondos de Pensiones (SAFP) (1996), *The Chilean Pension System*, SAFP, Santiago de Chile.

Vittas, D. (1995), 'Pension Funds and Capital Markets', mimeo, Financial Sector Development, World Bank.

World Bank (1994), *Averting the Old Age Crisis: Policies to Protect the Old and Promote Growth*, Oxford University Press, Oxford.

8. The Limits of Foreign Savings[*]

The current account deficits that this paper will address share three important common features. First, they are 'private-sector driven' in the (non-Ricardian) sense that they do not reflect government budget deficits. We look into four Asian and four Latin American countries that do not have public-sector deficits and that have received heavy capital imports over the 1990s. We thus ignore the public budget and assume full private capital mobility as given. We are thus obliged to view the current account not as a net export balance, as in the old elasticities approach, but as a private-sector savings–investment balance. Second (apart from shortly ahead of currency crisis), the current account deficits are 'overfinanced', implying a positive overall balance of payments and rising levels of foreign exchange reserves. Third, a part of the deficit is financed by capital flows that are largely determined by cyclical factors, as has been generally the case for an important share of the emerging-market flows of the 1990s (see, e.g., Calvo, Leiderman and Reinhart, 1996). Their cyclical determination makes these flows akin to reversal.

The abundance of private capital flows confronts many Asian and Latin American authorities with a specific transfer problem. They have to make the basic decision of whether to accept or resist the capital inflow, or how much to accept or how much to resist. We aim to inform that decision, from the perspective of long-term development. Advice on *how* (if any) foreign savings should be resisted (macroeconomic restraint, sterilized intervention, capital controls, *et al.*) will not be given here. Likewise, it is not intended to advise authorities on financial crisis prevention (excellent surveys now abound; see Goldstein, 1996, for example).

The chapter is structured as follows. First, the benefits of foreign savings (rather than of gross capital mobility per se) are reviewed along different theoretical strands in the literature. The potential benefits of foreign savings are growth enhancement through higher investment and consumption-smoothing through risk sharing. We thus provide capsule summaries of neo-

[*] Originally published in R. Hausmann and H. Reisen (eds), *Promoting Savings in Latin America*, IDB/OECD Development Centre, Paris 1997, pp. 233–264. An edited version was subsequently published as 'Net Capital Inflows: How Much to Accept, How Much to Resist?' in R. Glick (ed.), *Managing Capital Flows and Exchange Rates: Perspectives from the Pacific Basin*, Cambridge University Press, Cambridge (UK) 1998, pp. 289–321.

classical and new growth models as well as of the inter-temporal approach to the current account. Second, we present and calibrate various notions of long-term sustainability of debt-augmenting capital flows, in view of a country's inter-temporal solvency. Since large current account deficits will not be financed by foreigners forever, authorities need to know the required size and time profile of the subsequent adjustment back to payments balance. Third, since an unsustainable deficit is not necessarily an 'excessive' deficit, the size of the current account deficit does not give rise to normative judgements; what matters, by contrast, is the *source* of the deficit. We make a case for resisting part of foreign savings when unsustainable currency appreciation, excessive risk-taking in the banking system and a sharp drop in private savings coincide. The policy response has then to strike a balance between the benefits of consumption-smoothing and of financing viable investment versus the economic costs of excessive private borrowing. A case can be made that foreign direct investment is less likely than other capital flows to stimulate excessive private consumption and to cause a real appreciation problem.

THE BENEFITS OF (NET) CAPITAL INFLOWS

It will perhaps be surprising that the role for development that the economic literature assigns to foreign savings, rather than to capital mobility (and gross flows) per se, is fairly modest. This in stark contrast to the earlier 'two-gap' literature (Chenery and Bruno, 1962; McKinnon, 1964), according to which growth was not only limited by a country's ability to save, but also by foreign savings to buy necessary imported inputs. Since the abundance of foreign exchange (rather than the scarcity) motivates this paper, we omit discussion of the two-gap literature. We can immediately move from structuralist to mainstream economic thinking.

Neo-classical Considerations

In the neo-classical general equilibrium framework, the benefits of capital inflows into (capital-) poor countries are essentially derived from divergences in the marginal productivity of capital. Labour in advanced countries is equipped with better and more capital than the workers in developing countries, and capital can be used more productively by being sent south.

The simplest of the neo-classical models, the two-country Kemp–MacDougall model (see, e.g., Lal, 1990) can provide some basic insights about the benefit of capital inflows as well as the optimal size of these

inflows. Savings rates are constant and a fixed proportion of per capita income in both countries. The marginal product of capital is higher in the poor country than in the rich country in autarky, and is diminishing in both countries with rising capital–labour ratios. With perfect capital mobility, the poor country will benefit from capital inflows, until its marginal product of capital is equal to that of the rich country; both in turn determine (and are equal to) the world interest rate.

The size of the optimal net capital inflow rises with the difference between the autarkic marginal product of capital and the world interest rate, and falls the faster marginal capital productivity declines with a higher capital–labour ratio. The poor country gains per capita income – the marginal output of capital, times the capital inflow, minus the income payments on the capital stock located at home. (The rich country, of course, gains as well from the capital export: the output loss due to capital relocation is more than compensated by interest and dividend payments.) In the new, long-run equilibrium, output will grow at the same rate as in the closed economy.

The Kemp–MacDougall theory crucially assumes that the capital inflow is invested, not consumed, and that the capital ratio is raised by the inflow, until the steady-state capital ratio is reached. The inflow is not consumed, because the world interest rate exceeds the country's rate of time preference. This fulfils an important requirement of the full debt cycle, so that the deficits first incurred on trade and current accounts will give way to a trade surplus and later a surplus on current account. Concerns about debt stocks and the size of the financial and real transfer are unwarranted because they will adjust in a sort of automatic way. Foreign investors are assumed to bring in capital goods and take away part of the additional production, thereby resolving the transfer problem. The traditional neo-classical model thus seems more appropriate to describe FDI inflows than other capital flows.

Mere capital accumulation does not guarantee that a country will benefit from capital inflows; first, in the presence of sufficiently misguided policies, inflows can 'immiserize'; and, second, an upward-sloping supply of capital will mean that the cost of capital inflows rises at the margin. Even on standard neo-classical grounds, governments can be justified to resist part of the capital inflows.

Models of 'immiserizing' inflows have been developed by Bhagwati (1973), Johnson (1967), and Brecher and Diaz Alejandro (1977). Tariff-induced inflows of capital magnify the welfare losses due to distorted consumption and production patterns by stimulating capital accumulation in protected sectors and by attracting foreign capital into these sectors, if foreign capital receives the full (untaxed) value of its marginal product. As

Calvo (1996) suggests, drastic structural reform in most capital importing countries has made the 'immiserizing inflow' argument less relevant today in its original presentation. These reforms do not guarantee that countries have moved to Pareto optimum. Distortions persist that may stimulate private credit booms, for example, by maintaining high marginal tax rates with full deductability of interest payments. Moreover, distortions may be reintroduced in the case of a capital-outflow crisis.

There is also an 'optimum tariff'-type case for taxing capital inflows. Harberger (1985) suggests levying an optimal tax on foreign borrowing, if the recipient country faces an upward-sloping supply of credit, to equate its tax-inclusive average cost to the higher marginal cost. A related argument can be built for the group of capital-importing net debtor countries, if such a tax succeeds in improving their joint capital terms of trade by dampening interest rates.

Further evidence that capital inflows will not play a crucial role in the standard neo-classical framework comes from growth accounting (Krugman, 1993). Adding human capital accumulation to the standard Solow growth model, output growth can be written as

$$\dot{Y} = \alpha\dot{K} + \beta\dot{H} + (1 - \alpha - \beta)\dot{L} + \dot{\theta} \qquad (8.1)$$

where dots represent growth rates of output Y, physical capital K, human capital H and labour L, α and β are the physical and human capital shares in national income and θ is the growth rate of Solow residual. Mankiw, Romer and Weil (1992) have found that the three variables K, H and L of their augmented Solow model explain almost 80 per cent of the cross-country variation in income per capita of the full Summers/Heston country sample of 98 non-oil countries. Their estimates imply a physical capital share α of 0.31 and a human capital share β of 0.28. Taking an average capital–output ratio of 2.5 and an average current account deficit of 4 per cent of GDP (a stylized description of major capital importers), the Solow model would predict an increase in the growth rate of capital of 1.6 per cent; and the resulting increase in short-run growth of output would merely reach 0.50 per cent.

Implications of the Endogenous Growth Literature

Endogenous-growth models, unlike neo-classical models which imply decreasing returns to capital, are characterized by the assumption of non-decreasing returns to the set of reproducible factors of production. Equation (8.1) becomes an endogenous growth model if $\alpha + \beta = 1$, so that

$$\dot{Y} = \alpha\dot{K} + \beta\dot{H} \tag{8.2}$$

Equation (8.2) says that long-term growth can be explained entirely by growth in capital, without any appeal to a Solow residual. This implies external economies to capital accumulation: the elasticity of output with respect to capital greatly exceeds its share of GNP at market prices. Such externalities create a presumption that the benefits of capital inflows must be much higher than those stipulated by the standard neo-classical approach.[1] In the neo-classical growth model, countries benefiting from large inflows could see large increases in capital accumulation; their growth rates should peak on impact, to gradually reach the steady state. To change the growth rate of the capital recipient permanently, though, the inflow must not only lift the economy to a higher capital equipment (and income level), but it also has to change the economy's production function. In contrast with the Solow growth framework (where technological change is exogenously given), the new growth literature highlights the dependence of growth rates on the state of technology relative to the rest of the world. Despite the optimistic predictions of the endogenous growth model for the benefits of inflows, Cohen (1993) finds for a sample of 34 developing debtor countries that benefited from renewed access to the world financial markets in the 1970s, capital accumulation was actually less than for other developing countries, an observation which is not explained by endogenous factors – the initial output per capita and the initial stock of capital. Rather, capital accumulation failed to increase because much of the capital inflow leaked into consumption.

For foreign direct investment flows, in contrast to debt-creating flows, the optimistic assessment of endogenous growth has been validated recently by Borensztein, De Gregorio and Lee (1995). They find in a cross-country regression framework for 69 developing countries over the period 1970–89 that for each percentage point of increase in the FDI-to-GDP ratio, the rate of growth to the host economy increases by 0.8 percentage points. The contribution of FDI to long-term growth results from two effects. FDI adds to capital accumulation, because it stimulates domestic investment, rather than crowding out domestic investment by competing in domestic product markets or financial markets. The complementarity of FDI and domestic investment is explained by their complementarity in production and by positive technology spillovers. The second growth effect of FDI stems from the embodied transfer of technology and efficiency, provided the host country has a minimum threshold stock of human capital; FDI can increase the growth rate of the host economy only by interacting with that country's absorptive capacity.

FDI flows, then, have the potential to speed up convergence through two channels. First, by stimulating capital accumulation (rather than consumption), FDI raises the initial starting ratio of poor country to rich country GNP, R. Second, by helping change a country's production function through introducing higher efficiency, FDI flows raise a country's growth rate and the differential between the poor country and rich country growth rate, D. The time to convergence (of per capita income between rich and poor countries), t, can be written as a function of R and D:

$$t = - (\ln R) / D \qquad\qquad (8.3)$$

What difference for the time to convergence does a rise in the FDI-to-GDP ratio make? Assuming R to be a fourth, and taking the above results by Borensztein and co-authors to mean that a rise in the FDI ratio will increase the growth differential by 0.8 percentage points from 2 per cent to 2.8 per cent, the time needed for convergence declines from 69 years to 50 years, a decline of 27 per cent.

It is also interesting to compare what difference an FDI flow makes in the neo-classical compared with the endogenous growth model. In the neo-classical model, only the level of GNP is affected, not its growth rate. Assuming capital's share in income α to be 0.31 (Mankiw *et al.*, 1992) and a capital–output ratio of 2.5, the marginal product of capital is 12.4 per cent ($\alpha/K/Y$). An inflow worth 4 per cent of GNP that only raises the initial starting ratio of poor country to rich county GNP will raise R from 0.25 to 0.26, producing little reduction in the time to convergence (from 69 to 67 years).

The Inter-temporal Approach to the Current Account

In the models considered so far, the benefits of capital inflows are derived from net capital inflows that are fully invested and raise the level or the growth rate of GDP. However, the benefits of capital flows are not only derived from directing world savings to the most productive investment opportunities, but also from allowing individuals to smooth consumption over different states of nature by borrowing or diversifying portfolios abroad. Developing countries are likely to benefit greatly from the international pooling of country-specific risks that would result in inter-temporal smoothing of consumption levels.[2] First, poor countries tend to be more shock-prone than richer ones; second, since per capita income is low, any downside adjustment will hurt more than in countries with higher consumption levels. Table 8.1 illustrates the point for five Latin American countries (for which data were easily available).

Table 8.1　Gains from the elimination of consumption variability

Country	Annual per cent consumption gain[a]	Real GDP per capita, 1990[b] (US = 100)	Std. dev. of GDP growth[c]
Argentina	1.94	19	4.83
Brazil	1.80	14	5.43
Chile	2.75	22	6.34
Mexico	0.54	29	3.77
Venezuela	2.22	30	4.65

Notes:
a. Obstfeld (1993): The calculations assume that the logarithm of per capita consumption follows a random walk with trend and that individuals have generalized isoelastic utility functions with annual time discount factor 0.95, relative risk aversion parameter 1, and inter-temporal substitution elasticity 0.25.
b. Heston and Summers (1993); GDP is PPP adjusted.
c. IADB, *Annual Report 1995*; the observation period is 1970–92 for annual real GDP.

In principle, the inter-temporal approach to the current account can be helpful in answering the question of how much to accept (in terms of the size of the current account deficit) of capital flows offered by foreign investors. International capital mobility opens the opportunity to trade off present levels of absorption against future absorption; if saving falls short of desired investment, foreigners have to finance the resulting current account deficit, leading to a rise in the country's net foreign liabilities. The inter-temporal approach views the current account as the outcome of forward-looking dynamic saving and investment decisions (Obstfeld and Rogoff, 1994), which are driven by expectations of future productivity growth, interest rates and other factors. Finally, the approach is able, in principle, to provide a benchmark for defining 'excessive' current account deficits in the context of models that yield predictions about the equilibrium path of external imbalances (Milesi-Ferretti and Razin, 1996).

Without writing down the whole maximization problem for the representative consumer (among the many assumptions necessary to produce behavioural predictions are inter-temporal separability of preferences and perfect foresight; see Obstfeld and Rogoff, 1994), Table 8.2 collects some important predictions of the inter-temporal approach to the (first-period) current account from the two impulses that have figured prominently in the discussion on the determinants of recent capital flows to emerging markets.

Table 8.2   *Current account effects predicted by the consumption-smoothing approach*

Shock	Temporary			Persistent		
	Saving	Investment	Current account	Saving	Investment	Current account
Drop in world interest rates below permanent average rate						
– Net debtor countries	+	0	+	not applicable		
– Net creditor countries	–	0	–			
Rise in productivity						
– Country-specific	+	0	+	–	+	–
– Global	+	0	+	+	+	0

Sources: Discussions in Glick and Rogoff (1992), Obstfeld and Rogoff (1994) and Razin (1995).

Table 8.2 yields some important insights about how the 'equilibrium' current account of the developing-country recipients should have responded to the drop in world interest rates, or, alternatively, to the reform-induced rise of productivity:

– The capital-importing countries, being net foreign debtors, should have raised the saving rate in response to cyclical portfolio flows, which are interest-driven. The current accounts should have moved towards lower deficits (or into surplus) as people smooth consumption in the face of temporarily low interest payments. For net creditor countries, temporarily low interest rates would have resulted in opposite current account effects. If a net debtor country widens current account deficits in response to temporary interest rate reductions, the response may well destabilize rather than smooth the inter-temporal consumption path.

– Likewise, the inter-temporal approach does not necessarily predict widening current account deficits when capital flows are attracted by country-specific productivity surges. The 'equilibrium' response of the current account depends crucially on the expectation of whether the productivity surge is temporary or permanent. In both cases, the productivity surge will raise output immediately, but only a persistent rise in productivity will cause permanent income to rise. The reason is that only a permanent productivity surge will induce investment and a higher future capital stock. The rise in permanent income will also cause consumption to rise more than output, resulting in a strong current account deficit as a result of lower saving and higher

investment. A transitory increase in productivity, by contrast, should result in an opposite current account effect (a lower deficit), since there is no effect on investment and agents save part of any transitory increase of income (in the permanent income model of consumption).

– Productivity surges must not necessarily be interpreted as country-specific, but can be part of a broader global shock. A persistent productivity-enhancing shock common to all countries will raise the world rate of interest. This should dampen consumption in net debtor countries sufficiently to compensate for the consumption effects arising from higher permanent income brought about by higher investment. Since all countries cannot improve their current accounts, world interest rates rise until global savings and investment are balanced. A global transitory productivity shock will produce excess world saving and thereby exert downward pressure on interest rates. A temporary drop in world interest rates should result in lower current-account deficits for net debtor countries, as analysed above.

It is noteworthy that – among the capital-flow determinants discussed here – the inter-temporal approach predicts a widening of current account deficits (for net debtor countries) only if the country enjoys a permanent idiosyncratic productivity boom. However, the predictive power of the inter-temporal approach to the current account may remain very limited for developing countries, in spite of their higher financial openness. Heymann (1994) raises some important questions, notably in the context of recurrent episodes of private-sector overindebtedness: How plausible is the assumption of rational expectations during a period when there is a 'regime change' in the economy? How correct can forecasts be about the expected value of future prices and quantities, and how realistic and binding is the inter-temporal budget constraint to induce agents to plan according to these forecasts? Such questions raise deep doubts about the claim that 'The inter-temporal approach to the current account offers a viable framework for assessing macroeconomic policy' (Obstfeld and Rogoff, 1994).

The Evidence on Benefits

How much economic benefit have our sample countries derived from foreign savings? Have current account deficits been excessive in view of the benefits (on costs, see below)? Let us consult some data to confront the theories surveyed so far with them. Note that the standard neo-classical approach assumes that foreign savings are invested and that the investment will raise the country's capital ratio (with respect to labour). The country

will import foreign savings as a function of the difference between the efficiency and the borrowing cost of investment. Table 8.3 shows that all sample countries should have benefited from foreign savings in principle, given the strong difference between efficiency and cost measures. That difference is particularly strong for Thailand, Malaysia and Chile; it is weaker for Mexico, Peru and the Philippines, with Argentina and Indonesia in between. Strikingly, labour was only equipped with more capital where capital was most efficient (Argentina, Chile, Indonesia, Malaysia and Thailand). By contrast, the capital–labour ratio fell strongly in Mexico during the inflow period, excluding any benefits there on standard neo-classical grounds.

Table 8.3   *Efficiency, average borrowing cost and capital–output ratios (in per cent)*

Country	Efficiency[a] avg. 1987–94	Real interest cost[b] avg. 1988–94	First year of inflow	Capital–labour ratio[c] % change up to 1993
Argentina	18.9	3.5	1991	+8.0
Chile	24.4	3.8	1990	+21.2
Mexico	13.2	4.3	1989	−23.1
Peru	n.a.	3.2	1992	−1.0
Indonesia	20.4	3.0	1990	+18.1
Malaysia	22.7	2.9	1989	+24.0
Philippines	13.5	3.0	1992	+1.2
Thailand	27.8	3.3	1988	+40.6

Sources:
a. JP Morgan, *Emerging Markets Economic Outlook*, September 1995. Efficiency is defined here as the inverse of the investment rate to the real GDP growth rate.
b. World Bank, *World Debt Tables 1996*, Vol. 2. Defined as average terms of new commitments in US dollar terms minus US CPI inflation rate.
c. World Bank data files.

Figure 8.1 displays the Solow residual derived from estimating equation (8.1). We see marginal productivity rise during the inflow period, except in Peru, Indonesia and the Philippines (and in the G7 countries). The evidence gives some support for the presumption on standard neo-classical grounds, that foreign savings were highly beneficial if they were invested, above all in Thailand, Malaysia and Chile.

Figure 8.1   Solow residuals

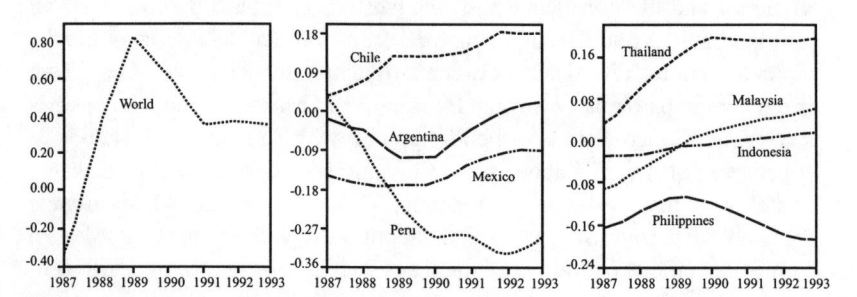

Sources: Author's calculations; IMF, National Accounts.

Table 8.4   Income growth and convergence

Country	PPP estimates[a] of GNP per capita (US=100)		Potential GDP growth rate since classified as 'open' by Sachs/Warner[b]		Actual GDP growth rate since first year of inflow until 1995[c]
	1990	1994	Year	Growth potential	
Argentina	21.9	33.7	1991	4.3	5.4
Chile	29.0	34.4	1976	4.2	6.4
Mexico	28.0	27.2	1986	1.8	1.7
Peru	12.7	13.9	1991	7.8	5.9
Indonesia	11.0	13.9	1970	6.1	7.1
Malaysia	27.6	32.6	1970	6.5	8.9
Philippines	10.9	10.6	1988	2.6	3.8
Thailand	21.6	26.9	1960	7.2	9.7

Sources:
a. World Bank, *World Development Report*, 1992 and 1996.
b. Peak-to-peak method; see text.
c. JP Morgan, *World Financial Markets*, various issues.

What happened to growth and convergence after the inflows started? Table 8.4 reports actually some decline for Mexico's and the Philippines' PPP adjusted per capita income, while the other recipient countries catch up strongly. We also observe, with the noticeable exception of Mexico and Peru, that the inflow period coincides with *actual* GDP growth rates that exceed our estimates of *potential* growth rates, which refer to the period since the sample countries have 'opened up' according to Sachs and Warner (1995). (The potential growth rates have been obtained by the simple peak-to-peak method, as will be explained below.) However, it is still too early to

arrive at any solid judgement on whether the recent capital inflows have raised efficiency and the growth rate permanently.

How well then does the inter-temporal approach explain actual current account balances in our eight sample countries? It is still too early, in view of the limited number of reliable observations of productivity developments in the sample countries for the recent capital-inflow period, to estimate investment and current-account equations for the individual sample countries.[3] We therefore present for the period 1988–93 panel estimates for the current-account equation

$$CA_t = b_0 + b_1 I_{t-1} + b_2 \Delta \theta^c_t + b_3 \theta^w_t + b_4 CA_{t-1} + b_5 TOT_t + b_6 r^w_t, \quad (8.4)$$

where *CA* is the current account deficit as a fraction of GDP, *I* is gross domestic investment as a fraction of GDP, θ^c and θ^w are domestic and global productivity (the Solow residual derived from Cobb–Douglas production functions), *TOT* is the terms of trade index, and r^w is the real US treasury bill interest rate (see Table 8.5, first panel).

Table 8.5   Panel estimates on current-account equations, 1988–93 (t-values in brackets)

---

1. $CA_t = b_1 I_{t-1} + b_2 \Delta \theta^c_t + b_3 \theta^w_t + b_4 CA_{t-1} + b_5 TOT_t + b_6 r^w_t$

    −0.2   −0.02   −0.06   +0.6   −0.001   +0.01
    (−0.87) (−0.14) (−1.7)   (2.52) (−1.02) (0.31)

Estimation: Fixed effect model using OLS framework;
    number of observations: 48; $R^2 = 0.59$; DW = 2.53

---

2. $BD_t = b_1 (S^{pr} - I)_t$

    −0.4 $R^2 = 0.84$; DW = 1.48; number of obs. = 48
    (−10.2)

    $CA_t = b_1 I_{t-1} + b_2 \Delta \theta^c_t + b_3 \theta^w_t + b_4 CA_{t-1} + b_5 TOT_t + b_6 r^w_t$

    −0.1   +0.1   −0.1   +0.5   −0.001   +0.003
    (−0.45) (1.16) (−2.54) (3.42) (−0.48) (0.89)

    $R^2 = 0.58$; DW = 2.62; number of obs. = 48

Estimation: Simultaneous equation system with GMM estimation (= 3 SLS).

Sources: Instrumental variable method was used; residuals were heteroskedastic-consistent.
Current account, gross domestic investment, terms of trade index: all World Bank data base.
US treasury bill interest rate minus change in CPI index/private savings: all IMF.
Domestic productivity, world productivity (GDP-weighted average for G7 countries) are Solow residuals from Cobb–Douglas production functions: all World Bank data base; national accounts.

The second panel estimate in Table 8.5 introduces a government budget reaction function similar to Summers (1988), where

$$BD_t = b_0 + b_1 (S^{pr} - I)_t \tag{8.5}$$

the government budget deficit BD_t responds to changes in the balance between private savings S^{pr} and investment (all variables as a fraction of GDP). Equation (8.5) can be taken as evidence of current-account targeting, so that equation (8.4) has to be estimated in a simultaneous equation system.

As seen in Table 8.5, there is a strong negative correlation between the size of the private current account and the size of the budget deficit. The results for the current-account equation are largely the same, however, in the direct and the simultaneous panel estimate. All parameters show the expected sign as predicted in Table 8.2, but only global productivity enters significantly among the determinants stressed by the inter-temporal approach.

The results in Table 8.5 lead to the tentative conclusion that econometric tests derived from the inter-temporal approach to the current account cannot explain actual current account deficits in major capital-flow recipient countries. This means either that the observed current account deficits have been excessive, or that the benchmark (derived from the inter-temporal approach) is ill-defined or insufficiently represented in our estimates. While global productivity (as defined in Table 8.5) stagnated during the observation period 1988–93, country-specific productivity surges were observed in Argentina, Chile, Malaysia, Mexico and Thailand. These countries could be predicted by the inter-temporal approach to run current account deficits, due to transitorily higher investment levels (and possibly lower saving rates), assuming that the productivity surges were permanent.

Table 8.6 explores the issue in more country detail by means of a simple shift analysis. The table (apart from the memo columns) is structured as Table 8.2 which summarized the main predictions of the inter-temporal model. As Table 8.6 shows, the observed shift in savings–investment balances often does not suit the theoretical predictions:

–   Argentina and Peru engage in excessive private consumption. Only a permanent rise in productivity, which should give rise to higher investment rates, or a temporary drop of actual output below potential could have justified the observed rise in private consumption rates. There is, however, no rise in observed investment rates, while actual output has been rising strongly.

- The Mexican story is slightly different, because output growth remained extremely low during the inflow period. There was some moderate rise in investment rates, but most of the switch in the current account balance was due to a private consumption boom. That boom could partly be justified by higher public savings, current income levels below potential, and expectations of higher permanent income (as indicated by higher investment); but the size of the switch in private consumption is clearly excessive.

Table 8.6   Saving–investment balances in selected countries

Country	Change in annual averages as % of GDP from first year of inflow to 1994 against 1986 to first year of inflow[b]				Memo:		
	Current account	Investment	Saving	Private consumption	First year of inflow	Year when CA deficit peaked	Peak CA deficit,[a] % of GDP
Argentina	−2.1	+0.4	−1.7	+4.2	1991	1994	3.5
Chile	+1.3	+4.3	+5.6	−0.2	1990	1993	2.1
Mexico[c]	−5.3	+1.8	−3.5	+5.8	1989	1994	7.8
Peru	−2.5	−0.8	−3.4	+3.9	1992	1995	6.4
Indonesia	+1.1	+4.6	+5.7	−4.3	1990	1996	4.0
Malaysia	−8.2	+8.8	+0.6	+2.4	1989	1995	8.5
Philippines	−2.4	+3.5	+1.1	+3.6	1992	1994	4.5
Thailand	−5.4	+11.8	+6.4	−5.6	1988	1995	8.3

Sources:
a. JP Morgan, *World Financial Markets*, Second Quarter 1996; data for 1995 are estimates and for 1996 forecasts.
b. Based on national account data; saving rates were derived as residual; IMF, *International Financial Statistics*.
c. IMF, *World Economic Outlook*, May 1995.

- There is also a rise in private consumption, as a fraction of GDP, in Malaysia and the Philippines. The rise is compensated by a sufficient rise in public savings and validated by higher investment rates (indicating expectations of higher permanent income levels). It should be noted, however, that the rise in the Philippine investment rate goes along with a fall in the Solow residual (Figure 8.1) during the inflow period.

- Chile, Indonesia and Thailand respond to capital inflows with a drop in private consumption rates, although their output growth rises on impact above potential, although public savings rise (implying no Ricardian offset), and although a strong rise in investment rates and rising

productivity would quite solidly warrant expectations of a higher permanent income. Note finally that Indonesia and Chile reduce their external deficit as a result of strong increases in savings. Indonesia is different from Chile and Thailand, however, in one respect: productivity (Figure 8.1) declines during the inflow period, suggesting a future drop in the country's investment rate and current account deficit.

The evidence suggests two lessons, one for theorists and one for practitioners. The insight for theory is that the inter-temporal approach fails to predict the macroeconomic responses of most capital-flow recipient countries. In the case of Chile, the existence of effective capital controls may provide a part of the explanation for the failure of the inter-temporal approach (which assumes full capital mobility). In the case of the other sample countries (for which full openness can be assumed), 'excessive' private consumption (Argentina, Mexico, Peru) and 'excessive' savings responses (Thailand) must be explained by the determinants not captured by the consumption-smoothing approach.

The insight for the practitioners is that current account deficits were excessive in Mexico and are probably more in Peru by 1996. Malaysia's and Thailand's deficits, although high, cannot be labelled as 'excessive', however. They are used for investment which exploits high efficiency and rising total factor productivity; moreover, foreign savings are so far supported by rising national savings in these countries.

LONG-TERM SUSTAINABILITY

Debt Dynamics

It is a common fallacy to confuse unsustainability with undesirability. Foreign savings must not necessarily be resisted because they finance a current account deficit that is unsustainably large. In particular during reform episodes, a deficit may represent a sound stock adjustment from financial assets into real assets in the case of an investment boom, because the expected profitability of real assets has improved. The corresponding deficit in the current account will inevitably be temporary, yet desirable. This is a valuable lesson from the inter-temporal approach.

Nonetheless, a large deficit will not be financed by foreigners forever; there will at some point inevitably have to be adjustment back to payments balance. It is thus not only important to know the *sources* of the current account deficit (see below), but also the *size* and the *time profile* of the

balancing adjustment. And that makes long-term sustainability of the current account deficit a benchmark of which authorities should be aware.

Building on work by Milesi-Ferretti and Razin (1996) and Edwards, Steiner and Losada (1995),[4] let us first consider an economy in steady state, with liabilities as a fraction of the country's GDP that foreigners are willing to hold in equilibrium, denoted by *d*. *d* can be seen as an 'equilibrium portfolio share'. Note that foreign direct investment is *not* governed by portfolio considerations; multinational companies seek to internalize agglomeration benefits by concentrating (rather than diversifying) their FDI flows. Consequently, FDI flows will not be covered by the subsequent discussion on long-term sustainability. In equilibrium, i.e. with *d* to be held constant, the country can accumulate net liabilities, equal to both the current account deficit plus net accumulation of international reserves, as a fraction of GDP, *CA* and *FX*, in proportion to its long-run GDP growth, γ.

$$CA + \Delta FX = \gamma d \qquad (8.6)$$

Long-run GDP growth also exerts two indirect effects on the steady state current account that is consistent with a stable debt-to-GDP ratio. First, as the economy expands, the desired level of international reserves will also grow. The literature on the demand for international reserves has empirically identified two different determinants (Heller and Khan, 1978). The first is the level of imports (not the import ratio, which is ambiguous), with an elasticity of demand for reserves close to unity. The second is the variability in the balance of payments which, by creating uncertainty, increases the demand for reserves. We ignore the uncertainty in the balance of payments, which is difficult to forecast; yet, it can in principle be incorporated into the analysis, by making predictions about the coefficient of variation from the time trend in the foreign reserve ratio. Denoting real annual import growth by η, the change in the desired reserve ratio can be written as

$$\Delta FX = [(1 + \eta)/(1 + \gamma)]FX - FX \qquad (8.7)$$

Incorporating (7) into (6) yields

$$\gamma d = CA + [(\eta - \gamma)/(1 + \gamma)]FX \qquad (8.8)$$

A second channel through which GDP growth indirectly impacts on debt dynamics is the Balassa–Samuelson effect. In the long run, *relative* growth will lead to real exchange rate appreciation, largely driven by the evolution of productivity differentials between the traded and non-traded goods in the

domestic economy and in the rest of the world. Real exchange rate appreciation per unit of GDP growth, denoted by ε, reduces both debt and foreign exchange reserves as a fraction of GDP, so that equation (8.8) is enlarged to

$$(\gamma + \varepsilon)d = CA + [(\eta + \varepsilon - \gamma)/(1 + \gamma)]FX \qquad (8.9)$$

Equation (8.9) describes the steady-state current account deficit that can be sustained over the long run if the debt ratio remains constant and desired reserves are raised in proportion to import growth:

$$CA = (\gamma + \varepsilon)d - [(\eta + \varepsilon - \gamma)/(1 + \gamma)]FX \qquad (8.9')$$

Table 8.7 provides numerical examples of equation (8.9') for four Latin American and four Asian countries. The variables d (total external debt/GDP) and FX (international reserves/GDP) refer to 1995 estimates as given in JP Morgan, *World Financial Markets* (29 March 1996). The variables γ, ε, and η, ideally, should be estimated on the basis of best guesses about *future* trends.

For γ, we estimate the potential real GDP growth rate for two periods, for 1960–95 and for the countries' respective period of 'openness' as classified by Sachs and Warner (1995). Since GDP can be seen as the result of a transformation of key factors of production, a theoretically appropriate way to estimate potential GDP is to feed the available volume of factor inputs in the business sector into a numerically specified production function. However, even small estimation errors for the individual parameters of the production function (output elasticities; rate of technical progress; degree of slack) can add up quickly to produce rather implausible estimates for potential output. We thus opt for a very simple approach, which only uses actual GDP data as input for the derivation of potential GDP estimates, the so-called *peak-to-peak method*.

In a first step, we identified the peak of actual GDP in each cycle and connected these data points by interpolation. The procedure is applied for two different observation periods, for 1960–95 (for Malaysia 1970–95) and from the countries' opening until 1995. For Argentina and Peru, Sachs and Warner (1995) classify the year of opening as 1991, for the Philippines 1988, for Mexico 1986 and for Chile 1976; in the other cases the observation periods coincide. We use annual GDP data, except for Peru and the Philippines where good quarterly data are available and where the reform period is relatively short. The resulting GDP series can be seen as an approximation of the highest attainable level of output at any given point in time.

Table 8.7 Debt-related current account deficits in steady state

Country	CA =	$(\gamma+\varepsilon)d^*$		$[(\eta+\varepsilon-\gamma)/(1+\gamma)]FX^*$	Memo: d	FX
Argentina	0.016	(0.043+0.007)0.5	—	[0.318+0.007−0.043]/1.043]0.035	0.33	0.050
Chile	0.020	(0.042+0.006)0.5	—	[0.069+0.006−0.042]/1.042]0.114	0.34	0.220
Mexico	−0.006	(0.018+0.000)0.5	—	[0.126+0.000−0.018]/1.018]0.140	0.68	0.058
Peru	0.038	(0.078+0.009)0.5	—	[0.152+0.009−0.078]/1.078]0.065	0.51	0.127
Indonesia	0.030	(0.061+0.004)0.5	—	[0.073+0.004−0.061]/1.061]0.099	0.54	0.088
Malaysia	0.017	(0.065+0.014)0.5	—	[0.111+0.014−0.065]/1.065]0.396	0.42	0.291
Philippines	0.006	(0.026+0.001)0.5	—	[0.112+0.001−0.026]/1.026]0.166	0.59	0.087
Thailand	0.028	(0.072+0.010)0.5	—	[0.133+0.010−0.072]/1.072]0.197	0.48	0.192

Note:
* See text for explanation.

In a second step, we calculated the average ratio of actual GDP to the highest attainable GDP for each cycle – a measure for the 'normal' degree of slack in the eight economies – and applied this ratio to the series of highest attainable GDP to derive estimates for potential GDP. The *annual growth rate* of potential GDP is then obtained by regressing the series of potential GDP on a time trend. The results show largely plausible parameter values, except possibly for Mexico and the Philippines where the opening of the economy actually seems to have reduced the growth rate of potential GDP relative to the total observation period. For want of any better estimates, the growth rates of potential GDP obtained for the period since reform are used in Table 8.7.

For ε, we rely on Larraín (1996) who has estimated with the Instrumental Variables Method the determinants of real exchange rates (viz. the dollar) for a sample of 28 Asian and Latin American countries through the period 1960–90. The impact of GDP relative to the US level on real exchange rates is corrected for other determinants, namely government spending, degree of openness and terms of trade. The calculation of ε, the annual 'equilibrium' real exchange rate appreciation is not only driven by the annual growth rate of potential GDP, but also by the country's relative income level. Since the relationship between real exchange rates and relative GDP levels is non-linear, a given estimate for the growth rate of potential GDP will lead to more real equilibrium exchange rate appreciation at higher relative income levels; witness the difference, for example, between Malaysia and Indonesia.

Finally, estimates about the future annual real import growth rate, η, are simply extrapolated out of the reform-period sample for each country. Argentina's annual import growth may seem implausibly high, but it has to be recognized that Argentina is still a very closed economy in terms of the import ratio *m* and that the potential for natural trade (Mercosur) is far from exhausted.

Table 8.7 displays the calibration of equation (8.9') for the long-run equilibrium current account ratio which holds debt and reserve levels steady in terms of GDP. Since a high debt ratio can be sustained by a larger deficit in the current account than a smaller debt ratio, we assume for all sample countries that foreign investors are comfortable with tolerating a debt ratio of 50 per cent. This is at about the level in Peru or Thailand, countries about which the financial press has started to worry recently. Likewise, for the foreign exchange reserves we assume a target level of half the import ratio (six months of imports) for all countries. Note that because of low estimates of potential growth rates, neither Mexico nor the Philippines can afford a steady-state deficit in the debt-related current account.

Table 8.8 considers a hypothetical adjustment of the current debt–GDP ratio to 0.5 and of foreign exchange reserves to a target level of half the import–GDP ratio. The resulting 'transitional' current account deficits vary largely across countries. To reach the targeted debt–GDP and reserve levels within five years, Mexico would have to run a current-account *surplus* worth more than 5 per cent of GDP (excluding the part financed by FDI). Chile, by contrast, could enjoy a five-year period of current-account *deficits* (plus FDI) of 5 per cent of GDP to find herself at the imposed levels of debt stocks and foreign exchange levels.

Table 8.8   *Transitional current account deficits (five-year adjustment to*
$d^*=0.5$ *and* $FX^*=0.5m$*)*

Country	1/5CA	=	$d^*-(1-\gamma-\varepsilon)d$	–	$[FX^*-((1-\eta-\varepsilon)/1+\gamma)FX]$
Argentina	0.0367	=	0.1865	–	0.0027
Chile	0.0515	=	0.1763	+	0.0813
Mexico	−0.0516	=	−0.1678	–	0.0902
Peru	0.0136	=	0.0344	+	0.0338
Indonesia	−0.0045	=	−0.0049	–	0.0173
Malaysia	−0.0087	=	0.1132	–	0.1569
Philippines	−0.0330	=	−0.0741	–	0.0908
Thailand	0.0032	=	0.0594	–	0.0435

* See text for explanation.

Table 8.9   *Various concepts of current account balances (in per cent of*
GDP)

	Memo: Actual 1994	Cyclical correction	–	FDI	=	Residual	Memo: Steady-state	Memo: Transitional
Argentina	−3.5	−3.0	–	0.4	=	−2.6	−1.6	−3.7
Chile	−1.5	−1.5	–	3.6	=	+2.1	−2.0	−5.2
Mexico	−7.8	−7.1	–	2.2	=	−4.9	+0.1	+5.2
Peru	−4.5	−3.5	–	4.7	=	+1.2	−3.8	−1.4
Indonesia	−1.6	−0.4	–	1.3	=	+0.9	−3.0	+0.5
Malaysia	−5.9	±0.0	–	6.5	=	+6.5	−1.7	+0.9
Philippines	−4.4	−4.3	–	1.5	=	−2.8	+0.6	+3.3
Thailand	−5.9	−1.1	–	3.1	=	+2.0	−2.8	−0.3

Note:
The cyclically corrected deficit corrects imports for the difference in actual and potential GDP.

Table 8.9 displays the various concepts for actual, cyclically corrected, FDI-corrected, steady-state and transitional current deficits for the year 1994 (the last year for which FDI data were available). Then, taking account of FDI and cyclical correction (the residual), current account deficits were higher than steady-state deficits in Argentina, Mexico and the Philippines. By contrast, high-deficit countries such as Malaysia and Thailand were clearly within long-term sustainable ranges.

PROBLEMS WITH EXCESSIVE CURRENT ACCOUNT DEFICITS

The benefits of foreign savings – consumption-smoothing and growth of income – will not materialize when current account deficits represent excessive current consumption or when foreign funds are misallocated. A hard landing to payments balance will thus be unavoidable. We have first to recall, however, some arguments of those who think that excessive consumption and unsound investment surges are unlikely to happen in the absence of public-sector deficits and distortions.

The Lawson Doctrine

Commenting on concerns over the UK balance of payments in a speech to the IMF, the UK Chancellor Nigel Lawson concluded in September 1988 (a year before a deep crisis with falling output and surging unemployment set in): 'we are prisoners of the past, when UK current account deficits were almost invariably associated with large budget deficits, poor economic performance, low reserves and exiguous net overseas assets. The present position could not be more different'. What came to be internationally known as the Lawson doctrine, is a proposition that has been most eloquently expressed by Max Corden (1977; and, with some qualifications, 1994):

> The current account is the net result of savings and investment, private and public. Decentralized optimal decisions on private saving and investment will lead to a net balance – the current account – which will also be optimal. There is no reason to presume that governments or outside observers know better how much private agents should invest and save than these agents themselves, unless there are government-imposed distortions. It follows that an increase in a current account deficit that results from a shift in private sector behaviour should not be a matter of concern at all. On the other hand, the public budget balance is a matter of public policy concern and the focus should be on this. (Corden, 1994)

The fact, however, that large current account deficits reflected primarily a private-sector saving–investment imbalance did not prevent private capital markets from attacking currencies in Chile (early 1980s), in the UK and the Nordic countries (late 1980s) and in Mexico and Argentina (mid-1990s). So what was wrong with the Lawson doctrine?

– *First*, in a forward-looking rational-expectations framework, current account balances are always the result of private-sector decisions, with or without public-sector deficits. With Ricardian equivalence, a public budget deficit will immediately stimulate private savings to pay for future taxes. People who subscribe to the Lawson doctrine are thus saying that they do not believe in Ricardian equivalence (they believe in optimal private-sector decisions, but not in rational expectations). In fact, the Ricardian offset coefficient has been estimated to average 0.5 for developing countries (Edwards, 1995); other things being equal, a deterioration in the current account worth 5 per cent of GDP thus would require the public-sector deficit to worsen by 10 per cent of GDP.

– *Second*, current private-sector liabilities are often contingent public-sector liabilities. Foreign creditors may force governments, as happened in Chile after 1982, to turn private-sector debt into public-sector obligations. Furthermore, private-sector losses tend to be absorbed eventually by the public sector, either in terms of tax revenue forgone or through costly resolutions of banking crises, in particular when financial institutions are deemed 'too large to fail'. Balance-of-payments and financial crises are often caused by common factors, such as domestic financial liberalization, implicit deposit insurance or exchange rate-based stabilization plans (Kaminsky and Reinhart, 1996).

– *Third*, observed and expected returns to saving and investment are distorted by various market failures: (a) private borrowers do not internalize the rising marginal social cost of their private borrowing that arise from the upward-sloping supply of foreign capital (Harberger, 1985); (b) excessively optimistic expectations about permanent income levels after major changes in the policy regime lead to over-borrowing, because financial market institutions fail as efficient information conduits between depositors and borrowers (McKinnon and Pill, 1995). Financial market bubbles add to such boom mentality by discouraging private savings through the wealth effect.

– *Fourth*, a movement into current account deficit may lead to an unsustainable appreciation in the real exchange rate. The appreciation is

in conflict with development strategies based on the expansion of exports and efficient import substitution, which centrally relies on a reliable and competitive exchange rate. Overvalued exchange rates cause sub-optimal investments which are costly to reverse, undermine active trade promotion, export diversification and productivity growth and breed capital flight. Large swings in real exchange rates, often a result of temporary capital flows, have been found to significantly depress machinery and equipment investment and thus long-run growth performance (Agosin, 1994).

– *Fifth* (as now also stressed by Corden, 1994), markets are concerned with country risk and do look at a country's total debt ratio. Therefore, the current account as a whole, and not just the sources of its changes, become relevant. Once debt ratios and current account deficits exceed certain levels (see above), decentralized decision making can lead to excessive borrowing from a national point of view (again, due to the Harberger externality), particularly when increased borrowing is for consumption rather than for investment.

Table 8.10 Corrections of private-sector driven current account deficits

Country	Year (period avg.)	Current acc. % of GDP	Real GDP growth % p.a.	Real priv. cons. % p.a. per cap.	RER appreciation % p.a.
Chile	1980	−7.1	7.8	1.5	22.0
	1981	−14.5	5.6	2.4	8.4
	1982	−9.5	−14.1	−12.4	−20.6
	1983	−5.6	−0.7	−5.1	−20.4
Mexico	1993	−6.5	0.6	−2.1	5.8
	1994	−7.8	3.5	3.7	−3.7
	1995	−0.3	−6.9	−9.2	−28.1
Argentina	1993	−2.9	6.0	1.2	7.4
	1994	−3.5	7.4	3.7	1.7
	1995	−0.8	−4.4	−9.2	0.4

Sources: IMF, *International Financial Statistics*; JP Morgan, *World Financial Markets*; own calculations.

Table 8.10 displays three hard-landing episodes in Latin America where the required switch in the current account went along with sharp drops in real GDP, even sharper cuts in private per capita consumption, and often strong depreciation in real exchange rates. During the bust, the benefits of

consumption-smoothing and growth enhancement through foreign savings
do indeed ring hollow.

Private Spending Booms

As defined above, large current account deficits may represent 'excessive'
private consumption, as was suggested above for Argentina, Mexico and
Peru. The empirical link between consumption booms, surges in bank
lending and subsequent banking crises is well documented (Gavin and
Hausmann, 1996). Therefore, payments deficits owing to private spending
booms suggest great risks to the public sector – risks of tax revenue losses
and costly bank crisis resolutions, as documented by Table 8.11.

Table 8.11 Episodes of systemic banking crises with heavy capital inflows

Country	Scope of crisis	Cost of rescuing banks, % of GDP
Argentina 1980–82	16% of assets of commercial banks; 35% of total assets of finance companies	55.3
Chile 1981–83	45% of total assets	41.2
Israel 1977–83	Entire banking sector	30.0
Finland 1991–93	Savings banks affected	8.2
Mexico 1995–?	Commercial banks past due to gross loan ratio reaches 9.3% in February 1995	12–15

Sources: Bank for International Settlements, *63rd Annual Report*, 1993; G. Caprio and D.
Klingebiel (1996).

While it seems obvious that such costs imposed on the public sector
suggest that governments engage in some stabilizing measures to moderate
private spending booms (restrictive fiscal policies or credit restrictions for
private borrowers), it is less straightforward that the resistance to large
current account deficits is part of such measures. Distortions should be
corrected at the source; the twin payment and banking crises seem to
originate in either domestic financial deregulation, implicit deposit
insurance, or protracted exchange rate-based stabilization plans:

- Since the 1980s, the link between banking crises and balance-of-payments crises has strengthened. Kaminsky and Reinhart (1996) trace 71 balance-of-payments crises and 25 banking crises during the period 1970–95; while they report only 3 banking crises vs 25 balance-of-payments crises during 1970–79, they find 22 banking crises vs 46 payments crises over 1980–95. They find that financial liberalization (which has occurred mostly since the 1980s) plays a significant role in explaining the probability of a banking crisis preceded by a private lending boom. A banking crisis, in turn, helps to predict a currency crisis. There is also clear evidence for the OECD countries that quick and extensive financial deregulation has tended to lower household savings by lessening liquidity constraints (Blundell-Wignall and Browne, 1991). While most of that drop in private savings could be interpreted as a temporary stock adjustment to a higher consumption path, there is evidence that household saving rates have remained low, unless financial deregulation occurred gradually or had already occurred in the 1950s and 1960s (Andersen and White, 1996).

- Information asymmetries, reinforced by the lack of institutions that monitor and supervise credit risk, produce moral hazard and adverse selection. Firms with a high risk–return profile have an incentive to borrow heavily, as their exposure is limited by bankruptcy laws. Consumers incur excessive debt when they feel that their debt is not comprehensively monitored. In principle, banks and other intermediaries may attempt to reduce credit risk through credit rationing. This would set a limit to the extent to which liberalization can ease liquidity constraints. But when the government insures deposits against adverse outcomes, it alters how the banking system views the risks associated with making loans – it introduces moral hazard. This results in higher bank lending, which in turn can underpin excessively optimistic expectations about the success of reform (McKinnon and Pill, 1995).[5]

- Exchange rate-based stabilization plans have often been accompanied by a boom in bank lending, which in turn has fuelled a boom in consumption spending. Unlike under money-based stabilization, disinflation produces a rise in real-money balances, as a result of central bank intervention to peg the currency and of higher money demand as domestic wealth holders convert their assets back into domestic currency. The unsterilized intervention on the foreign exchange market is fully intermediated into the banking system. This allows a boom in credit to agents who have been rationed previously as a result of

inflation and financial repression (Sachs *et al.*, 1996; Reisen, 1993). Subsequently, overvaluation due to inflation inertia will cause recession and a deterioration of bank assets as a result of non-performing loans and lower asset prices.

While the source of these private spending booms is domestic and not the fact that they are financed by foreign savings, we have to ask whether foreign savings do worsen the boom (Corden, 1994). In the absence of foreign capital inflows, the spending boom would manifest itself not in a current account deficit, but in higher interest rates. The critical question, then, is what kind of investment would be crowded out by the rise in domestic interest rates. With ineffective bank supervision (as a result of too rapid financial deregulation, for example), the average productivity of borrowing may decline as risk-averse investors withdraw from the pool of potential borrowers. The failure to finance productive investment would be the cost of the decision not to accept capital inflows; the excess of the risk-adjusted domestic interest rate over the world interest rate would be a measure of the distortion created by that decision. The result on the decision whether to accept or resist inflows would be ambiguous.

In the McKinnon–Pill model the closed-economy financial market failure is reflected in higher financial yields, but its effect on quantities – borrowing and consumption – is ambiguous, depending on offsetting income and substitution effects. Excessively optimistic expectations about future permanent income levels, resulting in both over-consumption and over-investment, are financed by excessive borrowing from the rest of the world. The distortion (crazy expectations; boom mentality) is reinforced by foreign savings. The McKinnon–Pill solution to the distortion is similar to a Pigou–Harberger tax (nominally, a reserve requirement on foreign deposits) so as to incite the optimal choice between consumption-smoothing and excessive borrowing.

The first-best solution to the boom distortion triggered by exchange rate-based stabilization is to announce, at the start of the stabilization plan, that a peg will be temporary, to be followed by more nominal exchange rate flexibility. While this is easier said than done, it will not do away with the immediate remonetization and real exchange rate appreciation that characterize the first phase of disinflation. Temporary support from selective controls on short-term capital controls may well be needed (Hausmann and Reisen, 1996).

The Real Appreciation Problem

If the scope for sterilized intervention is limited or exhausted[6] and if foreign savings are partly spent on nontradables, a protracted current account deficit will be associated with real appreciation of the exchange rate. But there is no mechanical link between the size of the deficit and the size of appreciation. To the extent that the shift in the current account balance represents higher investment, the increased resource transfer is likely to be spent on additional imports of capital goods and intermediate goods. In such a case, the real transfer will be 'effected' largely through the transfer of purchasing power, with little effect on relative prices. But when the current account deficit largely represents a consumption boom, the transfer of purchasing power will not solve the real transfer problem by itself, since a large part of the additional purchasing power is likely to fall on nontradables. In such cases, a shift in relative prices – a real appreciation of the exchange rate in the recipient country – will be necessary. This lesson from the inter-war transfer debate is fully supported by Table 8.12.

Table 8.12   Consumption, import structure and real exchange rate appreciation

Country	Change in domestic saving rate since inflows started (from Table 8.6)	Degree of undervaluation (US=100) Current vs PPP-adj. income per cap.			Catch-up effect	Residual (change minus catch-up effect)
		1990	1994	Change		
Argentina	−1.7	50	93	+43	8	35
Chile	+5.6	31	40	+9	3	6
Mexico	−3.5	32	60	+28	0	28
Peru	−3.4	42	59	+17	1	16
Indonesia	+5.7	24	24	±0	1	−1
Malaysia	+0.6	38	41	+3	7	−4
Philippines	+1.1	31	35	+4	0	4
Thailand	+6.4	30	35	+5	5	0

Sources: World Bank, *World Development Report,* 1992 and 1996; Larraín (1996).

The table suggests that the real appreciation problem only appeared when capital inflows were mostly consumed rather than invested, as was noted for Argentina, Mexico and Peru. The degree of 'unwarranted' appreciation (the residual) is derived from data in the UN Income Comparison Project, as reported in the World Bank's *World Development Reports.* What is known

as the Balassa–Samuelson effect, is that poor countries tend to be 'cheap' in PPP terms, since services tend to be cheaper in poor countries. In fact, there is a strong non-linear correlation between the PPP-adjusted per capita income of a country relative to the US and the deviation of the currency below PPP (Reisen, 1993). In 1990, neither Argentina nor Peru had been 'cheap' countries in PPP terms as determined by their comparative per capita income. Since then, however, their currencies have strongly appreciated, as did the Mexican peso until 1994. Only a small part of that appreciation (in Mexico's case, none) is due to the 'catch-up' effect: the fact that relative growth (compared with US levels) will lead to trend appreciation of the real exchange rate. The table again employs the results obtained by Larraín (1996). The 'residual' appreciation is likely to be in conflict with development strategies based on the expansion of exports and efficient import substitution, which centrally relies on a reliable and competitive exchange rate, similar to the 'Dutch disease' effects of a major discovery of natural resources (Edwards and van Wijnbergen, 1989).

Is Foreign Direct Investment Special?

From 1970 to 1982, Singapore ran a current account deficit worth 12.1 per cent of GDP on average; in the early 1970s, the deficit peaked at around 20 per cent of GDP several times. Almost half of the corresponding net capital inflows consisted of foreign direct investment (FDI). Real GDP growth averaged more than 8.6 per cent per year over the period; the domestic saving rate doubled from 21 per cent in 1970 to more than 40 per cent in 1982; a balance-of-payments crisis never developed. Such anecdotal evidence is supported by Frankel and Rose (1996), who find in a panel of annual data for over 100 developing countries from 1971 through 1991 that a high ratio of FDI to debt is associated with a low likelihood of a currency crash. This raises the question whether FDI is special with respect to its macroeconomic implications. There is a strong presumption that indeed it is:

–   First, foreign direct investment is largely determined by non-cyclical considerations. Being rather governed by long-term profitability expectations, it is less subject to sudden shifts in investor sentiment. While on an annual basis, large fluctuations of foreign-direct-investment *flows* are regularly observed, foreign-direct-investment *stocks* are largely illiquid and irreversible.[7] Foreign direct investment, which is little dependent on financial market sentiment, has bad-weather qualities. This observation is reinforced by Mexico's capital

account in 1995, which showed only a slightly reduced net inflow of foreign direct investment.

– Second, the Harberger externality does not apply to foreign direct investment. Even if the supply schedule of FDI was upward-sloping, FDI is likely to produce positive external spillovers, comparable to agglomeration benefits. This conjecture implies that higher inflows of FDI will carry positive externalities, by improving the host country's production function (Borensztein *et al.*, 1995). Moreover, returns on FDI are state-contingent and sovereign risk seems to apply less than to other forms of foreign capital inflows. As a result, foreign investors do not observe an upper limit of engagement, in contrast to debt ratios and the like.

– Third, to the extent that FDI is not induced by privatization (which represents, other things being equal, just a change in ownership), FDI inflows will exert less upward pressure on the real exchange rate, minimizing the risk of 'Dutch disease' (see Table 8.13). Since FDI is likely to crowd in domestic investment and to the extent that it is 'green plant' investment, it will stimulate a corresponding movement in the demand for foreign exchange by stimulating imports. Moreover, by stimulating investment rather than consumption, FDI creates an *ex ante* home goods excess supply in the recipient country; equilibrium in the home goods market requires a depreciation of the real exchange rate to stimulate the demand for home goods (Artus, 1996).

Table 8.13   Foreign direct investment and privatization, 1990–94

	Latin America	East Asia (excl. China)
Net private capital inflows, $ bn	173.8	110.0
– of which: raised through privatization	22.2	3.8
Net foreign direct investment inflows, $ bn	71.3	47.2
– of which: raised through privatization	13.0	2.0
'Traditional' foreign direct investment, $ bn	58.3	45.2
% of 'traditional' FDI in net inflows	33.5	41.1

Sources: World Bank, *World Debt Tables 1996*; own calculations.

CONCLUSIONS

This chapter has first surveyed several theoretical strands in the economic literature for their hypotheses regarding the benefits of *net* capital inflows (as opposed to capital mobility and gross capital flows). Perhaps surprisingly, in the current context of heavy portfolio flows and non-binding foreign exchange constraints (which were emphasized earlier on by the two-gap literature), the benefits of large net inflows are mostly found to be small.

Even if net capital inflows were fully invested rather than consumed, neo-classical growth models do not promise grandiose benefits. The resulting rise in the capital ratio will only affect short-term growth, not a country's long-term growth rate, as long as capital flows do not affect the production function. But even such modest benefit may not be realized, when capital flows are immiserizing due to distortions, or when the rising marginal costs of foreign borrowing are not appropriately factored in by the economic agents. Endogenous growth models promise more (but they do not promise large capital flows to capital-poor countries when marginal capital returns are non-decreasing). The requirement for high benefits is, however, that capital flows carry externalities that improve a country's efficiency, externalities which can only be exploited when a certain level of human capital is already present in the country.

The inter-temporal approach to the current account identifies circumstances that justify welfare-enhancing current account deficits. Among the determinants for recent capital flows to emerging markets, however, the approach predicts a large current account deficit only when a country-specific productivity surge will raise permanent income. Permanent productivity increases and technological spillovers emphasized by the new growth literature are most likely embodied in foreign direct investment inflows to a largely undistorted economy.

We here provide illustrations of references against which to judge the size of actual current account deficits to determine their long-term sustainability. It was found that actual deficit numbers alone cannot provide information about long-term sustainability. Any judgement would need to consider debt–GDP ratios (current versus tolerated by investors), official foreign exchange reserves (current versus targeted), the potential GDP growth rate, import growth, the Balassa–Samuelson effect, and the structure of capital inflows. Sustainability considerations do not make sense for FDI flows, as long as there is no widely held notion about the sustainability of net foreign liabilities for the stock of FDI invested in a country.

The size of the current account deficit does not give rise to normative judgements; a deficit worth 3 per cent of GDP may be 'excessive' in one

country, while a deficit worth 12 per cent of GDP may be justified for another country. What distinguishes such deficits is not so much whether they are driven by public-sector or private-sector decisions, since there is some evidence for a Ricardian offset and since private debt is a contingent public-sector liability. What matters for governments is, by contrast, the source of the current account deficit. Some foreign savings should be resisted when they are seen to finance excessive consumption or unproductive investment.

How much foreign savings should be resisted in such a case? The answer depends primarily on the nature of the source that ultimately gives rise to a spending boom and on the structure of the capital inflow. Private spending booms mostly originate in prior domestic deregulation, in the interaction of implicit or explicit deposit insurance with an existing boom mentality, and in disinflation brought about by exchange rate-based stabilization. Resisting foreign savings is thus not necessarily a first-best policy response. If more nominal exchange rate flexibility, effective prudential regulation and bank supervision and gradual domestic financial reform succeed in keeping private savings rates stable and productive investment financed, all the better. If, by contrast, unsustainable currency appreciation, excessive risk-taking in the banking system and a sharp drop in private savings coincide, there is a case for resisting foreign capital inflows. The policy response has then to strike a balance between the benefits of consumption-smoothing and financing viable investment and the risks of excessive borrowing.

A case can be made for the open economy to accept all foreign direct investment, unless it creates new distortions as a result of new trade restrictions and as long as it can be absorbed by the existing stock of human capital. Foreign direct investment has staying power; it is little constrained by considerations of sovereign risk and portfolio limits from the perspective of the investor; and by crowding in domestic investment and having a minor initial effect on consumption (possibly unless privatization-induced), foreign direct investment is unlikely to generate a real appreciation problem.

NOTES

1. However, if returns to capital are constant, then the rate of return on capital will not be decreasing in the capital–labour ratio. There is thus no incentive in the endogenous-growth model for capital to flow from rich to poor countries, because returns on capital need not be larger in poor countries (Krugman, 1993).
2. The benefits of portfolio diversification are particularly present in the case of fully-funded pensions. Ageing industrial countries can escape part of the demographic problems by investing in emerging markets, while poor countries can diversify away some of their idiosyncratic risks stemming from higher exposure to country-specific shocks by investing some of their pension assets in industrial countries (Reisen, 1994a, 1997).

3. Individual country estimates for the period 1970–90, following the reduced-form regression in Glick and Rogoff (1992), do not find a significant impact of domestic productivity on changes in the current account. It should be noted, however, that Glick and Rogoff are only able to obtain a low level of explanatory power in their estimates on current-account determinants for even the industrial countries. The R^2 in their individual country time-series regressions range between 3 and 49 per cent, indicating an incomplete model.
4. We ignore interest payments on outstanding debt and the resource transfer (the non-interest current account) here to keep the focus on the sustainable current account deficit. The loss of information is minor to the extent that average interest costs do not vary largely across the sample countries.
5. In other words, bank lending supports excess credibility of liberalization and stabilization programmes. Earlier, when liberalization was seen as temporary (a hypothesis which does not seem apt to describe existing policy regimes in the capital-importing countries), it was *lack* of credibility which could explain temporary spending booms as residents exploited a 'window of opportunity' (Calvo, 1987).
6. On sterilized intervention in Asia and Latin America, see Reisen (1994b).
7. Using quarterly balance-of-payments flow data for changes in *net* claims of FDI, portfolio equity, 'long-term' and 'short-term' flows, Claessens *et al.* (1995) find that capital-account labels do not provide any information about the volatility of the flow. In particular, they argue that FDI and long-term flows are not more persistent than others. However, the primary policy concern here is with *reversals* of foreign investment of large magnitude, a concern not addressed by Claessens and co-authors who base their analysis on quarterly time-series properties of net, rather than gross, inflows.

REFERENCES

Agosin, M.R. (1994), 'Saving and Investment in Latin America', *UNCTAD Discussion Papers,* No. 90.

Andersen, P.S. and R.W. White (1996), 'The Macroeconomic Effects of Financial Sector Reforms: An Overview of Industrial Countries', mimeo, Bank for International Settlements, Basle.

Artus, P. (1996), 'Le financement de la croissance par endettement extérieur', *Document de travail No. 1996-05/T*, Caisse des dépôts et consignations, Paris.

Bank for International Settlements (1993), *63rd Annual Report*, Washington, DC.

Bhagwati, J.N. (1973), 'The Theory of Immiserizing Growth: Further Applications', in M.B. Connolly and A.K. Swoboda (eds), *International Trade and Money*, Toronto University Press, Toronto.

Blundell-Wignall, A. and F. Browne (1991), 'Macroeconomic Consequences of Financial Liberalisation: A Summary Report', *ESD Working Paper*, No. 98, Organisation for Economic Co-operation and Development, Paris.

Borensztein, E., J. De Gregorio and J.-W. Lee (1995), 'How Does Foreign Direct Investment Affect Economic Growth?', *NBER Working Paper*, No. 5057, National Bureau of Economic Research, Cambridge, MA.

Brecher, R.A. and C.F. Diaz Alejandro (1977), 'Tariffs, Foreign Capital, and Immiserizing Growth', *Journal of International Economics*, 7.4.

Calvo, G. (1987), 'On the Costs of Temporary Policy', *Journal of Development Economics*, 27.

Calvo, G. (1996), 'Varieties of Capital-Market Crises', *Working Paper No. 15*, Center for International Economics, University of Maryland at College Park.

Calvo, G., L. Leiderman and C. Reinhart (1996), 'Inflows of Capital to Developing Countries in the 1990s', *Journal of Economic Perspectives*, 10.2.

Caprio, Jr., G. and D. Klingebeil (1996), 'Bank Insolvency: Bad Luck, Bad Policy, or Bad Banking?', The World Bank, Washington, DC.

Chenery, H.B. and M. Bruno (1962), 'Development Alternatives in an Open Economy: the Case of Israel', *Economic Journal*, 57.

Claessens, S., M.P. Dooley and A. Warner (1995), 'Portfolio Capital Flows: Hot or Cold?', *The World Bank Economic Review*, 9.1.

Cohen, D. (1993), 'Convergence in the Closed and in the Open Economy', in A. Giovannini (ed.), *Finance and Development: Issues and Experience*, Cambridge University Press, Cambridge.

Corden, W.M. (1977), *Inflation, Exchange Rates and the International System*, Oxford University Press, Oxford.

Corden, W.M. (1994), *Economic Policy, Exchange Rates and the International System*, Clarendon Press, Oxford.

Edwards, S. (1995), 'Why are Saving Rates So Different Across Countries?: An International Comparative Analysis', *NBER Working Paper*, No. 5097, National Bureau of Economic Research, Cambridge, MA.

Edwards, S., R. Steiner and F. Losada (1995), 'Capital Inflows, the Real Exchange Rate and the Mexican Crisis of 1994', mimeo, The World Bank, Washington, DC.

Edwards, S. and S. van Wijnbergen (1989), 'Disequilibrium and Structural Adjustment', in H. Chenery and T.N. Srinivasan (eds), *Handbook of Development Economics*, Vol. 2, Elsevier, Amsterdam.

Frankel, J. and A.K. Rose (1996), 'Currency Crashes in Emerging Markets: Empirical Indicators', *NBER Working Paper*, No. 5437, National Bureau of Economic Research, Cambridge, MA.

Gavin, M. and R. Hausmann (1996), 'The Roots of Banking Crises: The Macroeconomic Context', *Working Paper Series 318*, Inter-American Development Bank, Washington, DC.

Glick, R. and K. Rogoff (1992), 'Global versus Country-Specific Productivity Shocks and the Current Account', *NBER Working Paper*, No. 4140, National Bureau of Economic Research, Cambridge, MA.

Goldstein, M. (1996), 'Presumptive Indicators/Early Warning Signals of Vulnerability to Financial Crises in Emerging-Market Economies', mimeo, Institute for International Economics, Washington, DC.

Harberger, A. (1985), 'Lessons for Debtor-Country Managers and Policymakers', in G.W. Smith and J.T. Cuddington (eds), *International Debt and the Developing Countries*, The World Bank, Washington, DC.

Hausmann, R. and H. Reisen (eds) (1996), *Securing Stability and Growth in Latin America: Policy Issues and Prospects for Shock-Prone Economies*, Organisation for Economic Co-operation and Development, Paris.

Heller, H.R. and M.S. Khan (1978), 'The Demand for International Reserves Under Fixed and Floating Exchange Rates', *IMF Staff Papers*, 25.4, Washington, DC.

Heston, A. and R. Summers (1993), *The Penn World Table: An Extended Set of International Comparisons, 1950–1988*, Cambridge, MA.

Heymann, D. (1994), 'En la interpretacion de la cuenta corriente', *Economia Mexicana*, 3.1.

Johnson, H. (1967), 'The Possibility of Income Losses from Increased Efficiency or Factor Accumulation in the Presence of Tariffs', *Economic Journal*, 77.

Kaminsky, G. and C.M. Reinhart (1996), 'The Twin Crises: The Causes of Banking and Balance-of-Payments Problems', *Working Paper No. 17*, Center for International Economics, University of Maryland at College Park.

Krugman, P. (1993), 'International Finance and Economic Development', in A. Giovannini (ed.), *Finance and Development: Issues and Experiences*, Cambridge University Press, Cambridge.

Lal, D. (1990), 'International Capital Flows and Economic Development', in M. Scott and D. Lal (eds), *Public Policy and Economic Development: Essays in Honour of Ian Little*, Clarendon Press, Oxford.

Larraín, G. (1996), 'Productividad del gasto publico y tipo de cambio real', in F. Morande (ed.), *Estudios empiricos de tipo de cambio real in Chile*, CEP/ILADES Georgetown University, Santiago de Chile.

McKinnon, R. (1964), 'Foreign Exchange Constraints in Economic Development and Efficient Aid Allocation', *Economic Journal*, 74.

McKinnon, R. and H. Pill (1995), 'Credible Liberalizations and International Capital Flows', mimeo, Stanford University.

Mankiw, N.G., D. Romer and D.N. Weil (1992), 'A Contribution to the Empirics of Economic Growth', *Quarterly Journal of Economics*, 107.2.

Milesi-Ferretti, G.M. and A. Razin (1996), 'Sustainability of Persistent Current Account Deficits', *NBER Working Paper*, No. 5467, National Bureau of Economic Research, Cambridge, MA.

Obstfeld, M. (1993), 'International Capital Mobility in the 1990s', *NBER Working Paper*, No. 4534, National Bureau of Economic Research, Cambridge, MA.

Obstfeld, M. and K. Rogoff (1994), 'The Intertemporal Approach to the Current Account', *NBER Working Paper*, No. 4893, National Bureau of Economic Research, Cambridge, MA.

Razin, A. (1995), 'The Dynamic-Optimizing Approach to the Current Account: Theory and Evidence', in P. Kenen (ed.), *Understanding Interdependence: The Macroeconomics of the Open Economy*, Princeton University Press, Princeton, NJ.

Reisen, H. (1993), 'Integation with Disinflation: Which Way?', in R. O'Brien (ed.), *Finance and the International Economy*, 7, The Amex Bank Review Prize Essays, Oxford University Press, Oxford.

Reisen, H. (1994a), 'On the Wealth of Nations and Retirees', in R. O'Brien (ed.), *Finance and the International Economy*, 8, The Amex Bank Review Prize Essays, Oxford University Press, Oxford.

Reisen, H. (1994b), *Debt, Deficits and Exchange Rates*, Edward Elgar Publishing Limited, Aldershot.

Reisen, H. (1997), 'Liberalizing Foreign Pension Fund Investment: Positive and Normative Aspects', *World Development*, Vol. 25.7, July, pp. 1173-1182.

Sachs, J. and A. Warner (1995), 'Economic Reform and the Process of Global Integration', *Brookings Papers on Economic Activity*, 1.

Sachs, J., A. Tornell and A. Velasco (1996), 'Financial Crises in Emerging Markets: The Lessons from 1995', *NBER Working Paper*, No. 5576, National Bureau of Economic Research, Cambridge, MA.

Summers, L. (1988), 'Tax Policy and International Competitiveness', in J.A. Frenkel (ed.), *International Aspects of Fiscal Policies*, University of Chicago Press, Chicago.

World Bank (1992, 1996), *World Development Report*, Washington, DC.

Part 3

Capital Flows

Capital Flows

The third part of this collection expands on issues – the management of capital inflows by developing-country authorities – which formed the core of my first book published by Edward Elgar, *Debt, Deficits and Exchange Rates* (1994). For the macroeconomic policymakers in the concerned capitals, the (re)discovery of the emerging markets in the early 1980s by private investors has been a mixed blessing. Unsustainable real exchange rate appreciation, excessive risk-taking in ill-supervised domestic banking systems that intermediated the foreign inflows, speculative booms in real estate, and surges in private consumption, are a few elements of the flip side to the rediscovery of the emerging world by private capital flows that chase the best mix of risk and return.

The next essay originally goes back to a Distinguished Lecture invitation by the Pakistan Society of Development Economists to their Eleventh Annual General Meeting in April 1995. A revised version was presented at the Fifth Seminar on International Finance organized by the Asian Development Bank and the Hong Kong Monetary Authority several months later. In coping with the macroeconomic risks arising from capital inflows, Asia has been a 'latecomer' to problems that Latin America had experienced early on, partly as a result of greater financial openness in the latter region. The essay draws five policy lessons from the heavy-inflow episode of the 1990s: identify the origin of rising foreign exchange reserves; identify the limits of foreign debt; discourage above-limit, short-term inflows; observe the trade off between price stability and competitiveness; and design policies to target monetary aggregates and exchange rates, including fiscal policy, sterilized intervention, reserve requirements and exchange rate management.

The essay on Moody's and Standard and Poor's (as the important *pars pro toto* of the sovereign credit rating industry), written jointly with Guillermo Larraín and Julia von Maltzan, reflects the demise of public aid and the rise of private capital flows to the developing world. No one has expressed this observation better than the *International Herald Tribune* (23 February 1995): 'In the 1960s, the most important visitor a developing country could have was the head of AID, the US agency that doles out foreign aid. In the 1970s and 80s, the most important visitor a developing

country could have was from the IMF, to help restructuring the economy. In the 1990s, the most important visitor a developing country can have is from Moody's Investors Service Inc.'. The essay, which was first presented at the 1997 Annual Meeting of the American Economic Association in New Orleans, deals with the question that rating agencies react to events rather than anticipating them. Credit rating agencies had been conspicuous among the many who failed to predict Mexico's economic 1994–95 crisis (unlike your author in his 1993 Amex Prize essay 'Integration with Disinflation: Which Way?'). While the essay cautions against overestimating the influence that credit ratings exert on the assessment of sovereign risk by the financial markets, it also finds a highly significant short-run announcement effect when negative reviews of emerging-market sovereign bonds are published. Thus, credit rating agencies can potentially assist in dampening excessive private inflows into emerging markets.

The three major currency crises over the 1990s – Scandinavia 1991–93, Mexico 1994–95, South-East Asia 1997–99 – have hit countries with strong macroeconomic fundamentals but weak domestic financial systems and hence weak private-sector balance sheets. The third essay shows that a deeper cause of recurrent emerging-market crises is the loosening of portfolio discipline in weak domestic financial systems as a result of 'disorderly' financial opening and heavy short-term capital inflows. Developing countries are therefore advised to pay close attention to indicators of financial vulnerability, in particular to short-term debt levels as a fraction of foreign exchange reserves, as well as to currency and maturity mismatches in private-sector balance sheets. The essay points to the avenues that should be pursued to avoid vulnerability to speculative currency attacks.

The 1997–98 Asian crisis ranks already among the most notable of the many crises in financial history, affecting many key emerging markets beyond the region. The resulting policy challenges have given urgency to the debate on a coherent approach to financial globalization. The fourth essay aims at informing that debate. It evaluates several suggestions for crisis resolution and crisis prevention, both on a global scale and with respect to host-country policies. Progress towards a less crisis-prone international financial system will hinge on how to correct the excessive risk-taking by banks; regulatory distortions which bias bank lending towards the short-term must be corrected. Emerging markets should aim at raising the quality of inflows. Chile-type regulatory measures, however, will only be effective if supported by a culture of transparency and enforcement as well as by macroeconomic policies consistent with raising the share of long-term inflows.

9. Managing Volatile Capital Inflows: The Experience of the 1990s[*]

THE NATURE OF CAPITAL FLOWS IN THE 1990s

Several econometric studies (reviewed in IMF, 1994) suggest that cyclical external factors account for some 30 to 50 per cent of the variation in private capital flows to developing countries, playing a greater role in Latin America than in Asia. The implicit warning that these studies carry, namely that a rise in OECD-country interest rates would lead to a halt or even reversal of capital flows, was partly confirmed by the $40 billion reserve loss of Mexico and by net outflows from dedicated emerging market funds during 1994.

The macroeconomic adjustment to a sudden reversal of foreign capital flows can be extremely painful. There are at least four major reasons why governments and central banks should care about the sustainability of the capital flows which their economies can tap abroad:

– First, it is increasingly acknowledged that global capital markets suffer from three major distortions: the problem of asymmetric information causes herd behaviour among investors and, in good times, congestion problems; the fact that some market participants are too big to fail causes excessive risk-taking; finally, the global financial markets feature multiple equilibria, unrelated to 'fundamentals'. It is questionable, therefore, whether the financial markets will discipline governments into better policies; even if they were to do so, the social and economic costs may be excessive.

– Second, any shortfall in capital inflows will require immediate cutbacks in domestic absorption to restore external balance. The savings–investment balance is more likely to be achieved through cuts in investment than through higher savings in the short term, compromising future output levels. Current output levels fall to the extent that rigidities

[*] Originally published in *Asian Development Review*, Vol. 14, No. 1, 1996, pp. 72–96.

prevent resource reallocation, so that contractionary disabsorption effects outweigh expansionary substitution effects.

–   Third, the expansion of domestic credit connected with unsterilized capital inflows may not be sound enough to stand the rise in domestic interest rates and the fall in domestic asset prices that go with a reversal of these inflows (Rojas-Suarez and Weisbrod, 1994). The resulting breakdown of domestic financial institutions provides incentives for monetary expansion and fiscal deficits incurred by the public bail-out of ailing banks.

–   Fourth, temporary capital flows may lead to an unsustainable appreciation in the real exchange rate. The appreciation is in conflict with development strategies based on the expansion of exports and efficient import substitution, which centrally relies on a reliable and competitive exchange rate. Overvalued exchange rates cause sub-optimal investments which are costly to reverse, undermine active trade promotion, export diversification and productivity growth and breed capital flight (Fischer and Reisen, 1993). Large swings in real exchange rates, often a result of temporary capital flows, have been found to significantly depress machinery and equipment investment and thus long-run growth performance (Agosin, 1994).

For industrialized countries, Turner (1991) recently examined the volatility of different capital-account items in order to arrive at a distinction between permanent versus temporary and autonomous versus accommodating flows. For the period 1975–1989, the capital flows that were most closely correlated with financing requirements were classified as the most accommodating, and the most accommodating types of capital flows closely corresponded to the most temporary flows, proxied by their standardized variability (coefficient of variation) over the period 1975–1988. Finally, Turner made a ranking of four capital-account items, ranging from the most autonomous and permanent to the most accommodating and temporary (i.e. volatile) flows: (i) long-term bank lending; (ii) foreign direct investment; (iii) portfolio investment, and (iv) short-term bank flows.

A closer inspection of different capital-account items tends to confirm Turner's results:

–   Long-term bank lending includes essentially syndicated Euro-loans, amounting to more than $200 billion in 1994. The OECD (1995) reports the average maturity of the recorded euro-credits. A striking observation is that the average maturity on these syndicated loans to borrowers from

OECD countries is *shorter* than to borrowers from developing countries. During the 1990s, the average maturity for OECD borrowers has oscillated between 5 and 6 years, while borrowers from developing countries enjoyed average maturities of between 6 and 9 years. The longer maturities for developing country borrowers are explained by the high proportion of long-term project loans in syndicated lending.

– Foreign direct investment is largely determined by non-cyclical considerations. Being rather governed by long-term profitability expectations, it is less subject to sudden shifts in investor sentiment. While on an annual basis, large fluctuations of foreign direct investment *flows* are regularly observed, foreign direct investment *stocks* are largely illiquid and irreversible. Foreign direct investment, which is little dependent on financial market sentiment, has bad-weather qualities. This observation is reinforced by Mexico's capital account in 1995, which showed only a slightly reduced net inflow of foreign direct investment.

– Portfolio investment is a mixed bag with respect to its stability. Investment by pension funds and life insurance companies can be taken as long-term investment, since these funds follow a buy-and-hold strategy rather than a trading strategy in the emerging stock markets. Unlike banks and most other investors, pension funds and life insurers benefit from regular inflows of funds on a contractual basis and from long-term liabilities (with no premature withdrawal of funds), which together imply little liquidity risk (Davis, 1995). As long as these funds are underinvested in the emerging stock markets (as measured by their percentage share in world stock market capitalization) and as long as the emerging stock markets display a comparatively low return correlation vis-à-vis the OECD stock markets, developing countries can expect further equity-related capital flows from pension funds and life insurers (Reisen, 1994a). In order to tap these flows, developing countries must strive for investment grading by the major credit rating agencies.

– Equity-related investment by domestic residents with overseas holdings, by private foreign investors and from managed funds (country funds and mutual funds) is largely governed by cyclical determinants and oriented at short-term returns. In the course of the early 1990s, the decline in returns on riskless assets in the US and other OECD countries has led, not to an acceptance of falling returns, but to a growing tolerance of risk. Mainly via mutual funds, this has brought much speculative money to the emerging stock markets. The mutual funds have to publish regular (by now, even daily) asset prices and can suffer large redemptions at any time

when there is bad news. What is more, with the need to have sufficient cash to pay off clients redeeming their holdings, a widespread crisis such as happened after the devaluation of the Mexican peso in late 1994 forces fund managers to sell in markets totally unrelated to the origin of the crisis.

– Any other portfolio investment, in particular bond-related, should be considered as volatile. Borrowing through corporate or government bonds, the most important component of Latin American capital inflows in the 1990s (see below), is largely governed by interest rate differentials and thus akin to reversal. The average maturity of Latin American international bonds has fallen below 4 years during the 1990s so that a high part of outstanding bonds can be fairly rapidly withdrawn; moreover, a concerted response to sustain external financing is difficult to organize as claims are dispersed among numerous bond holders (Griffith-Jones, 1994).

– Short-term bank lending and borrowing facilities (such as euro medium-term notes and euro-commercial paper) are particularly cyclical and volatile. Developing countries interested in sustained growth should be wary whenever firms and banks incur these borrowings.

Using quarterly balance-of-payments flow data for changes in *net* claims of FDI, portfolio equity, 'long-term' and 'short-term' flows, Claessens *et al.* (1995) find that capital-account labels do not provide any information about the volatility of the flow. In particular, they argue that FDI and long-term flows are not more persistent than others. However, the primary policy concern here is with *reversals* of foreign investment on a large magnitude, a concern not addressed by Claessens and co-authors who base their analysis on quarterly time-series properties of net, rather than gross, inflows.

THE 1990s CAPITAL FLOWS: ASIA AND LATIN AMERICA IN PERSPECTIVE

Putting the 1990s surge of capital flows into a broad regional perspective may be useful for two reasons: first, Asia and Latin America compete in international capital markets, and second, Asia may offer valuable policy lessons to Latin America and vice versa. However, country policies and experiences vary within the two regions, requiring to supplement the regional perspective with a more country-specific analysis.

Table 9.1   Two episodes of high capital flows, Asia and Latin America
(annual averages)

	1978–82		1990–93	
	Asia	Latin America	Asia	Latin America
Gross capital inflows, $ bn of which (per cent)	19.3	36.5	74.7	36.7
. FDI	15.0	15.1	37.1	33.5
. Portfolio	3.6	4.9	14.2	68.1
. Other 'long term'	53.9	63.6	21.7	−32.1
. Other 'short term'	27.5	16.4	27.0	30.5
Net capital inflows, $ bn	15.8	26.3	46.6	23.8
Reserve accumulation	6.9	0.6	31.0	18.0

Source: IMF, *World Economic Outlook*, October 1994; own calculations.

Many observers have been drawn to an overly optimistic interpretation on the capital flows of the early 1990s by some regularities between Asia and Latin America and by some differences to the flows that preceded the debt troubles of the 1980s. Unlike in the 1980s, capital flows were not pulled in by deficit-running government budgets and public enterprises, but essentially by private investors and private firms. Unlike in the 1980s, when bank lending prevailed in both regions, risk capital has been flowing to both regions as portfolio and direct investment. As a share of gross capital flows, FDI rose from 15 per cent during 1978–82 to 35 per cent during 1990–93 in both regions (see Table 9.1). Another similarity between both regions is the size of *net* capital flows in terms of their gross domestic products and the high percentage share of these net flows that have gone into foreign exchange reserves. But beneath the surface, some important differences loom large for the composition and sources of capital flows:

– First, although the share of FDI in gross capital inflow is only slightly higher in Asia than in Latin America, its *nature* differs between the two regions. In Latin America it has mainly taken the form of debt/equity swaps and privatization, which do not necessarily generate additional capital formation. In Asia, by contrast, foreign direct investment has mostly been in the form of acquisitions or the setting up of new

enterprises (BIS, 1994). The different composition of FDI may determine its macroeconomic consequences: in Asia it is more likely to add to domestic investment and it is also more likely to be skewed towards export production (rather than construction of shopping malls, for example) than in Latin America.

- Second, the *share and the nature* of portfolio flows differ markedly between the Asian and Latin American capital accounts. In Asia, portfolio flows accounted for just 14.2 per cent of gross capital inflows, compared with a corresponding percentage share of 68.1 per cent in Latin America. Around three quarters of portfolio investment to Latin America were borrowings in international capital markets, while only a quarter consisted of equity-related flows (Group of Thirty, 1994). Not only is the equity-related share of portfolio flows higher in Asia than in Latin America, but it is also likely to come from more stable sources. Pension funds and insurance companies often limit their investment towards those countries which have been assigned investment-grade credit ratings by rating agencies such as Moody's and Standard & Poor's. Currently, only Chile and Colombia in Latin America carry the investment grade stipulated by the portfolio allocation guidelines of pension funds, while in Asia the grade is enjoyed by China, Indonesia, Korea, Malaysia, Chinese Taipei and Thailand. This explains why UK pension funds (for which such a breakdown is available), had by 1993 invested 4.6 per cent of their assets in Asia, compared with only 0.6 per cent in Latin America.

- A third difference in the composition of capital flows is that lending classified as 'long term' by the IMF constitutes a fifth of Asia's gross inflows while it has been negative in Latin America, thanks to Brady-type debt reduction and limited new lending. On the other hand, Latin American firms and banks tapped short-term borrowing facilities slightly more than did borrowers from Asia.

The fact that it is difficult in practice to distinguish between permanent and temporary capital inflows confronts the policymaker in the recipient country with a *specific transfer problem*. He or she has to make the basic decision *whether to accept or resist the capital inflow* (Williamson, 1994), or how much to accept and how much to resist. (A third possibility is to induce a transfer as Mexico did in 1994 by offering dollar-linked short-term government paper and by selling foreign exchange reserves to defend the exchange rate as investor confidence started to wane.)

Table 9.2   *External financing of major capital flow recipients, avg. 1989–94, in per cent of GDP*

	Current account deficit	Reserve accumulation	Direct foreign investment	Net other financing
	(1) +	(2) =	(3) +	(4)
China, People's Rep. of	−0.5	0.8	2.6	−2.3
India	1.5	0.8	0.2	2.1
Indonesia	2.3	0.8	1.2	1.9
Korea, Rep. of	0.0	0.4	0.3	0.1
Malaysia	2.6	6.4	6.9	2.1
Philippines	4.2	1.8	1.1	4.9
Thailand	5.8	3.2	2.3	6.7
Avg. Asia	2.3	2.0	2.1	2.2
Argentina	1.5	0.6	1.7	0.4
Brazil	−0.1	1.1	0.3	0.7
Chile	0.7	3.6	2.5	1.8
Colombia	0.4	1.5	1.5	0.4
Mexico	5.3	0.3	1.4	4.2
Peru	3.3	2.4	0.3	5.4
Avg. Latin America	1.4	1.5	1.3	1.6

Sources: JP Morgan, *Emerging Markets Economic Outlook*, 16 December 1994; World Bank, *World Debt Tables 1994*; own calculations.

Table 9.2 shows that on average both regions accepted around half of the transfer accomplished by a current account deficit in the balance of payments, while the other half went into the build-up of foreign exchange reserves. But the regional averages hide important country differences. In Asia, Indonesia, the Philippines and Thailand accepted most of the inflows by running current account deficits; in Latin America, Mexico, Argentina and Peru belong to this group. By contrast, Malaysia and Chile have resisted most of the transfer by building up foreign exchange reserves (and sterilizing them, see below).

MACROECONOMIC PREREQUISITES AND THE USE OF CAPITAL FLOWS

The choice whether to accept or resist the transfer should not only be guided by the composition and volatility of capital flows, but can be based on two different economic theories. The first is the *sequencing literature* which recommends linking the acceptance of capital inflows to the progress in fiscal and monetary stabilization, domestic financial liberalization, prudential supervision and trade liberalisation (Edwards, 1990; Fischer and Reisen, 1993). Fiscal consolidation is a necessary prerequisite because it obviates the temptation to finance unsustainable budget deficits a bit longer thanks to inflows and because regular tax revenues obviate the need for governments to rely on the implicit taxation of domestic financial intermediation. Moreover, government budgets need to allow for the contingency that subsequent capital outflows will force up domestic interest rates that worsen the fiscal balance (Turner, 1995). Low inflation and inflationary expectations prior to heavy capital inflows obviate the temptation to use the exchange rate regime (a nominal peg, an active crawl, or a pure float) to help speed up the disinflationary process with heavy capital inflows: the costs of misallocation involved by the inevitable real currency appreciation which is due to inertial inflation is largely documented (Fischer and Reisen, 1993). The risk that capital flows are skewed towards nontradables is also increased by the extent of price distortions in the local economy; to avoid 'immiserizing' capital inflows (Brecher and Diaz-Alejandro, 1977), domestic financial liberalization, trade liberalization and solid export diversification had better precede a period of heavy capital inflows. Strict regulatory and supervisory policies are important for minimizing moral hazard (including corruption, fraud and excessive risk-taking) in the banking system and for ensuring the health and viability of domestic banks. We all know, however, that such prudential requirements are rarely fulfilled in the developing world. Turner (1995) argues rightly, therefore, that in the absence of strict supervision, developing country banks may need to be better capitalized than they need be in the major OECD countries. Well-capitalized banks will be able to withstand the emergence of bad debts and sharp fluctuations in real interest rates, and the value of domestic assets held as capital. Over longer periods, the Feldstein–Horioka observation of a close match between national investment and saving rates does also hold for the developing world. Notwithstanding the tremendous rise in international securities transactions and in global foreign exchange trading, the integration of asset markets for the broader categories of world saving and wealth remains limited (Reisen, 1996). Therefore, another important prerequisite not emphasized enough in the sequencing debate, is a high domestic savings ratio.

Table 9.3 shows that Asia (in particular East Asia) and Latin America differed with respect to the macroeconomic prerequisites for capital inflows to raise efficiency and growth without compromising stability. First, with fragile public finances, Latin America has in the past relied much more than Asia did on inflationary finance, as witnessed by seigniorage as a percentage of GDP during the 1970s and 1980s. While most of the heavy capital importers had reduced their budget deficits by the early 1990s, at least India and Brazil did not yet fulfil the fiscal requirements for sustainable capital inflows for the size of their budget deficits, and the Philippines looked fragile for the relative size of her public debt. Second, again in striking contrast, the heavy capital flows of the 1990s have coincided with slightly higher inflation levels in Asia, while capital flows have gone along with falling inflation levels in Latin America, thanks to heavy real appreciation of currencies. Third, prior to the 1990 flows, black market premia in Latin America have largely exceeded those in Asia, indicating a higher anti-export bias and the risk of immiserizing capital inflows in Latin America. Export promotion has been more deeply anchored in Asia than in Latin America, as witnessed by the much more dynamic export growth; again this may indicate that the damage done to the diversification and fostering of exportable production when volatile real exchange rates undermine the confidence in the government's commitment for active trade promotion is much greater in Latin America than in (East) Asia. A final striking difference is the level of gross domestic savings. In Asia, they are mostly solidly in the 30-plus range as a percentage of GDP, in Latin America they are far below. Note the important country outliers within the two regions, though (Chile, Philippines).

The second body of theory on which to base the decision whether to resist or accept inflows is derived from the mechanics of the debt cycle. The mobilization of external savings has been the classic role for capital flows to developing countries, where the relative capital shortage should offer higher returns than in the developed world. According to the *debt cycle hypothesis*, rarely validated empirically, external savings raise domestic investment and growth, which in turn stimulates saving which eventually contributes to the elimination of net foreign debt. Such a virtuous circle hides five requirements, again rarely complied with in practice (Devlin *et al.*, 1994):

– First, external capital flows should consistently augment investment, rather than being diverted to consumption.

– Second, the investment must be efficient.

Table 9.3   Prerequisites for the 1990s episode, Asia and Latin America

	Avg. seigniorage 1970–88	Gov't budget 1988–93	Public debt 1994	Avg. black market premium	Export growth, US $	Gross domestic savings, avg. 1989–91
	% of GDP	% of GDP	% of GDP	Post-trade reform up to 1992	avg. p.a., 1980–92	% of GDP
China, People's Rep. of	n.a.	-2.6	n.a.	88.0	11.9	33
India	1.5	-7.4	45	23.8	5.9	24
Indonesia	1.4	-0.6	39	8.9	5.6	37
Korea, Rep. of	1.6	0.5	22	3.0	11.9	36
Malaysia	1.3	-3.7	58	0.0	11.3	33
Philippines	1.0	-3.3	96	4.6	3.7	20
Thailand	1.0	3.3	16	1.2	14.7	34
Argentina	4.2	-5.9	22	21.1	2.2	19
Brazil	2.3	-46.9	40	51.7	5.0	24
Chile	3.7	2.0	18	16.1	5.5	28
Colombia	2.1	-0.4	22	12.9	12.9	24
Mexico	3.1	-3.2	32	10.3	1.6	20
Peru	3.6	-4.0	42	11.5	2.5	17

Sources: Seigniorage: Easterly, Rodriguez and Schmidt-Hebbel (1994); Government data: JP Morgan, *Emerging Markets Outlook*, Dec. 1994; Black market premium: Dean, Desai and Riedel (1994); Exports: World Bank, *WDR 1994*; Savings: World Bank, *World Tables*, 1994.

- Third, the country must invest in tradables (or trade-related infrastructure) in order to be able to create a trade surplus to accommodate the subsequent switch in transfers required to service the debt.

- Fourth, an aggressive domestic savings effort is called for, with the marginal savings rate exceeding the country's average savings rate.

- Fifth, the virtuous circle requires capital exporters willing to provide stable and predictable flows at terms in line with the recipient country's factor productivity.

Table 9.4 shows that generally the ingredients for the virtuous circle of capital flows are more likely to be found in Asia than in Latin America. Other than in the Philippines, the Asian capital importers did not divert external savings into higher consumption (shares of GDP). In particular in India, Indonesia and Thailand, the private sector responded to inflows by augmenting investment (shares of GDP), and in Malaysia and again Thailand, government consumption was considerably reduced in the wake of capital inflows. By contrast, the Latin American capital importers did divert the flows on aggregate into higher consumption shares, with the exception of Chile and Colombia. In Mexico and Peru, private consumption boomed, and in Argentina and Brazil government consumption was raised by more than four percentage points of GDP. These findings imply that Latin America, unlike Asia, did not raise the marginal savings rate above the average savings rate when capital flows rolled in.

While since 1988 investment efficiency as measured by incremental capital output ratios is reported by the Group of Thirty (1994) as 'quite comparable' for the two regions, investment and growth rates have been considerably higher in Asia than in Latin America. Machinery and equipment investment, rather than construction investment, has not only been shown to explain importantly long-run growth performance, i.e. growth *rates* (De Long and Summers, 1991), but also more likely, investment in tradables necessary for later debt service. Table 9.4 displays a striking difference for the two regions here, with equipment investment averaging 13.8 per cent of GDP over 1989–91 in Asia, compared with just 8.8 per cent in Latin America.

Table 9.5 points to a final striking regional difference in the use and effects of capital inflows. In Asia, inflation levels generally increased (with the mild exception of Malaysia and the Philippines), reflecting the reluctance of policymakers to accommodate capital inflows with an upward float of the exchange rate and the subsequent incapacity to fully control domestic monetary aggregates. In Latin America, Argentina, Mexico and Peru used exchange rate policy and capital flows to rapidly lower inflation levels;

Table 9.4 Macroeconomic indicators, Asia and Latin America, % of GNP

	Change in private consumption avg. 1989–93 vs avg. 1985–89	Change in gov't consumption avg. 1989–93 vs avg. 1985–89	Equipment investment avg. 1989–91	Real GDP growth, % p.a. 1994	Short-term external debt end 1994
China, People's Rep. of.	−1.5	0.1	n.a.	11.5	2.4
India	−4.2	−0.3	12.5	6.0	3.2
Indonesia	−4.3	−0.6	n.a.	7.0	13.2
Korea, Rep. of	−0.7	0.5	12.8	8.0	5.6
Malaysia	2.0	−1.7	n.a.	8.6	8.6
Philippines	1.8	1.4	10.6	4.7	12.1
Thailand	−3.7	−1.8	19.3	8.5	15.7
Argentina	−1.1	4.3	3.6	5.8	3.4
Brazil	−2.3	4.0	n.a.	4.3	6.4
Chile	0.0	−1.7	8.6	6.3	6.7
Colombia	−0.3	0.5	8.2	4.8	5.2
Mexico	3.6	0.2	9.6	3.1	16.5
Peru	7.7	−1.7	9.7	12.7	15.0

Sources: IMF, *International Financial Statistics*; *Emerging Markets Investor*, March 1995; JP Morgan, *Emerging Markets Outlook*, December 1994; UN, *National Accounts.*

Table 9.5 Exchange rate regimes and real exchange rates, 1990s

	FX regime	Annual CPI inflation Dec. 92 – Dec. 94	Real exchange rate[1] CPI/US-CPI 1990=100 Sept. 94	Real effective exchange rate, trade-weighted WPI-based, 1990=100 Sept. 94
China, People's Rep. of	Adjustable peg	8.8–27.0	75.9	n.a.
India	Adjustable peg	8.0–9.4	75.7	78.7
Indonesia	Passive crawling peg	5.0–10.0	105.3	97.0
Korea, Rep. of	Managed peg	4.5–6.3	101.6	82.0
Malaysia	Managed peg	4.9–4.2	108.9	106.2
Philippines	Managed floating	8.2–7.8	126.9	103.2
Thailand	Managed peg	3.0–4.6	111.4	98.4
Argentina	Currency board	17.5–3.4	168.8	107.2
Brazil	Passive crawling peg	1149–936	130.5	105.4
Chile	Target zone	12.7–9.0	119.0	115.1
Colombia	Managed floating	25.1–22.0	133.9	119.5
Mexico	Active crawling peg	11.9–7.0	122.2	111.6
Peru	Floating	56.7–16.0	122.0	96.4

Notes:
1. Nominal US dollar exchange rate adjusted for local versus US consumer prices. Index numbers higher than 100 denote appreciation.

Sources: IMF, International Financial Statistics; Emerging Markets Investor, November 1994.

Argentina and Mexico anchored the exchange rate and inflation expectations at the US dollar, while Peru followed the domestic monetarist approach with a full float (as did the Philippines). The real exchange rate, comparing the exchange rate adjusted rise in local consumer prices relative to the United States, appreciated almost 70 per cent in Argentina and more than 20 per cent in the Philippines, Brazil, Colombia, Mexico and Peru over the 1990s.

The real exchange rate is an important relative price for determining the relative consumption of and investment into tradables versus non tradables. The real exchange rate thus helps predict *future* problems to generate a trade surplus but it does not, however, indicate changes in *current* external competitiveness which are better denoted by the *real effective exchange rate*. The latter indicator is an index of the country's trade-weighted average value against the currencies of its principal trading partners, adjusted for relative price changes based on indexes most closely measuring the prices of domestically produced finished manufactured goods. With exchange-rate based disinflation or a nominal appreciation of the exchange rate, producer prices generally fall more rapidly than do consumer prices which include non-tradables not exposed to world market competition. Another reason is often the consolidation of government budgets implying withdrawal of various subsidies that enter the consumer price index but not the producer price index. Finally, any productivity surges will be reflected in falling producer prices, but not immediately in falling consumer prices. The real effective exchange rate has nowhere appreciated more than 20 per cent over the 1990s, quite in contrast to earlier experiences in the Southern Cone of Latin America. Note, however, that the relative competitive position has deteriorated in Colombia, Chile, and Mexico and, thanks to discretionary devaluation, improved in the People's Republic of China and India.

POLICY LESSONS OF THE 1990s FOR THE NEXT EPISODE OF HEAVY INFLOWS

After a short episode of monetary tightening in the OECD area during the years 1994–95, falling interest rates in OECD countries have not failed to push heavy flows of cyclical money into the emerging markets again. This section aims at drawing advice from recent experiences for finance ministries and central banks on how to proceed in dealing with the supply of temporary capital.

Identify the Nature of the Shocks

Let us assume that the authorities first observe a rise in foreign exchange reserves. Such rise must not necessarily be due to a flattening of the supply side curve of foreign capital. Frankel (1994) has recently analysed three different sources of the disturbance, i.e. the rise in foreign exchange reserves within the traditional IS/LM framework. He distinguishes three sources of rising foreign exchange reserves:

1) An improvement in the trade balance caused by prior devaluation, as in the Colombian case of the early 1990s and as now experienced in Mexico. Improving terms of trade or superior productivity growth may also cause reserve inflows through a trade balance surplus.

2) A domestic monetary disturbance, which can be either a contraction in domestic money supply or an increase in demand for money, which could be in response to a domestic exchange-rate-based stabilization programme.

3) Finally, as is the focus in this paper, a drop in external interest rates and asset returns, as happened in the OECD area at the start of the 1990s.

Frankel (1994) shows convincingly that an attempt to discern the nature of the disturbance is likely to be most useful in deciding the appropriate macroeconomic response. An improvement of the *trade balance* that tends to persist will result in an appreciation of the real exchange rate, either through nominal appreciation of the currency or through monetary accommodation. When the underlying cause of the trade imbalance is the excess of domestic spending over production, as in the United States, the trade balance can only be restored by adjusting private or public spending through changing savings, budget deficits or investment.

When a rise in foreign exchange reserves results from an increase in *demand for money*, the optimal response is monetary accommodation to that rise in demand. A sterilization attempt would entail needlessly high interest rates and a contraction of economic activity. When the shock originates in *domestic monetary contraction*, the optimal response is very much governed by the country's degree of financial openness. A completely open economy will only allow the option to let the currency float upwards if monetary contraction is to be sustained. But restrictions on short-term inflows open the option to avoid nominal appreciation and to sterilize capital inflows in order to keep the money supply on target.

The final case is an *exogenous fall in world interest rates*. The resulting capital inflows cause the domestic currency to appreciate in real terms, unless there is sterilized intervention on the foreign exchange market. The nominal exchange rate appreciates when it is flexible as in Peru and the Philippines; the domestic price level rises when the nominal rate is pegged, as happened in Hong Kong over the early 1990s. With either fully floating or pegged exchange rates, the real exchange rate appreciation resides in the failure of the monetary authorities to supply the mix of assets which foreign and domestic investors are now demanding. The authorities do nothing in the floating-rate case; they issue money in exchange for foreign assets in the pegged-rate case; they should issue bonds instead, by engaging in sterilized intervention (Kenen, 1993). Sterilized intervention in the 1990s inflows has been practised most aggressively in Chile and Malaysia.

Identify the Limits of Foreign Indebtedness

Only very rough rules of thumb are available to set a prudent limit to the size of capital flows that can be accepted (Williamson, 1994). While in 1994 many observers started to realize that Mexico's current account deficit was reaching a level that would be unsustainable (8 per cent of GDP), there was no theory behind such observation. In practice, the inter-temporal budget constraint does not help, because many poor countries have been allowed to run deficits for an almost unlimited time period. Some capital flows, such as foreign direct investment inflows, are less vulnerable to withdrawal and are not debt-creating; but they cannot be fully ignored either since they also generate a need for foreign exchange earnings to service remittances. Economists therefore, when asked to assess prudent limits for current account deficits, tend to recur to a debt-dynamics equation:

$$d_t = d_{t-1} (i^* - n) + c_t \qquad (9.1)$$

where the debt/GDP ratio rises when the interest rate on existing debt, i^*, exceeds GDP growth, n, or by the amount of the non-interest current account deficit as a fraction of GDP, c_t. The relevant interest rate here is the effective rate, which is the weighted average across all kinds of debt, creditors, and currency denominations. Equity-related inflows can be incorporated in principle, by imputing the dividend yield rather than the effective interest rate.

A prudent limit for current account deficits can be derived from here. It is obvious that the size of the sustainable deficit depends very much on the effective interest rate and on the country's growth rate. With more concessional flows or equity-related inflows, a bigger deficit ratio can be sustained; the same holds for a high-growth country. An often-quoted rule of

thumb (Williamson, 1994) for the net debt/GDP ratio is that it should not exceed 40 per cent. Once the country has reached that level, the non-interest current account as a fraction of GDP should prudently not (at least for long) exceed the difference between its growth rate and the effective interest rate. Here we have a major difference between, say, Mexico and Thailand whose current account deficit reached also 8 per cent of GDP in 1994. Table 9.6 gives a stylized account of that difference, assuming a debt/GDP ratio of 40 per cent (which in fact has been reached in both countries).

Table 9.6   The sustainable debt-related current account deficit and GDP growth

0.4	(Interest (service, % of (external debt (1)	−	Dollar inflation[a] (2)	−	Real annual GDP growth potential[a] (3)	)) =)	Sustainable non-interest current acc. deficit[b] (4)
Mexico	6.7		3.0		4.5		0.8
Thailand	6.9		3.0		8.5		4.6

Notes:
a. assumed.
b. on debt-creating flows, with no increase in the debt/GDP ratio.

Source: World Bank, *World Debt Tables 1994–95*; own calculations.

Table 9.6 demonstrates that there is nothing automatically unsustainable about a country running a high current account deficit relative to GDP, as long as it is matched by a high growth rate. Inclusive of interest payments, Thailand can run a deficit on its current account in the order of 4.6 per cent of GDP (adding 40 per cent of interest payments to the non-interest deficit), while Mexico can only afford a current-account deficit of 3.0 per cent of GDP to hold the debt/GDP ratio at a constant 40 per cent. Likewise, a low-income country such as Pakistan can run a higher deficit on its current account than Mexico, even when its growth potential is similar, because her average interest cost will be around two percentage points lower thanks to a high share of concessional capital inflows.

Discourage Above-limit Short-term Inflows

Capital market failures can call for direct measures to discourage capital inflows. In particular developing-country borrowers are faced with a supply curve of foreign savings that is horizontal until a certain net debt position (the level of which is unknown *ex ante*) but, at some point, turns steeply upward. As Chile experienced in the early 1980s and Mexico did now, private market participants do not internalize the social cost of their borrowings abroad (Harberger, 1985) and that market failure, not unlike the congestion externality in road traffic, justifies capital controls on short-term inflows, such as a tax on short-term external credits. The underlying paradigm is that the monetary authorities (a) pursue longer-term objectives than do private agents operating in financial markets, and (b) they are better informed about future macroeconomic trends and their long-term effects on the economy (Zahler, 1992). Before resorting to capital controls, however, the monetary authorities should eliminate any remaining subsidies to inward investment, such as free deposit insurance (Williamson, 1994).

One cannot be dogmatic on the benefits of completely unrestricted capital flows; even the major market participants agree. JP Morgan (1995, 12) notes in its *Emerging Markets Economic Outlook*: 'Most countries in Asia explicitly restrict short-term inflows and limit foreign borrowing by residents. The two most successful economies in Latin America – Chile and Colombia – do likewise'.

Chile, after having phased out the subsidies provided to inward investment by debt–equity swaps, imposed a 20 per cent reserve requirement against foreign holdings of bank deposits which was raised to 30 per cent in 1992. Further, a tax of 1.2 per cent was imposed on short-term external credits. Colombia imposed a 3 per cent tax on transfers from abroad in 1991. Malaysia reimposed foreign exchange control measures in early 1994, limiting banks' holdings of foreign funds that were not trade-related or intended for investment in plant, equipment, or inventory stocks. Thai mutual funds have been prohibited from purchasing non-Thai assets. Even Singapore prohibits short or long Singapore dollar positions unless the documentation can be produced for the underlying trade transaction, and portfolio controls still apply to Singaporean financial institutions. Korea and Chinese Taipei have never lifted certain foreign exchange controls, and Chinese Taipei placed a ceiling on foreign holdings of listed Taiwanese shares (Reisen and Yèches, 1993; Glick and Moreno, 1994; Greenwood, 1994). Asia also restricts equity inflows more than does Latin America, again with the exception of Chile. Table 9.7 confirms the restrictedness of Asian stock markets by comparing the regions' global market weights (IFC global index) with those where foreigners are free to invest (IFC investible index).

Foreign exchange controls, however, have their well-publicized drawbacks. First, if they could be enforced effectively, this is done at the cost of interfering with the international integration of financial markets; such interference invites misallocation of resources because the country's residents face other prices and returns (generally, lower) for a given asset than do people elsewhere and because the controls may preclude the benefits (important in poor countries) of consumption smoothing. Second, the effectiveness of capital controls tends to erode over time since people find ways to evade them which in turn risks triggering an ever tighter net of capital controls being imposed by the authorities.

Table 9.7   Stock market investibility, 1993

	Stock market weights (%) within emerging markets	
	Global	Investible
Asia	63.7	42.5
Latin America	31.1	48.8
– Chile	3.5	1.6
Other emerging	5.4	8.7

Source: IFC, *Emerging Markets Factbook 1994.*

Observe the Trade-off between Price Stability and Competitiveness

What should be done when stabilization of the domestic price level does not precede an open capital account? It is tempting for the monetary authority either to let the currency purely float in order to control monetary aggregates or to resort to exchange-rate based disinflation by means of an active crawl or by means of a currency-board arrangement. Although theoretically elegant, such exchange-rate regimes carry considerable risks of generating an unsustainable overvaluation as a result of volatile capital flows (for an early warning on Mexico's overvaluation, see Reisen, 1993a).

The complication for exchange rate management arises because inflation tends to be built into expectations, via implicit (or even explicit) indexation in goods and labour markets. This makes goods prices and labour costs sticky, while financial markets tend to be forward-looking. This asymmetry between the labour market and financial markets raises stabilization costs by producing real exchange rate overshooting. If the government which wants to bring down inflation firmly believes in domestic monetarism, as it did in New

Zealand from 1984 to 1988 and recently in Peru, it will dismantle controls and opt for a clean float. With a clean float of the exchange rate and no capital controls, the effectiveness of monetary policy is enhanced by both domestic demand (tight credit) and foreign demand (strong currency). However, the effectiveness of monetary policy has an immediate and often persistent cost in terms of external competitiveness (Joumard and Reisen, 1992).

In developing countries exchange rate pegs translate easily into overvalued real exchange rates. Capital inflows tend to be powerless to arbitrage away large interest rate differentials vis-à-vis industrial countries. To be sure, interest rates embody country risks (higher than in OECD countries) and real overvaluation fuels the exchange risk premium. But there are institutional factors, too, which explain the much-observed lack of interest rate convergence towards world levels (Fischer, 1993).

With positive nominal interest rate differentials against the world financial markets (reflecting microeconomic causes or the ongoing stabilization effort), a credible peg can induce excessive portfolio inflows which easily exceed the sterilization capacity of the central bank. The resulting excess demand can, in principle, be eliminated by fiscal or income restraint. In many developing (and some industrial) countries, however, the opposite is likely to happen because excessive inflows tend to undermine support for restrictive policies. When exchange rate pegs help to bring down inflation, the disinflation performance is often unsustainable (Larraín and Reisen, 1994). Exchange-rate based disinflation starts to succeed only once the implied overvaluation dampens domestic wages and prices, helped by growing unemployment and appreciation. The subsequent correction of excess unemployment and overvaluation will inevitably imply a return to higher levels of inflation.

The high degree of international capital market integration attained over the last ten years often places governments in a situation where they pursue too many targets with too few policy instruments. While this dilemma calls for setting clear priorities, it has to be realized that the policy trade-offs involved are radically different from a situation with only limited capital mobility. That change has immediate implications for the choice of the appropriate exchange-rate regime. In the 1980s still, the policy to anchor inflationary expectations on a stable currency (such as the US dollar) was largely guided by the desire to raise the credibility of the policymaker. The 1990s have clearly shown, however, that pushing too hard (aiming to disinflate too quickly) to establish the credibility of the policymaker may well destroy the credibility of the policy. It is thus wise not to be overambitious and single minded with inflation targets in the low-level single-digit rate when capital flows in. The experiences in the early 1980s and 1990s in much

of Latin America and Asia provide a case for targeting money *and* real exchange rates simultaneously.

Policies to Target Money and Exchange Rates

In view of volatile capital flows, the authorities should (and many do) aim at restraining the inflationary and/or risky domestic credit expansion and the unsustainable real exchange rate appreciation associated with these flows. In other words, I assume that the authorities will not be prepared to accept either a pure float of their currency or an irrevocable currency union – the two extremes between which Obstfeld (1995) sees no comfortable middle ground any more with integrated capital markets.

Neither of these two extremes can appeal to emerging-market authorities. Given the thinness of their exchange and other financial markets, a pure float seems impracticable for most developing countries; domestic monetary aggregates constitute an unreliable anchor for countries under financial reform; and flexible exchange rates are likely to overshoot their long-run level with sticky prices. For a number of reasons supported by the criteria developed in the theory of optimum currency areas (notably, the relatively small degree of regional trade integration) and by the Balassa–Samuelson theory on the productivity-related divergence of real exchange rate trends (Reisen and van Trotsenburg, 1988), a currency union is not quite yet within sight anywhere in Asia or Latin America. Thus, we are bound to occupy the middle ground between these two extremes. What are the options?

Fiscal policy

With an open capital account, the traditional Mundell assignment has monetary policy acquire a comparative advantage in dealing with external balance, while fiscal policy serves to maintain internal balance. Fiscal demand management can rely on a macro effect and a composition effect (Corbo and Hernández, 1994). By tightening government consumption, the interest rate can be lowered and thus choke off some of the capital inflows attracted by positive interest differentials. The composition effect also helps to avoid an appreciation of the real exchange rate as most of the government consumption tends to be spent more on the nontradable sector, unlike private consumption. However, an activist fiscal policy requires sound government finances; and the government budget may be too inflexible to adjust to macro policy needs in time.

Sterilized intervention

When the rise of foreign exchange reserves is identified to originate abroad, central banks are advised to absorb such rises (to resist nominal appreciation),

while simultaneously reducing domestic credit in order to avoid an inflationary increase in the money supply (Frankel, 1994; Reisen, 1994b). As the Mexican authorities learned in 1994, sterilized intervention is an asymmetric policy which provides useful short-term relief in the case of excessive *inflows*, but is rapidly ineffective in the case of *outflows* when foreign exchange reserves fall to zero. Many economists are dismissive of sterilized intervention, however.

First, while there is agreement among economists that nonsterilized intervention (just as any other monetary policy) can affect nominal exchange rates, the effectiveness of sterilized intervention is much more controversial. Changing the composition of central bank assets without changing their aggregate size, it is often argued, cannot be an effective policy to influence the relative price between two monies. Such agnosticism ignores the *portfolio-balance* channel; in the case of capital inflows, the corresponding rise in the central bank's net foreign assets will be sterilized by a rising supply of domestic-currency bonds. If domestic and foreign bonds are imperfect substitutes (due to currency or sovereign risk), investors will require a higher expected return on domestic bonds to hold their larger outstanding stock; the currency will tend to depreciate. But to the extent that sterilization drives short-term interest rates higher, it may perpetuate excessive capital inflows and real appreciation for a while.

A second objection to sterilized intervention, particularly raised in the Latin American context (Calvo, Leiderman, and Reinhart, 1993), stems from the alleged fiscal costs. This objection is based on two arguments: (a) to dampen the appreciation, the central bank typically has to swap low-yield foreign exchange for high-yield domestic bonds; the accumulated interest differential can become an important fiscal (or quasi-fiscal) burden; (b) sterilized intervention deprives the government of a reduction in its debt-service burden by preventing the decline in the domestic interest rate that normally accompanies a capital inflow. Both arguments are unlikely to hold in present value terms if the capital inflow and exchange rate appreciation are correctly assessed as temporary. With risk premiums in domestic interest rates sufficiently small, the short-term fiscal losses derived from swapping low-yield foreign exchange for high-yield domestic bonds should be partly offset by a subsequent capital gain derived from the appreciation of foreign exchange reserves. Governments might also want to follow a suggestion laid out by Dornbusch and Park (1995): create low-coupon, local-currency, long-term bonds exclusively for foreigners for sterilization purposes to discourage short-term inflows and to lower sterilization costs. Finally, the authorities can swap government excess savings (originating, say, in social security funds or public enterprises) held with banks into (and out of) government bonds

(Reisen, 1993b). This practice can be considered as a generalized form of sterilized intervention.

Reserve requirements

By imposing reserve requirements on bank deposits, the Central Bank reduces domestic credit expansion following a capital inflow by directing banks to hold cash or deposits at the central bank. As the reserve requirements – provided they exceed the level of reserves voluntarily held by the banks – drive a wedge between lending rates (which rise) and savings returns (which drop), they constrain additional inflows of foreign capital as well as the quantity of deposits and of loans. Rojas-Suarez and Weisbrod (1994) show that the decision whether to sterilize inflows (in the sense described above) or to raise reserve requirements should be linked to the strength of the central bank relative to that of the commercial banks as the decision implies a choice on where to concentrate resources. They conclude that, with a weak banking system, the central bank should opt to sterilize by issuing liabilities directly to the public rather than imposing reserve requirements; the latter weaken the banks as borrowers are diverted to lenders who may escape such reserve requirements.

Some exchange-rate flexibility

Except when extremely open and when fighting hyperinflation, countries are advised to cope with volatile capital flows through some exchange rate flexibility. First, flexible exchange rates will allow to accommodate with nominal appreciation rather than with higher inflation the trend appreciation of the real equilibrium exchange rate which reflects superior productivity growth and the corresponding rise in relative prices for nontradables (the Balassa–Samuelson effect). Second, widening the band of permissible exchange rate fluctuations can reinforce the perception of foreign investors and domestic exporters that the inflow-related appreciation is temporary. Such perception will dampen short-term inflows by raising the currency risk premium in local interest rates while avoiding discouragement of investment in the tradable sector. The flexible crawling peg complemented by a wide band has been successfully managed in Chile and Israel (Helpman, Leiderman and Bufman, 1994). By contrast, fixed exchange rates (including currency-board systems) and active crawling pegs are an invitation to speculative, self-fulfilling attacks even with restrictive fiscal and monetary policies (Obstfeld, 1995).

In the foreseeable future, the middle ground between a pure float and monetary surrender will probably be more comfortable for Asia's and Latin America's economies than for the members of the European Monetary System, as long as capital accounts are not fully open, as there is a general

lack of access to foreign funds and as governments retain influence on their domestic financial institutions. But with heavy capital flows, no single policy will be sufficient to simultaneously target money and exchange rates and to aim for external as well as internal balance.

REFERENCES

Agosin, Manuel R. (1994), 'Saving and Investment in Latin America', *UNCTAD Discussion Papers*, No. 90, UNCTAD, Geneva.

BIS (Bank for International Settlements)(1994), *64th Annual Report*, Bank for International Settlements, Basle.

Brecher, Richard and Carlos Diaz-Alejandro (1977), 'Tariffs, Foreign Capital, and Immiserising Growth', *Journal of International Economics*, Vol. 7, No. 4, pp. 317–322.

Calvo, Guillermo, Leonardo Leiderman and Carmen Reinhart (1993), 'Capital Inflows and Real Exchange Rate Appreciation in Latin America: The Role of External Factors', *IMF Staff Papers*, Vol. 40, No. 1, pp. 108–150, Washington, DC.

Claessens, Stijn, Michael P. Dooley and Andrew Warner (1995), 'Portfolio Capital Flows: Hot or Cold?', *The World Bank Economic Review*, Vol. 9, No. 1, pp. 153–174.

Corbo, Vittorio and Leonardo Hernández (1994), 'Macroeconomic Adjustment to Capital Inflows: Latin American Style versus East Asian Style', *World Bank Policy Research Working Paper*, No. 1377, Washington, DC.

Davis, E. Philip (1995), *Pension Funds: Retirement-Income Security and Capital Markets: An International Perspective*, Oxford University Press, Oxford.

Dean, J., S. Desai and J. Riedel (1994), 'Trade Policy Reform in Developing Countries since 1985', *World Bank Discussion Paper*, No. 267, Washington, DC.

De Long, Bradford and Lawrence H. Summers (1991), 'Equipment Investment and Economic Growth', *Quarterly Journal of Economics*, Vol. 56, No. 2, pp. 445–502.

Devlin, Robert, Ricardo Ffrench-Davis and Stephany Griffith-Jones (1994), 'Surges in Capital Flows and Development: An Overview of Policy Issues', in R. Ffrench-Davis and S. Griffith-Jones (eds), *Coping with Capital Surges: Latin American Macroeconomics and Investment*, Lynne Rienner, Boulder and London.

Dornbusch, Rudiger and Yung Chul Park (1995), 'Financial Integration in a Second Best World', in *idem* (eds), *Financial Opening: Policy Lessons for Korea*, Korea Institute of Finance, Seoul, pp. 12–53.

Easterly, W., C. Rodriguez and K. Schmidt-Hebbel (1994), *Public Sector Deficits and Macroeconomic Performance*, The World Bank, Washington, DC.

Edwards, Sebastian (1990), 'The Sequencing of Economic Reform: Analytical Issues and Lessons from Latin American Experience', *The World Economy*, Vol. 13, No. 1, pp. 1–14.

Fischer, Bernhard (1993), 'Impediments in the Domestic Banking Sector to Financial Opening', in H. Reisen and B. Fischer (eds), *Financial Opening: Policy Issues and Experiences in Developing Countries*, OECD, Paris, pp. 119–132.

Fischer, Bernhard and Helmut Reisen (1993), *Liberalising Capital Flows in Developing Countries: Pitfalls, Prerequisites and Perspectives*, OECD Development Centre, Paris.

Frankel, Jeffrey (1994), 'Sterilization of Money Inflows: Difficult (Calvo) or Easy (Reisen)?', *IMF Working Paper*, WP/94/159, Washington, DC.

Glick, Reuven and Ramon Moreno (1994), 'Capital Flows and Monetary Policy in East Asia', *Pacific Basin Working Paper*, No. PB 94-08, Federal Reserve Bank of San Francisco.

Greenwood, John (1994), 'Exchange Rate Regimes and Monetary Stability in Asia', *Asian Monetary Monitor*, Vol. 18, No. 4, pp. 1–9.

Griffith-Jones, Stephany (1994), 'European Private Flows to Latin America: The Facts and the Issues', in R. Ffrench-Davis and S. Griffith-Jones (eds), *Financial Opening: Policy Lessons for Korea*, Korea Institute of Finance, Seoul.

Group of Thirty (1994), *Latin American Capital Flows: Living with Volatility*, Group of Thirty, Washington, DC.

Harberger, Arnold C. (1985), 'Lessons for Debtor-Country Managers and Policymakers', in G.W. Smith and J.T. Cuddington (eds), *International Debt and the Developing Countries*, The World Bank, Washington, DC, pp. 236–257.

Helpman, E., L. Leiderman and G. Bufman (1994), 'A New Breed of Exchange Rates: Chile, Israel and Mexico', *Economic Policy*, 19, pp. 259–306.

IMF (International Monetary Fund)(1994), *World Economic Outlook*, October 1994, Washington, DC.

Joumard, Isabelle and Helmut Reisen (1992), 'Real Exchange Rate Overshooting and Persistent Trade Effects', *The World Economy*, Vol. 15, No. 3, pp. 375–388.

Kenen, Peter (1993), 'Financial Opening and the Exchange Rate Regime', in H. Reisen and B. Fischer (eds), *Financial Opening: Policy Issues and Experiences in Developing Countries*, OECD, Paris, pp. 237–262.

Larraín, Guillermo and Helmut Reisen (1994), 'Disinflation with Unemployment in Latin America: Sustainable?', in D. Turnham *et al.* (eds), *Social Tensions, Job Creation and Economic Policy in Latin America*, OECD, Paris, pp. 129–144.

Obstfeld, Maurice (1995), 'International Currency Experience: New Lessons and Lessons Relearned', *Brookings Papers on Economic Activity*, 1995:1, pp. 119–220.

OECD (1995), *Financial Market Trends*, No. 60, OECD, Paris.

Reisen, Helmut (1993a), 'Integration with Disinflation: Which Way?', in R. O'Brien (ed.), *Finance and the International Economy*, 7, The Amex Bank Review Prize Essays, Oxford University Press, Oxford, pp. 128–145.

Reisen, Helmut (1993b), 'Southeast Asia and the "Impossible Trinity"', in *International Economic Insights*, Vol. 4, No. 3, pp. 21–23.

Reisen, Helmut (1994a), 'On the Wealth of Nations and Retirees', in R. O'Brien (ed.), *Finance and the International Economy*, 8, The Amex Bank Review Prize Essays, Oxford University Press, Oxford, pp. 86–107.

Reisen, Helmut (1994b), 'The Case for Sterilised Intervention in Latin America', in H. Reisen, *Debt, Deficits and Exchange Rates: Essays on Financial Interdependence and Development*, Edward Elgar, Aldershot (UK) and Brookfield (US), pp. 205–228.

Reisen, Helmut (1996), 'Developing-Country Savings and the Global Capital Shortage', in OECD, *Future Global Capital Shortages: Real Fact or Pure Fiction?*, Paris.

Reisen, Helmut and Axel van Trotsenburg (1988), 'Should the Asian NICs Peg to the Yen?', *Intereconomics* (July/August), pp. 172–77.

Reisen, Helmut and Hélène Yèches (1993), 'Time-Varying Estimates on the Openness of the Capital Account in Korea and Taiwan', *Journal of Development Economics*, Vol. 41, No. 2, pp. 285–305.

Rojas-Suarez, Liliana and Steven R. Weisbrod (1994), 'Financial Market Fragilities in Latin America: From Banking Crisis Resolution to Current Policy Challenges', *IMF Working Paper*, WP/94/117.

Turner, Philip (1991), 'Capital Flows in the 1980s: A Survey of Major Trends', *BIS Economic Papers*, No. 30, Bank for International Settlements, Basle.

Turner, Philip (1995), 'Capital Flows in Latin America: A New Phase', *BIS Economic Papers*, No. 44, Bank for International Settlements, Basle.

Williamson, John (1994), 'The Management of Capital Inflows', Institute for International Economics, Washington, DC, mimeo.

Zahler, Roberto (1992), 'Monetary Policy and an Open Capital Account', *CEPAL Review*, No. 48, United Nations Economic Commission for Latin America and the Caribbean, Santiago, Chile.

10. Emerging-market Risk and Sovereign Credit Ratings[*]

INTRODUCTION

Credit rating agencies were conspicuous among the many who failed to predict Mexico's 1994–95 economic crisis. While the 20 December devaluation of the peso rocked the world financial markets, until 22 December Standard and Poor's had Mexico's sovereign debt only one step below an investment grade rating with a 'positive outlook'. The Mexican crisis has thus produced the sentiment that rating agencies react to events rather than anticipating them and raised questions about how seriously investors should take sovereign ratings on developing countries.

Our paper aims at broader empirical content for judging whether the two leading rating agencies lead or lag market events with respect to sovereign risk. The evidence will be based on announced as well as implemented ratings of sovereign bonds from the two major rating agencies for 26 OECD and non-OECD countries and their impact on yield spreads relative to US treasury bonds. The next section will present a discussion on the potential of the rating industry to attenuate boom–bust cycles with overborrowing in the international capital markets. The subsequent section will describe the country sample, the data and the methodology. We then present the econometric evidence on the interaction of sovereign yield spreads and changes in country ratings. We take two approaches: first, we perform Granger Causality tests (Granger, 1969) based on an unbalanced panel data set with yearly observations for the period 1988–95; second, we examine the daily reaction of sovereign yield spreads on rating change announcements and implemented rating changes between 1987 and 1996. The final section concludes.

---

[*] Originally published as OECD Development Centre Technical Paper No. 124, April 1997.

SOVEREIGN EMERGING-MARKET RISK AND THE RATING INDUSTRY

The Mexican crisis of 1994–95 has again demonstrated the vulnerability of emerging-market economies to financial crises associated with the reversal of excessive private capital inflows. The boom–bust cycle with overborrowing can be explained, *inter alia*, by negative Harberger externality (Harberger, 1985): private borrowers do not internalize the rising marginal social cost of their private borrowing that arises from the upward-rising supply of foreign capital. In principle, the credit rating industry could help mitigate such congestion externality in world capital markets.

Governments generally seek credit ratings not only to ease their access to international capital markets, but also because these assessments affect the ratings of other borrowers of the same nationality. Many investors, in particular institutional investors, prefer rated over unrated securities, partly as a result of domestic prudential regulation. Sovereign yields also tend to rise as ratings worsen, reflecting the rise in the default risk premium (Cantor and Packer, 1996). The increase in the cost of borrowing, along with the threat of reduced availability of credit, would then provide the incentive for both the public and private sector to abstain from excessive capital inflows. By reducing the negative Harberger externality, early changes in sovereign ratings could help to impose market-based financial discipline. Cantor and Packer (1996) have recently claimed that 'credit ratings appear to have some independent influence on yields over and above their correlation with other publicly available information' (p. 34). This finding would imply that the ratings lead rather than lag the financial markets, by acquiring advance knowledge or superior information that has subsequently been conveyed to market participants.

Several considerations, however, suggest that there is little room for the credit rating industry to reduce congestion externalities with respect to sovereign emerging-market risk. These considerations originate in the nature of sovereign risk, the information content of sovereign-risk ratings, and the industrial organization of the rating industry.

First, in the absence of a credible supranational mechanism to sanction sovereign default, the default risk premium is more determined by the borrower's willingness to pay than by his ability to pay (Eaton, Gersowitz and Stiglitz, 1986). This does not just result from the existence of informational asymmetries between borrowers and lenders, that can be particularly pronounced in the international context. The incumbent authorities can also not commit themselves or their successors credibly to using the foreign capital inflow for productive purposes or that future returns will be used to repay the foreign liability.

Pensions, Savings and Capital Flows

Second, therefore, the nature of information that a rating may convey is not the same for sovereign risk as it is for national risk. While rating agencies may receive inside information from domestic corporate borrowers that can be essentially defined as *private* (such as acquisition, expansion, new products and debt issuance plans), sovereign-risk ratings are primarily based on publicly available information (such as debt and foreign-reserve levels or political and fiscal constraints). Consequently, announced or implemented rating changes will rarely be 'uncontaminated' with other publicly-available news.

Third, the sovereign credit rating industry derives most of its fee income from governments which solicit ratings of their bond issues. The industry can be characterized as a duopoly where the two leading agencies – Moody's Investor Service and Standard and Poor's – fight for market share between each other as well as with smaller agencies. The fear of losing demand (and fee income) from governments which look for ratings on their securities may delay rating deteriorations in periods of excessive capital inflows. The high share of split ratings (indicating disagreement in the evaluation of sovereign risk) can be partly traced to the endeavour of small agencies to gain market share by rating more generously than the market leaders. Table 10.1 exemplifies the point.

Table 10.1 Split sovereign credit ratings of central government and central banks, January 1994

	Moody's	Standard and Poor's	Other agencies, avg.[a]
Avg. rating notches above Moody's	-	0.18	1.36
Highest rating difference with Moody's (notches)			
• above	-	2	3.2
• below	-	2	0.1
Number of observations	49	45	24
Market share, %	41.5	38.1	20.3

Note:

a. The average 'other agencies' includes 10 rating agencies. Consequently, the systematic bias in the rating level might not be relevant for individual agencies of this group.

Source: *Financial Times*, Credit Ratings International, 1995.

Whether the sovereign credit rating industry leads or lags the financial markets is not just of academic interest. In order to help mitigate boom–bust cycles with overborrowing, the industry – in particular the two leading agencies – would have to lead by acquiring advance knowledge or by superior analysis that is subsequently conveyed to market participants. If, by contrast, rating agencies lag market events, they might contribute to amplify boom–bust cycles. During the boom, improving ratings would reinforce euphoric expectations and stimulate excessive capital inflows; during the bust, downgrading might add to panic among investors, driving money out of the country and sovereign yield spreads up.

DATA, SAMPLE SELECTION AND METHODOLOGY

Our analysis presents the econometric evidence on the interaction between ratings (assigned or imminent) and yield spreads on sovereign government bonds, including those of emerging markets. This focus severely limits data availability because most emerging-market government securities have been rated only since the 1990s and are not regularly quoted on the financial markets.

Data and Sample Selection

The sample consists of the ratings of sovereign foreign-currency debt for the period early 1987 to mid-1996 which have been assigned by Moody's and Standard & Poor's. The rating history has been obtained directly from these two market leaders who cover some 80 per cent of sovereign credit ratings. We do not only analyse *implemented* rating assignments, but also *imminent* rating changes (when Moody's puts a country on *watchlist* and Standard & Poor's assigns a country with a positive or negative *outlook*). The data will be used for an annual Granger Causality test on 26 sovereign ratings from 1988 to 1995 and for a short-term event study on 78 rating announcements from 1987 to 1996.[1]

Although the two agencies use different symbols in assessing credit risk, every Moody's symbol has its counterpart in Standard & Poor's rating scale. This correspondence allows us to transform the rating notches[2] into numbers, either by way of linear or logistic transformation, representing two hypotheses about the sovereign risk implied by varying rating notches. A linear scale of transformation assigns the highest rating notch (Aaa for Moody's, AAA for Standard & Poor's) the number 20 and falls over the residual 19 notches to the lowest level of creditworthiness (C for Moody's, D for Standard & Poor's), equal to zero. The linear scale implies that

Pensions, Savings and Capital Flows

differences of ratings correspond one to one with differences in perceptions of country risk.[3] The logistic transformation, by contrast, implies the hypothesis that risk perceptions first deteriorate slowly as rating notches decrease, then deteriorate faster in a certain region of rating notches (where ratings fall from investment-grade to speculative-grade) and finally deteriorate slowly again as ratings reach the bottom of the classification (see Figure 10.1).

Figure 10.1   Numerical transformation of sovereign ratings

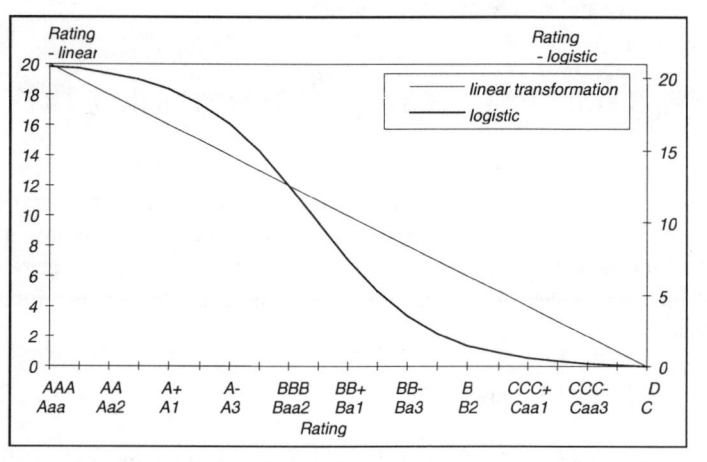

Source: Author calculations.

The second core data needed for our analysis are fixed-rate dollar bond redemption yield spreads on central government bonds above US treasury bond yields. Excluding currency risk, dollar bond spreads can be assumed primarily to reflect country risk premia on government bonds of the same maturity.

The benchmark is for 10-year US treasury bonds. For our sample, more than 70 per cent of the government bonds observed are of 10-year maturity; for the rest (except Brazil where maturity is 20 years), we took bonds of shorter maturity. The inclusion of shorter maturities introduces differences in yield spreads which are related to the yield curve; fortunately, the shorter maturities apply only for the period 1992–95 when the US yield curve remained relatively stable. Transaction price data on government bonds, in particular for the emerging markets, are not easily available. The major problem is that the government bonds are not actively traded, being mostly held by long-term institutional investors or by central banks. Among the full data set on government dollar bond yields, obtained from Datastream,

Bloomberg, JP Morgan, Merrill Lynch and the Federal Reserve Bank of New York, we filtered out by visual inspection all countries of which government bonds were not regularly priced, leaving us with a sample of 26 countries against a total of some 60 countries whose sovereign debt has been rated during part of the observation period. For every rating observation, we selected only one – the most regularly traded – government bond for each country, in order to maintain an equally weighted sample.

Apart from the two core data on ratings and dollar bond spreads, we use standard macroeconomic variables that determine country risk (see, e.g., Edwards, 1984) to correct our long-term analysis for such factors. In order to have a consistent data base that covers the full sample period, we took these variables from the DRI database (see Appendix 10.1).

Methodology

To examine whether the two rating agencies lead or lag financial markets, we proceed with two different methodologies. First, we perform *Granger Causality tests* based on an unbalanced panel data set with yearly averages for ratings and yield spreads during 1988–95.[4] Representing annual average of the yield spread by a vector Y, the average of the numerically transformed annual rating levels assigned by Moody's and Standard & Poor's by a vector X, and exogenous macroeconomic country risk determinants (see below) by a vector W_t, the Granger Causality test can be performed by the estimation equations

$$Y_{it} = \beta X_{it-1} + \mu W_{it-1} + \alpha_i + U_{it} \qquad (10.1)$$

$$X_{it} = \gamma Y_{it-1} + \eta W_{it-1} + \lambda_i + V_{it} \qquad (10.2)$$

where subscripts i and t denote countries and years respectively, where α and λ are country-specific intercepts (fixed effects), and U and V residuals.

If ratings would Granger cause dollar bond spreads, the estimation should find a feedback from X_{it-1} on Y_{it} (with $\beta > 0$). Simultaneously, Granger Causality requires that dollar bond spreads should not influence ratings $(\gamma = 0)$. Granger Causality would imply that the history of ratings matters for the evolution of yield spreads, but not vice versa. Were the rating agencies to lead (inform) the market, omitting X_{t-1} in the estimation equation (10.1) would alter the joint distribution of the vector W_{t-1}, while omitting Y_{t-1} in equation (10.2) would not alter the joint distribution of W.

The vector W represents the determinants of default cited in the literature on sovereign credit risk (e.g. Edwards, 1984). These variables are also repeatedly cited in rating agency reports as determinants of sovereign

ratings (Cantor and Packer, 1996), with the expected impact on ratings in parentheses:

- total foreign debt as a percentage of exports (−)

- central government spending as a percentage of GDP (−)

- annual rate of consumer price inflation (−)

- current account deficit as a percentage of GDP (−)

- real rate of annual GDP growth (+)

- savings as a percentage of GDP (+)

- default history, represented by a dummy, if the country has defaulted on its foreign-currency liabilities since 1970 (−).

Since a considerable amount of capital flows to the emerging markets is determined by global cyclical factors (Calvo, Leiderman and Reinhart, 1996), our vector W includes also the 10-year US treasury bond yield. We assume that a rise in the US treasury bond yield will tend to raise yield spreads, since it will cause a return of foreign capital to the industrial countries.

Second, we undertake an *event study* to investigate the short-run impact of press releases where the two leading agencies announce imminent or implemented rating changes on sovereign bonds. The event-study method analyses the yield spread response of sovereign dollar bonds in an observation window spanning from 40 trading days before the press release (day 0) to 40 trading days after. Usually (e.g. Hand, Holthausen and Leftwich, 1992) the method would focus on 'abnormal' excess returns after correcting yield spreads in a market model that relates the country-specific yield to the respective benchmark (in our case, JP Morgan's global government bond index or JP Morgan's emerging markets bond index plus). Alternatively, the event study can use *relative* yield spreads (the yield spread as a fraction of the benchmark yield) to study the response to rating announcements. In both cases, the response of yield spreads is subsequently subject to test-statistic which follows a t distribution. The null hypothesis for the sovereign bond market is that rating announcements will not lead to significant changes in yield spreads, since these announcements are 'contaminated' with other publicly available news.

RESULTS

Granger Causality

We perform the Granger Causality test by estimating equations (10.1) and (10.2) in an unbalanced panel of 114 observations for 26 countries, of which 10 are classified as emerging-market economies by the International Finance Corporation. The structure of Granger Causality tests would require the application of a dynamic model, which can be estimated efficiently by using a general methods of moments (GMM) (see, e.g., Ahn and Schmidt, 1995).[5] Since the GMM estimator would require a high number of instrument variables, which would entail an important loss of degree of freedom for our estimates, we are forced to use the less efficient maximum likelihood (ML) estimator in a panel model of fixed effects.[6] We make the usual assumptions of a fixed-effect model in a one-way error component regression (Baltagi, 1995). We obtain heteroskedasticity-robust standard errors by using the White estimator. We first estimate equations (10.1) and (10.2) by using four lags for each variable and subsequently reduce the number of explanatory variables by using the Schwartz Bayesian criterion.

Table 10.2 Granger Causality test statistics (from panel regressions)

Equation	(10.1)	(10.2)
Dependent variable	Yield spread	rating
Period	1988–95	1988–95
F-statistic	11.13***	9.04***
	$F(2,97)$	$F(1,93)$
P-value	0.000	0.000
Adjusted R^2	0.920	0.966
SER	0.565	0.311
Observations	114	114

Notes:
*** Significant at the 1 per cent level. The F-statistic tests whether the coefficient of the rating variable in eq. (10.1) and of the yield spread variable in eq. (10.2) differs significantly from zero when comparing the unrestricted with the restricted equation where the rating, resp. the yield spread variable has been excluded.

Table 10.2 presents the statistics of the Granger Causality test, using the logistic transformation of ratings into numbers which produced slightly more significant estimates than the linearily transformed ratings. The

underlying estimation equations are (10.1) and (10.2) (see Appendix 10.2 for more detailed results). The results show a two-way causality between ratings and yield spreads and reject Granger Causality of both ratings and yield spreads. While the estimation equation (10.1) leads to reject the hypothesis $\beta = 0$, equation (10.2) rejects the hypothesis $\gamma = 0$. This result means that ratings cause yield spreads and vice versa.

While the adjusted R^2 in Table 10.2 points to a high explanatory power of the model underlying equations (10.1) and especially (10.2) and while the *t*-statistics of the underlying parameters are generally significant, we cannot exclude multicollinearity problems in our vector **W** variables.[7]

Event Study

We next investigate how dollar bond spreads respond to Moody's and Standard & Poor's announcements of changes in their sovereign assessments. Our analysis is based on 78 rating events between 1987 and 1996,[8] of which 42 events affected the emerging markets; 8 ratings were put on review for possible downgrade and 14 for possible upgrade; 25 of the announcements report actual rating downgrades and 27 actual upgrades. Figure 10.2 visualizes the average movements of relative yield spreads – yield spreads divided by the appropriate US treasury rate – around the day 0 of the 78 rating announcements.

In general, Figure 10.2 shows clearly that a change in the risk assessment by the two leading rating agencies is preceded by a similar change in the market's assessment of sovereign risk. The pattern is particularly clear when countries have been put on review for possible downgrade or upgrade. During the 29 days preceding a review for possible downgrade, relative spreads rise by about 25 percentage points – a result which is heavily influenced by Mexico's *tesobono* crisis and the tequila effect on Argentina. Likewise, the 29 trading days before a country is put on positive outlook by one of the two agencies, the relative yield spread falls on average by eight percentage points. Moreover, once a country's rating has been put on review for a negative or positive outlook, the market trend appears to reverse. This pattern clearly recalls the common bourse wisdom to buy on the rumour and to sell on the fact.

For actual rating changes, Figure 10.2 displays a somewhat different observation. Only shortly ahead of the agency announcement can a market movement clearly be discerned, when a downgrade (upgrade) is preceded by a modest rise (drop) in yield spreads. After the rating has been changed, the market appears to vindicate the agencies' assessment over the next 30 trading days with a respective movement in relative yield spreads.

Figure 10.2   78 Rating events and sovereign yield spreads, 1990–96

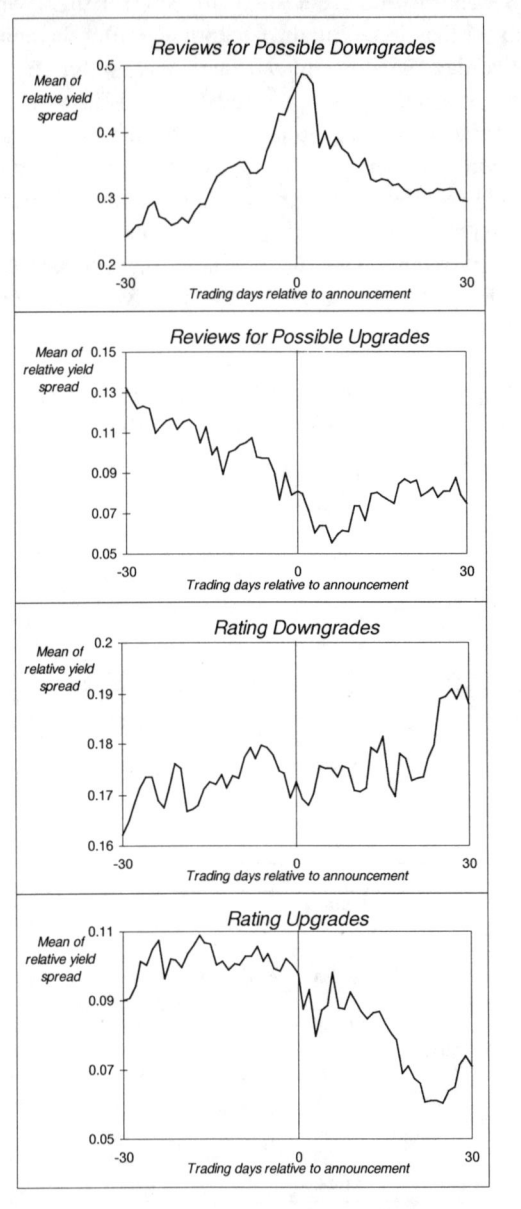

Sources: Bloomberg, Datastream, DRI, JP Morgan, Merrill Lynch, Moody's, Standard & Poor's.

Pensions, Savings and Capital Flows

To capture the immediate effects of rating announcements, Table 10.3 presents the results of our event study for several time windows – three windows each for the 29 trading days before and after the announcement as well as a two-day window (day 0 and day 1) for the date of the announcement. Ideally, the event study should investigate 'abnormal' excess returns after correcting dollar bond spreads in a market model that relates the country-specific yield to an appropriate benchmark. This procedure would require that the signs of the 'abnormal' excess returns are homogeneous with the direction of each announced change in the agencies' rating. Since this requirement did not hold for our sample,[9] Table 10.3 displays the change of the mean of the relative yield spreads and the respective *t*-statistic.[10]

Table 10.3 Short-term impact of the full sample of rating announcements (mean change of relative yield spreads)

	Full sample					
	Full sample			Emerging markets		
No. of announcements	51			31		
Trading days	Cumulative mean change	*t*-statistic	% with right sign	Cumulative mean change	*t*-statistic	% with right sign
−30 to −21	0.013	0.98		0.021	1.60*	
−20 to −11	0.015	1.17		0.022	1.67**	
−10 to −1	0.015	1.12		0.025	1.89**	
0 to + 1	0.009	1.53*	54.9	0.014	2.44***	58.1
+2 to +10	−0.019	−1.66**		−0.032	−2.76***	
+11 to +20	−0.007	−0.56		−0.014	−1.07	
+21 to +30	0.009	0.66		0.009	0.73	

	Moody's					
	Full sample			Emerging markets		
No. of announcements	22			12		
Trading days	Cumulative mean change	*t*-statistic	% with right sign	Cumulative mean change	*t*-statistic	% with right sign
−30 to −21	0.009	0.73		0.007	0.54	
−20 to −11	0.015	1.20		0.018	1.47*	
−10 to −1	−0.013	−1.08		−0.021	−1.66*	
0 to + 1	0.007	1.20	50.0	0.011	2.04**	58.3
+2 to +10	−0.008	−0.75		−0.008	−0.75	
+11 to +20	−0.004	−0.33		−0.008	−0.61	
+21 to +30	0.018	1.45		0.021	1.70	

Table 10.3 (continued)

	Standard & Poor's					
	Full sample			Emerging markets		
No. of announcements	29			19		
Trading days	Cumulative mean change	*t*-statistic	% with right sign	Cumulative mean change	*t*-statistic	% with right sign
−30 to −21	0.015	0.80		0.033	1.77**	
−20 to −11	0.015	0.83		0.026	1.39*	
−10 to −1	0.034	1.83**		0.055	2.96***	
0 to +1	0.010	1.23	56.7	0.017	2.02**	58.0
+2 to +10	−0.027	−1.64*		−0.050	−3.04***	
+11 to +20	−0.008	−0.41		−0.016	−0.87	
+21 to +30	0.000	0.01		−0.001	−0.04	

	Investment grade						Speculative grade		
	Full sample			Emerging markets			Full sample		
No. of announce-ments	39			19			12		
Trading days	Cumulative mean change	*t*-statistic	% with right sign	Cumulative mean change	*t*-statistic	% with right sign	Cumulative mean change	*t*-statistic	% with right sign
−30 to −21	0.00007	0.01		−0.0002	−0.03		0.0009	0.01	
−20 to −11	−0.001	−0.11		−0.007	−0.94		0.004	0.07	
−10 to −1	−0.001	−0.16		−0.002	−0.22		−0.0004	−0.01	
0 to +1	0.003	0.89	51.3	0.006	1.61*	52.6	−0.011	−0.38	66.7
+2 to +10	−0.0006	−0.09		0.002	0.25		−0.012	−0.21	
+11 to +20	0.003	0.33		0.002	0.28		0.0005	0.01	
+21 to +30	0.010	1.32		0.01	1.72		0.060	0.92	

Notes:
* Significant at the 10 per cent level; ** Significant at the 5 per cent level; *** Significant at the 1 per cent level.

Sources: Bloomberg, Datastream, JP Morgan, Merrill Lynch, Moody's, Standard & Poor's; own calculations.

Table 10.3 replicates quite closely Cantor and Packer (1996) to see whether dollar bond spreads respond to rating announcements. Note, however, that our analysis fully captures events following Mexico's *Tesobono* crisis up to 1996, unlike Cantor and Packer whose tests are based on observations up to 1994 only. Moreover, our more recent observation period implies that our country sample represents relatively more emerging-market observations. Nevertheless, our sample weakens Cantor and Packer for the full sample of rating events: the impact of rating announcements on dollar bond spreads is not significant.[11] However, that impact is highly significant only (at the 1 per cent level) for rating announcements on emerging-market sovereign bonds. Within the announcement window

(day 0–1), a rating event on emerging-market sovereign bonds moves the relative yield spread by 1.6 percentage points, more than for the full sample (0.7 percentage points). The change in the yield spread during the rating announcement is larger than the change in the preceding 29 trading days on a daily basis; but it is subsequently reversed, indicating a degree of market overshooting.

Roughly 55 per cent of the full sample and 64 per cent of the emerging-market sample of rating events are associated with the expected change in the yield spread.[12] Moody's and Standard & Poor's perform equally well. Disaggregation of announcements for investment-grade across speculative grade finds, in contrast to Cantor and Packer, a significant impact only for investment-grade, emerging-market securities.

To explore the announcement effect of rating events in more detail, Table 10.4 reports the median changes of relative yield spreads for four rating announcement categories: downgrade outlook/watchlist change announcements, upgrade outlook/watchlist change announcements, assigned rating downgrades, and assigned rating upgrades. The statistical significance of our results suffers obviously from that disaggregation; however, the distinction into different announcement categories allows us to originate the source of significant announcement effects that we reported in Table 10.3.

Table 10.4 reports a significant change of the yield spread in the expected direction during the announcement period (day 0–1) only when a country is put on review for a possible downgrade. For emerging-market securities, the negative announcement has a strong and significant effect on relative yield spreads, which rise by 11.3 percentage points. There is also a strong market anticipation in the 19 trading days before that rating event as spreads rise by 2 percentage points on a daily basis. Also significantly, part of the rise in relative yield spreads is reversed in the month following the announcement that an emerging-country rating has been put on review with a negative outlook (the reversal may indicate economic policy reactions by the authorities concerned). Even when including the weak significance for rating upgrades in emerging markets, our results contrast with Cantor and Packer who find significant results only for positive announcements. However, we are in line with most other studies using stock market data finding a significant price response to downgrades but not to upgrades (Goh and Ederington, 1993).

Table 10.4 Short-term impact of various rating announcement categories (mean change of relative yield spreads)

	OUTLOOK / CREDITWATCH: downgrade				OUTLOOK / CREDITWATCH: upgrade			
	Full sample		Emerging markets		Full sample		Emerging markets	
No. of announcements	8		4		10		8	
Trading days	Cumulative mean change	t-statistic	Cumulative mean change	t-statistic	Cumulative mean change	t-statistic	Cumulative mean change	t-statistic
−30 to −21	0.019	0.36	0.02	0.44	−0.028	−1.02	−0.030	−1.10
−20 to −11	0.087	1.66*	0.17	3.30**	−0.019	−0.69	−0.019	−0.68
−10 to −1	0.10	1.85*	0.205	3.93***	−0.016	−0.58	−0.017	−0.62
0 to +1	0.042	1.78**	0.083	3.57**	0.0026	0.21	−0.0003	−0.02
+2 to +10	−0.13	−2.88**	−0.26	−5.63***	0.00028	0.01	0.001	0.06
+11 to +20	−0.046	−0.89	−0.103	−1.97*	0.012	0.43	0.015	0.54
+21 to +30	−0.011	−0.21	−0.033	−0.64	−0.0035	−0.13	−0.003	−0.10

	RATING: downgrade				RATING: upgrade			
	Full sample		Emerging markets		Full sample		Emerging markets	
No. of announcements	17		8		16		11	
Trading days	Cumulative mean change	t-statistic	Cumulative mean change	t-statistic	Cumulative mean change	t-statistic	Cumulative mean change	t-statistic
−30 to −21	0.015	1.25	0.035	2.85**	0.006	0.40	0.006	0.36
−20 to −11	−0.008	−0.62	−0.016	−1.30	−0.005	−0.31	−0.00002	−0.001
−10 to −1	−0.006	−0.48	−0.015	−1.22	−0.003	−0.18	−0.003	−0.20
0 to +1	0.003	0.56	0.005	0.87	−0.007	−0.97	−0.008	−1.06
+2 to +10	0.004	0.34	0.008	0.75	0.007	0.44	0.012	0.80
+11 to +20	0.007	0.55	0.014	1.15	−0.009	−0.57	−0.014	−0.81
+21 to +30	0.011	0.94	0.021	1.76*	−0.01	−0.61	−0.009	−0.54

Notes:
* Significant at the 10 per cent level; ** Significant at the 5 per cent level; *** Significant at the 1 per cent level.

Sources: Bloomberg, Datastream, JP Morgan, Merrill Lynch, Moody's, Standard & Poor's; own calculations.

Finally, it is noteworthy that Table 10.4 reports a slow but rising market response when rating downgrades are actually implemented. The rise in the dollar bond spread in response to a downgrade on emerging-market sovereign bonds becomes significant only 20 trading days after the rating event. The slow response may reflect the reorientation of portfolios by institutional investors which are often guided by prudential regulation that discourages the holding of low-rated securities.

CONCLUSION

First, our Granger Causality test cautions against overestimating the independent long-run impact that sovereign credit ratings exert on the financial-market assessment of sovereign risk. The financial market and the two leading rating agencies appear broadly to share the same model in that assessment. As indicated by the explanatory power of the equations that underlie the causality test, dollar bond spreads and a set of default determinants seem to explain somewhat better the level of credit ratings than vice versa. The mutual interaction between sovereign yield spreads and ratings may be characterized by the nature of sovereign risk (requiring assessments on present and future willingness rather than only ability to pay), the information content of sovereign risk ratings ('contaminating' rating changes with other publicly-available news) and the industrial organization of the rating industry (introducing an upward bias in sovereign ratings).

Second, contrary to our expectations but in line with earlier studies, our event study finds a highly significant announcement effect – obviously muted by strong market anticipation – when emerging-market sovereign bonds are put on review with negative outlook. The result may surprise, beyond the above considerations, because the rating of these bonds is fairly new to the industry; this lack of experience is reflected by a high degree of split ratings. Negative rating announcements seem also to be effective in the aftermath of rating deteriorations (possibly not fully captured by the length of our observation window), as investors are incited to reorient their portfolios. Positive rating events, by contrast, do not seem to have a significant announcement effect on dollar bond spreads.

Third, these findings imply that the sovereign rating industry has the potential to help dampen excessive private capital inflows into the emerging markets with negative rating announcements. Positive announcements, by contrast, do not seem to exert a significant impact on sovereign risk assessments and thus are unlikely to add to the Harberger externality. For two reasons, even this conclusion must be cautioned however. The

econometric analysis of rating decisions seems sensitive to the sample period chosen. Even if rating agencies have the potential to dampen excessive inflows, our analysis does not provide information on whether the agencies would provide negative rating announcements in time.

NOTES

1. The sample countries include Argentina, Austria, Australia, Belgium, Brazil, Canada, Chile, Colombia, Czech Republic, Denmark, Finland, Germany, Hungary, Indonesia, Ireland, Italy, Korea, Malaysia, Mexico, New Zealand, Norway, Philippines, Poland, Portugal, Spain, South Africa, Sweden, Switzerland, Thailand, Turkey, UK, USA, and Venezuela.
2. A rating notch is the one-level difference on a rating scale.
3. An alternative transformation form could be a linked function with a 'structural break' when the sovereign bond passes non-investment grade to investment grade.
4. Unfortunately, monthly data for variables such as government spending are not available for all countries.
5. The estimation of this model leaves us with two alternatives. One is to use an ANOVA based general least square (GLS) estimator for an unbalanced panel. The GLS estimator uses the true variance covariance matrix. It is possible to obtain an unbiased, but not optimal estimator for the matrix with the ANOVA method. Secondly, we can use instrumental variables to capture the dynamic of a balanced model. In the latter case we would be using a general methods of moments (GMM) estimator which is an efficient instrument variable estimator as shown in Ahn and Schmidt (1995). As both methods cannot be used simultaneously, we decided to use the method for dynamic models, the GMM estimator.
6. This results from F and Hausmann tests which tested for alternative model specification simple OLS, the Var model (variation of slopes and intercepts across the country units), and the Between model.
7. Further research will work with the principal component model in order to reduce the number of regressors and multicollinearity. This would allow to use a GMM estimator for a simultaneous equation model with endogenous variables.
8. Between 1987 and 1996, we observe 126 precisely dated rating events by the two leading rating agencies, of which 48 cannot be used for our analysis for lack of regular trading of the underlying sovereign bond.
9. We constructed market models that regressed country-specific yields on the JP Morgan Global Government Bond Index (for OECD countries) and on the JP Morgan Emerging Market Bond Index Plus to calculate 'normal' returns. Although our market models yielded very high R^2, the signs of the 'abnormal' excess returns (actual yields minus 'normal' yields) were not in line with the direction of rating changes.
10. Using daily changes of the mean of the relative yield spreads and their standard deviation over the 60 days period surrounding the announcement, we constructed a test statistic which is *t*-distributed, following Holthausen and Leftwich (1986).
11. Because positive rating announcements should be associated with negative changes in spread, we multiply the changes in the relative spread by −1 when rating announcements are positive.
12. The number in parenthesis is a test-statistic which is based on a binomial distribution with *p* equal to 0.5.

Appendix 10.1 Source and description

Variable rating announcements	Source	used	Period	Definition	Problem	Countries
Standard & Poor's	Standard & Poor's	×	1987–1995 monthly	Rating & outlook		OECD and non-OECD
		×	1990–1996 daily	Rating & outlook		OECD and non-OECD
Moody's	Moody's	×	1986–1994 daily	Rating & creditwatch		non-OECD
Government bonds	Datastream, Bloomberg	×	1987–1995 annual, quarterly, monthly	In general government bonds with maturity of 10 years, but some have also maturities of 3, 5, 7 or 20 years.		Argentina, Austria, Australia, Belgium, Brazil, Canada, Chile, China, Colombia, Denmark, Finland, Germany, India, Indonesia, Ireland, Italy, Korea, Malaysia, Mexico, New Zealand, Norway, Philippines, Portugal, Spain, Sweden, Switzerland, Thailand, Turkey, UK, USA, Venezuela.
	Bloomberg, Datastream, JP Morgan, Merrill Lynch, Cantor & Packer	×	1990–1996 daily	In general government bonds with maturity of 10 years, but some have also maturities of 3, 5, 7 or 20 years.		Argentina, Brazil, Canada, Colombia, Czech Republic, Denmark, Finland, Hungary, Ireland, Italy, Korea, Malaysia, Mexico, New Zealand, Poland, South Africa, Sweden, Turkey.
Bond benchmarks						
Emerging markets bond index plus	JP Morgan	×	1991–1996 daily	Weighted index of several emerging markets bonds.		Index
Global government bond index	JP Morgan	×	1990–1996 daily	Weighted index of government bonds from OECD.		Index
US Treasury	Datastream	×	1987–1995 annual, quarterly, monthly	5 indices of US government bonds with maturities of 3, 5, 7, 10 or 20 years.		USA

Appendix 10.1 (continued)

Variable	Source	used	Period	Definition	Problem	Countries
Macro-economic variables						
Consumer price index	DRI	×	1987–1995 annual	Percent change from previous year	Eastern Europe is missing.	
	IMF		1987–1994 annual		1995 missing.	
	JP Morgan		1990–1995 annual		Only some emerging markets and some OECD countries, consistent with other sources.	
Current account balance/GDP	DRI	×	1987–1996 annual	Negative number indicates a deficit.	Eastern Europe is missing.	
	OECD		1987–1995 annual		Non-OECD missing.	OECD
	World Bank		1987–1993 annual	Negative number indicates a deficit.	1994, 1995 missing.	All countries
	JP Morgan		1987–1996 annual	Negative number indicates a deficit.	Only some emerging markets and some OECD countries, not always consistent with other sources.	Emerging markets + some OECD
External debt	JP Morgan	×	1987–1996 annual	Including short-term debt	Only some emerging markets and some OECD countries, not always consistent with other sources.	Emerging markets
	OECD	×	1987–1995 annual	Stock of foreign liabilities	Belgium, Ireland, Portugal, Spain missing.	

Appendix 10.1 (continued)

Variable	Source	used	Period	Definition	Problem	Countries
rating announcements						
External debt	World Bank – Debt Tables		1987–1995 annual		Not always consistent with other sources.	
External debt/GDP	JP Morgan	×	1987–1996 annual	Including short-term debt	Only some emerging markets and some OECD countries.	Emerging markets
External debt/exports	JP Morgan	×	1987–1996 annual	Including short-term debt	Only some emerging markets and some OECD countries.	Emerging markets
GDP	DRI	×	1987–1995 annual	Nominal in US$	Eastern Europe is missing.	
	OECD		1987–1995 annual		Non-OECD missing.	OECD
GDP per capita	DRI		1987–1995 annual	Nominal in US$	Eastern Europe is missing.	
GDP growth	DRI	×	1987–1995 annual	Real change from previous year	Eastern Europe is missing; 1994, 1995 missing.	
	World Bank		1987–1993 annual			All countries
Government spending/GDP	DRI	×	1987–1995 annual	Government spending divided by GDP	Eastern Europe is missing.	
	IMF		1987–1994 annual		Not existing for all countries.	
	World Bank		1987–1993 annual			All countries

214

Appendix 10.1 (continued)

Variable	Source	used	Period	Definition	Problem	Countries
rating announcements						
Investment ratio	DRI	×	1987–1995 annual	Domestic investment divided by GDP	Eastern Europe is missing. 1994, 1995 missing.	
	World Bank		1987–1993 annual	Domestic investment divided by GDP	Not consistent for all countries, often missing thus incomplete.	All countries
	IMF		1987–1994 annual			
Real effective exchange rate index	JP Morgan	×	1987–1995 annual		Not existing for all countries.	
Saving ratio	DRI	×	1987–1995 annual	Domestic saving divided by GDP	Eastern Europe is missing.	
	IMF		1987–1994 annual	Residual	Not consistent for all countries, often missing thus incomplete.	
	World Bank		1987–1993 annual	Domestic saving divided by GDP	1994, 1995 missing.	All countries

Appendix 10.2　Granger Causality coefficients

No. of observations	114		114	
No. of countries	26		26	
Adj. R^2	0.933		0.966	
SER	0.516		0.311	
Dependent variable		yield spreads		Rating
Rating	*RS(-2)*	−0.037	*RS(-1)*	0.126
		−2.09		7.76
	RS(-3)	0.132	*RS(-3)*	−0.044
		6.23		−0.89
Yield spreads			*YS(-1)*	−0.017
				−2.26
Real growth	*GG(-3)*	−0.108	*GG(-4)*	0.056
		−3.02		2.57
Current account / GDP	*CA(-2)*	−0.078	*CA(-2)*	0.078
		−2.19		4.03
			CA(-3)	0.019
				1.85
			CA(-4)	0.018
				1.83
Saving ratio	*SR(-1)*	−0.091	*SR(-3)*	−0.105
		−2.07		-3.06
	SR(-2)	0.090		
		1.61		
	SR(-3)	−0.114		
		−2.75		
US treasury bond 10 years	*UTR(-2)*	0.368		
		5.85		
	UTR(-4)	−0.078		
		−7.39		
Change of consumer price index	*CCP(-1)*	−0.076	*CCP(-4)*	0.051
		−1.68		3.71
	CCP(-4)	0.109		
		4.82		
Government spending / GDP	*GS(-1)*	−0.070	*GS(-1)*	0.098
		−1.65		5.01
			GS(-2)	−0.062
				−4.85
			GS(-3)	−0.059
				−5.06
			GS(-4)	0.060
				3.37

Appendix 10.2 (continued)

Real effective exchange rate index	*RERJ(-1)*	2.216	*RERJ(-1)*	1.664
		1.72		1.71
			RERJ(-2)	−1.779
				−1.21
			RERJ(-3)	1.551
				1.21
			RERJ(-4)	−2.438
				−2.20
External debts / exports	*EX(-1)*	−0.036	*EX(-2)*	0.060
		−3.27		14.95
	EX(-2)	0.006	*EX(-3)*	−0.016
		2.00		−6.93
	EX(-3)	0.009	*EX(-4)*	−0.008
		3.88		−2.57
	EX(-4)	0.005		
		1.75		

Sources: Bloomberg, Datastream, DRI, JP Morgan, Merrill Lynch, Moody's, OECD, Standard & Poor's; own calculations.

REFERENCES

Ahn, S. and P. Schmidt (1995), 'Efficient Estimation of Models for Dynamic Panel Data', *Journal of Econometrics*, 68.1, pp. 5–27.

Baltagi, B. (1995), *Econometrics Analysis of Panel Data*, John Wiley & Sons, Chichester.

Calvo, G., L. Leiderman and C. Reinhart (1996), 'Inflows of Capital to Developing Countries in 1990s', *Journal of Economic Perspectives*, 20.2, pp. 123–40.

Cantor, R. and F. Packer (1996), 'Determinants and Impact of Sovereign Credit Ratings', Federal Reserve Bank of New York, *Economic Policy Review*, 2.2, pp. 37–53.

Eaton, J., M. Gersowitz and J. Stiglitz (1986), 'The Pure Theory of Country Risk', *European Economic Review*, Vol. 30, No. 3.

Edwards, S. (1984), 'LDC Foreign Borrowing and Default Risk: An Empirical Investigation', 1976–80, *American Economic Review*, 74.4, pp. 726–734.

Goh, J.C. and L.H. Ederington (1993), 'Is a Bond Rating Downgrade Bad News, Good News, or No News for Stockholders?', *The Journal of Finance*, 158.5, pp. 2001–2008.

Granger, C.W.J. (1969), 'Investigating Causal Relations by Econometric Models and Cross-spectral Methods', *Econometrica*, 37, pp. 424–438.

Hand, J., R. Holthausen and R. Leftwich (1992), 'The Effect of Bond Rating Agency Announcements on Bond and Stock Prices', *The Journal of Finance*, 157.2, pp. 733–752.

Holthausen, R. and R. Leftwich (1986), 'The Effect of Bond Rating Changes on Common Stock Prices', *Journal of Financial Economics*, 17, pp. 57–89.

Harberger, A. (1985), 'Lessons for Debtor-Country Managers and Policy Makers', in G. Smith and J.T. Cuddington (eds), *International Debt and the Developing Countries*, World Bank, Washington, DC.

11. Domestic Causes of Currency Crises: Policy Lessons for Crisis Avoidance[*]

INTRODUCTION

The 1990s have witnessed three distinct regional currency crises: the European currency crisis of 1992–93, the Latin American crisis of 1994–95, and now the Asian crisis of 1997–98. Obviously, a major currency crisis every 24 months is too much for policymakers' comfort. The objective of exploring the causes of these crises, both domestic and international, is to make them less frequent and less severe.[1] In the process, we must avoid looking for 'causes' of currency crises in the victim countries alone. Rather, we need an integrated approach, based on realistic models of the benefits and risks of international capital flows between the rich and the developing countries (Table 11.1).

Table 11.1 Capital flows to Asian countries in crisis,[a] % of GDP

	1989–94[b]	1995–96[b]	1997
Net private capital flows	4.3	6.6	0.2
– net direct investment	1.2	1.1	1.1
– net portfolio investment	0.9	1.5	−0.6
– other net investment	2.2	4.1	−0.3
Net official flows	0.3	0.0	1.1
Change in reserves	2.0	1.3	−2.0

Notes:
a. Indonesia, Korea, Malaysia, Philippines, Thailand.
b. Annual averages.

Sources: IMF and Davies (1998).

---

[*] Originally published as OECD Development Centre Technical Paper No. 136, June 1998 and, in abridged form, as 'Heavy Foreign Flows, Weak Domestic Conduits: The Asian Crisis in Perspective' in Deutsche Bank Research, *Global Emerging Markets*, Vol. 1.2, August 1998, pp. 94–104.

The five countries most damaged by the Asian crisis – Indonesia, Korea, Malaysia, the Philippines and Thailand – received net private capital inflows worth 6.6 per cent of their combined GDP over the period 1995–96. In the second half of 1997, they suffered net outflows. The reversal from 1996 to 1997 constituted a swing of 11 per cent of their combined GDP. The biggest swing came from commercial banks who had extended loans well into 1997, despite earlier warnings on overexposure from the Bank for International Settlements (BIS) and the Institute of International Finance (IIF). There was also an important reversal of net portfolio investment. The only capital-account component proving to have staying power – just as during Mexico's 1994–95 crisis – was foreign direct investment flows. The Thai baht and the Korean won lost half of their value against the US dollar, and the Indonesian rupiah 80 per cent in the first months of the crisis, fanning a strong rise in non-performing loans in the local banking system and wiping out net capital for unhedged corporate borrowers. The reactive approach of the sovereign rating industry intensified panic by downgrading Asian borrowers to 'junk' status. Radelet and Sachs (1998), among many others, argue that the reversal in net capital flows, exchange rates and sovereign ratings in such a short period cannot be attributed to changes in the affected countries' fundamentals. The Achilles' heel of the global financial system seems to be the herd behaviour among commercial banks and portfolio investors (Wolf, 1998; Wyplosz, 1998), but for international financial investors to panic – as they did in Asia – requires weak fundamentals in the affected countries in the first place. This is what this paper will focus on.

Circumspection is required when writing about 'domestic causes' of currency crises. All too often, the isolated focus on characteristics found in countries which have fallen victim to a currency crisis yields 'causes' that are merely endogenous effects of massive net capital inflows. Current account deficits, overvalued exchange rates (in real terms), overinvestment in real estate and declining capital productivity all figure prominently in the list of culprits of Asia's crisis (see, e.g., Corsetti *et al.,* 1998). That view ignores, however, the endogeneity of such variables. Flows from capital-rich to capital-poor countries can only be effected with corresponding external deficits for the recipient countries, which are produced by a real appreciation of the exchange rate. The appreciation in turn reduces the relative incentive to invest in exportable production and tilts incentives towards nontradables, including real estate, whose relative price has to rise. Higher capital equipment to labour, a result of domestic investment financed by foreign savings, reduces the marginal return to capital.

This paper draws lessons from those emerging economies with excellent macroeconomic fundamentals that turned from financial-market darlings to

financial-crisis victims within months: Chile 1982, Mexico 1994 and now the five Asian victims. It will be argued that the 'root' cause for their currency crises resulted from the interaction of boom 'distortions', reinforced by exchange rate pegs that effectively promised super dollar returns, with the weakening of private-sector balance sheets as a result of heavy inflows, disorderly financial liberalization and weak domestic financial infrastructures. The paper first provides a short survey of the currency-crisis literature, then traces the process from boom to financial vulnerability, and finally draws conclusions for improving domestic financial systems (which should become a privileged target for aid flows), for exchange-rate policy and capital controls.

DOMESTIC INDICATORS OF EMERGING-MARKET CURRENCY AND BANKING CRISES: A CAPSULE SURVEY OF THE LITERATURE

'A sad commentary on our understanding of what drives capital flows is that every crisis spans a new generation of economic models. When a new crisis hits, it turns out that the previous generation of models was hardly adequate' (Rodrik, 1998, p. 5). The earliest models of currency crises, in particular the influential paper by former IMF chief economist Jacques Polak (1957) were based on the incompatibility of expansionary fiscal and monetary policies with fixed exchange rates. Excessive money creation would then 'leak out' through overall balance of payments deficits, until the shortage of foreign exchange reserves would force devaluation or impose controls on capital outflows. The attempts of investors to anticipate the inevitable collapse would generate a speculative attack on the currency when reserves fell to some critical level (Krugman, 1979; Flood and Garber, 1984). These 'first-generation' crisis models accounted well for the many currency crises in the 1970s and also for the 1982 developing-country debt crisis, but the models failed to explain Chile's 1982 crisis, the 1992 European crisis, the Mexican peso crisis 1994–95.

Table 11.2 shows that the 'first-generation' crisis model also fails to explain what happened in the five Asian crisis economies. Government budgets were balanced or moving into surplus (partly in appropriate fiscal response to higher net private capital flows). Growth in monetary aggregates was fairly high in all crisis countries, but cannot be described as runaway monetary expansion. Except in Thailand, inflation rates were coming down, nominal GDP growth was largely at levels corresponding to money creation, and all countries were at a stage of development where money demand was still growing.

The logic of the 'second-generation' crisis model (Obstfeld, 1994) does not apply to the Asian crisis either. This literature, developed in the aftermath of the European currency crises, stresses the trade-offs between the benefits of a credible exchange rate peg and the costs in terms of higher interest rates, higher unemployment or lower growth of defending the peg.

Table 11.2 'Traditional' crisis indicators

	Indonesia	Korea	Malaysia	Philippines	Thailand
Government budget, % of GDP					
– avg. 1990–94	0.4	−0.4	−0.7	−1.4	3.2
– avg. 1995–96	1.7	0.1	0.8	0.4	2.6
M2, annual growth					
– avg. 1990–94	19.4	18.0	21.4	20.6	16.7
– avg. 1995–96	27.2	15.7	20.9	23.7	14.8
Inflation rate, CPI					
– avg. 1990–94	8.8	5.3	4.1	11.1	4.6
– avg. 1995–96	8.7	4.7	4.4	8.3	5.8
Change in official foreign reserves, % of GDP (sterilized in parentheses)					
– avg. 1990–94	1.8	0.9	6.2	1.8	3.4
	(0.8)	(0.0)	(3.0)	(0.4)	(2.2)
– avg. 1995–96	2.0	0.4	1.3	2.6	0.6
	(1.0)	(0.4)	(0.0)	(1.8)	(0.0)
Real exchange rate appreciation, Accumulated %					
– 1990–94	8	9	14	38	11
– 1994–3/97	18	2	16	15	16
GDP growth, p.a.					
– avg. 1987–96	6.9	8.3	8.5	3.7	9.5
– EIU consensus expectations (7/97)	7.8	6.3	7.6	n.a.	6.8
Current account, % of GDP NIA definition					
– avg. 1990–94	−2.7	−1.5	−7.4	−4.5	−7.5
– avg. 1995–96	−3.8	−3.4	−9.7	−5.5	−9.1
– difference	−1.1	−1.9	−1.7	−1.0	−1.6
Efficiency[a]					
– avg. 1990–94	21.1	20.4	24.3	9.6	20.1
– avg. 1995–96	25.0	18.9	19.0	24.6	15.0

Note:
a. Defined here as GDP growth divided by the inverse of the investment rate of the preceding year.

Sources: Davies (1998), Corsetti *et al.* (1998), Radelet and Sachs (1998).

There was no such trade-off in the five Asian crisis countries before the crisis erupted. Past and expected growth was enviably high, interest rates and sovereign yield spreads were going down, not up, and unemployment was informal (as usual in developing countries). Traditional crisis models cannot explain the Asian crisis.

Nor do conventional flow explanations, which rely on current account sustainability or real overvaluation problems, explain the Asian crisis well. To be sure, there has been considerable appreciation of real effective exchange rates, in particular during the 1995–96 period. The effective appreciation resulted largely from the rise in the US dollar to which the Asian currencies were effectively pegged and from the depreciation of the yen, a key competitor currency. The inappropriateness of a dollar peg for the APEC currencies had long been recognized (Reisen and van Trotsenburg, 1988), although it had prevented beggar-thy-neighbour policies through competitive devaluations in the region, but in no way did the estimated overvaluation of the victim currencies reach Latin American or East European dimensions. On Goldman Sachs estimates (Davies, 1998), the estimated overvaluation did not exceed 5 per cent by mid-1997; by early 1998 Asian currencies were undervalued by up to 70 per cent on these estimates.

Current account deficits had been large in Malaysia and Thailand. That did not imply, however, that they were unsustainable in the sense of exploding total foreign debt/GDP ratios above sustainable thresholds (Reisen, 1998). Moreover, cyclically adjusted and corrected for underlying FDI cover, current account imbalances were not held to be excessive in the region, given the high past growth and expected growth potential. Rather than a (flow) crisis due to conventional current-account sustainability or real overvaluation problems, the Asian crisis seems primarily a capital-account crisis of stocks.

Broad aggregate efficiency numbers (as defined in Table 11.2) also fail to support the notion that capital flows reversed as investors perceived that they were not invested efficiently. While efficiency dropped somewhat in Korea, Malaysia and Thailand, that drop may at least partly be explained by a decline in marginal productivity of capital, as high net capital flows added to high domestic investment rates. In the two (capital-) poorest sample countries, Indonesia and the Philippines, capital efficiency actually rose during 1995–96 relative to the 1990–94 period.

As the speculative attacks of the 1990s, including the Mexican peso crisis, challenged the view that currency crises were due largely to the government's inability to achieve monetary and fiscal discipline, a number of researchers have turned to exploratory empirical models in order to identify crisis predictors. This literature points to indicators which are more

likely to be representative of the current Asian crisis than the indicators emphasized by the traditional currency crisis literature:

– In a panel of annual data for over 100 developing countries from 1971 to 1991, Frankel and Rose (1996) find that a high ratio of FDI to foreign debt inflows is associated with a low likelihood of a currency crash. Note here that this ratio deteriorated on average in the five crisis countries from roughly 1/2 over 1989–94 to 1/4 over 1995–96 (Table 11.1). By contrast, Frankel and Rose do not find evidence for the size of the current account deficit to predict currency crashes. It is interesting to recall that, from 1970 to 1982, Singapore ran a current account deficit worth 12.1 per cent of GDP on average; almost half of the corresponding net capital inflows consisted of FDI.

– Since the 1980s, the link between banking crises and balance-of-payments crises has strengthened. Kaminsky and Reinhart (1996) trace 71 balance-of-payments crises and 25 banking crises during the period 1970–95; while they report only 3 banking crises vs 25 balance-of-payments crises during 1970–79, they find 22 banking crises vs 46 payments crises over 1980–95. They find that financial liberalization (which has occurred mostly since the 1980s) plays a significant role in explaining the probability of a banking crisis preceded by a private lending boom. A banking crisis, they find, in turn helps predict a currency crisis. The Kaminsky and Reinhart findings are largely confirmed by Sachs, Tornell and Velasco (1996) who identify real exchange rates, bank loan growth (as an indicator of bank fragility) and the ratio of country M2 to reserves (indicating reserve adequacy) as significant crisis predictors. Banking crises, in turn, have been identified as being preceded by low growth, high real interest rates, high inflation, deteriorating terms of trade, explicit deposit insurance and by lax law enforcement (Demirgüç-Kunt and Detragiache, 1998).

It seems that the crisis prediction literature can partially, but not fully, account for the Asian crisis. It rightly points to the strong nexus between banking and currency crises, but low growth, high real interest rates and high inflation can definitely not be blamed. Table 11.3, by contrast, shows clearly that currencies become vulnerable to speculative attacks because of rising imbalances between real cash balances, short-term debt and official reserves. The importance of stock imbalances for vulnerability to speculative attacks had been driven home clearly already by the Mexican crisis (Calvo and Mendoza, 1996a). In Asia's crisis economies, in particular during 1995 and mid-1997, lending to the private sector had clearly paced

ahead of (fast) GDP growth. The two countries which experienced the highest net capital inflows – Malaysia and Thailand – also experienced the most rapid expansion in the commercial bank sectors.

Abundant foreign supply of capital (offered at rapidly falling sovereign yield spreads) and the greater ability of Asian non-bank and bank borrowers to tap the international financial markets interacted to fuel a rise in non-bank and bank foreign liabilities (toward BIS reporting banks). In terms of foreign assets, non-bank foreign liabilities exploded in Indonesia, Korea and Thailand, while bank foreign liabilities grew quickly in the Philippines and again Thailand during 1995 and mid-1997.

Table 11.3 Indicators of financial vulnerability

	Indonesia	Korea	Malaysia	Philippines	Thailand
Lending to private sector, % of GDP					
– end 1993	49	54	74	26	84
– end 1996	55	62	90	48	
Foreign liabilities/foreign assets (towards BIS reporting banks) a) non-banks					
– end 1994	9.9	5.9	1.9	0.9	5.3
– mid-1997	14.0	8.5	2.4	1.5	6.7
b) banks					
– end 1994	2.2	2.6	1.3	1.0	8.6
– mid-1997	2.8	2.7	1.8	2.6	12.4
Short-term foreign debt/reserves					
– mid-1994	1.7	1.6	0.3	0.4	1.0
– mid-1997	1.7	2.1	0.6	0.8	1.5
M2/reserves					
– end 1993	6.1	6.9	2.1	4.9	4.1
– end 1996	6.5	6.5	3.3	4.5	3.9

Sources: Corsetti *et al.* (1998), Radelet and Sachs (1998).

Rapid bank and non-bank foreign borrowing finally made Asian currencies vulnerable to attack. When short-term foreign debt starts to exceed official reserves (indicated by a ratio higher than one), each creditor knows that there are not enough liquid foreign exchange reserves, so there is a race to the exit. Table 11.3 indicates that such a situation clearly held for Indonesia and Korea already by mid-1994, and for Thailand thereafter. While Malaysia and the Philippines displayed a short-term debt/reserves ratio lower than one, they are financially open. Openness implies that M2/reserves becomes the relevant indicator for financial vulnerability, as

residents may try to obtain foreign currency for their domestic currency holdings. The M2/reserves ratio exceeded one by far in all five crisis countries, even though it had stopped growing over 1995–96 except in Indonesia and Malaysia.

FROM BOOM TO FINANCIAL VULNERABILITY

In the new global-markets era with intense capital mobility, yesterday's financial-market darlings, including new OECD entrants, have repeatedly become financial-crisis victims. The 'root' cause for emerging-market currency crises is the interaction of

- boom 'distortions' with excessively optimistic expectations by market participants, reinforced by exchange rate pegs in the presence of sustained interest differentials,

- with the loosening of portfolio discipline in weak domestic banking systems as a result of heavy capital inflows and disorderly financial liberalization.

This explanation seems to fit the crises in Chile 1982, Mexico 1994–95 and the ongoing Asian crisis well. In all three cases, market-friendly economic reform together with fiscal and monetary discipline went along with effective dollar pegs and financial liberalization.

Chile, Mexico and the South-East Asian countries were all widely celebrated as models of economic reform and high-growth performance before they crashed. Asia was the centre of admiration and rosy scenarios in the Asian Miracle Study by the World Bank (1993) and in the New Global Age Study by the OECD (1997). Governments in Europe incited their firms and banks to take a larger claim in the promising Asian economies. In fact, South-East Asia had not only been leading the world GDP growth league, but such growth had also been more stable than elsewhere in the developing world (Hausmann and Gavin, 1996). Asia's profound ignorance of Latin America's experience with currency crashes seemed no cause for concern. Chile's and Mexico's experience with twin payment and banking crises had originated in the explosive mix of domestic financial deregulation, implicit deposit insurance and super returns for foreign investors as a result of dollar pegs in the presence of sustained interest differentials (Reisen, 1997).

In South-East Asia, as in Chile and Mexico earlier, domestic financial reform, low levels of international interest rates (in particular in Japan) and excellent growth prospects contributed to a large increase in the supply of

loanable funds throughout the 1990s. Due to the existence of market and policy failures, that mix can easily explode into (1) overborrowing, (2) a banking crisis, and then (3) a full-blown currency crisis:

a) Private borrowers do not internalize the rising marginal social cost of their private borrowing that arises from the rising vulnerability to speculative attacks and the cost of fending these off (e.g. by increasing foreign reserves accordingly). This is the *Harberger externality*, a lesson already learned from Chile's 1982 crisis (Harberger, 1985).

b) Excessively optimistic expectations about 'permanent' income levels (e.g. after major changes in the policy regime, or new membership in a First World club) lead to overborrowing, because financial market institutions fail as efficient information conduits between depositors and borrowers (McKinnon and Pill, 1996). Financial market bubbles add to such a boom mentality through the wealth effect on current income. Firms with a high risk–return profile have an incentive to borrow and invest heavily, as their exposure is limited by bankruptcy laws or implicit guarantees (this is the focus of Krugman, 1998, but the theory is not new). Likewise, when the government insures deposits against adverse outcomes, it reduces incentives to ration credit and reduce credit risk. This results in higher bank lending, which in turn can underpin excessively optimistic expectations about future growth prospects.

c) Exchange rate pegs, in combination with sustained interest rate differentials (on which more below), tend to reinforce bank lending and spending booms. They constitute an incentive for offshore borrowing by creditworthy banks and non-banks as well as for foreign lenders. Central bank intervention on the foreign exchange market to peg the currency in view of net inflows, unless sterilized fully, is intermediated into the banking system. The exchange rate peg provides the incentive to allocate those funds disregarding currency and maturity risks, as these are being implicitly transferred to the central bank (Calvo and Mendoza, 1996b). Such incentives for currency and maturity mismatches may have been reinforced in Asia by its experience of sustained and stable growth. Catch-up growth should result in real exchange-rate appreciation (through the Balassa–Samuelson effect), explaining why short-term liabilities were foreign-currency denominated, unhedged. As growth went along with a high degree of stability, maturity mismatches (short-term debt for long-term investment) were ignored as well.

d) The persistence of high interest rate differentials after and despite financial opening can in theory be explained by sovereign risk premia, currency devaluation risk, inflation inertia or by structural determinants. However, bond yield spreads and syndicated loan rate spreads fell for South-East Asia well into mid-1997 (Cline and Barnes, 1997). Sovereign ratings by the leading rating agencies did not signal increased sovereign risk until after the crisis erupted (Reisen, 1998). With regard to exchange rates, the market failed to anticipate the extent to which currencies would depreciate, even once the crisis began (Radelet and Sachs, 1998). And high real interest rates could hardly reflect inflation inertia (as it often had done in Latin America), because inflation had been fairly low for years, except perhaps in the Philippines. This leaves us with microeconomic explanations of deviation from interest parity and persistently high domestic lending rates, just like those experienced by the Southern Cone countries in Latin America fifteen years earlier (Fischer and Reisen, 1993). The major structural determinants there were:

– the persistence of *segmented credit markets*, where creditworthy borrowers could tap global financial markets at low borrowing cost, while smaller and service-sector firms stayed confined to expensive domestic credit, with a corresponding concentration of bank loan portfolios;

– the existence of economic *conglomerates* (Chile's grupos, for example), with a group of firms organized around one or more domestic banks, resulting in weak portfolio discipline and overexposure by the conglomerate banks;

– *non-performing loans* and *distress borrowing*, as banks capitalize debt service on bad loans and increase interest charges on healthy borrowers, in order to avoid explicit bankruptcies of important borrowers that could result in a major bank run by depositors;

– *restricted entry* into the banking sector, in particular for foreign banks, resulting in oligopolistic structures and correspondingly large interest rate margins.

In the financially closed economy, the market and policy failures presented above are reflected in higher financial yields, but their effect on quantities – borrowing and spending – is ambiguous, depending on offsetting income and substitution effects (McKinnon and Pill, 1996). In the

open economy, by contrast, the boom distortion leads to excessive spending (consumption or investment), financed by excessive borrowing from the rest of the world. The McKinnon–Pill solution to the distortion is a reserve requirement on foreign deposits.

From a macroeconomic perspective alone, up to 1994 it was difficult to 'read' that Asia was heading for trouble. This is nicely shown by the IMF Occasional Paper No. 122 where the almost prophetic warnings by Folkerts-Landau and co-authors (1995) about the deteriorating credit quality and rising financial risks in the APEC countries were preceded (and to a certain extent discounted) by the macroeconomic analysis of Khan and Reinhart (1995), who concluded:

> The above discussion has highlighted that the risks associated with capital inflows create policy dilemmas. However, the overall picture is much more positive, as many Asian countries and a smaller number of Latin American countries have used these inflows to finance productive investment [sic!] and achieve higher growth ... to limit some of the risks associated with short-term flows, a reasonable sequencing of policies would consist in initially limiting the intermediation of those flows through sterilized intervention, greater exchange rate flexibility, and/or increased marginal reserve requirements, followed by a gradual monetization of these flows (that is, nonsterilized intervention), accompanied perhaps by an appreciation of the currency. (p. 29)

In fact, a purely macroeconomic analysis failed to identify Asia's vulnerabilities as there was fiscal restraint to constrain appreciation pressures, considerable sterilization of inflows and/or reserve requirements on foreign-currency deposits, no signs of CPI-adjusted real currency overvaluation, higher investment rates (rather than consumption) resulting from net inflows and a variety of capital inflow controls in the Asian crisis countries (Reisen, 1996). Only from 1995, real exchange rate misalignment developed as the dollar started to rise relative to the yen while the terms of trade (semiconductors, etc.) deteriorated. It was also only from 1995 that Asian domestic lending rates started to rise (after earlier converging towards international levels) and short-term borrowing become the dominant feature in Asian capital accounts. To be sure, most analysts had failed to perceive the extent to which portfolio discipline in the weak domestic financial systems had deteriorated as a result of heavy capital inflows and disorderly financial liberalization.

The failure of South-East Asia to adjust in a timely manner to changing external conditions and to domestic overheating was also rooted in the weak bank and non-bank balance sheets that had developed over the early 1990s. Currency devaluation would have drastically reduced the net worth of banks and non-banks as their foreign-currency liabilities were a multiple of foreign-currency assets already by the end of 1994, except in the Philippines

(Table 11.3). Increases in interest rates, and related declines in asset values that were heavily used as collateral for domestic lending, would have promoted a banking and financial crisis. As higher interest rates tend to intensify adverse selection problems in developing countries (Mishkin, 1996), they lead to a steep decline in domestic lending, investment and aggregate activity. Governments in Asia's crisis countries were not (yet) prepared to face these problems head on, and global financial markets were happy to provide enough money to delay the day of reckoning. A precise replay of Mexico (Calvo and Mendoza, 1996a).

Financial opening throughout Asia had encouraged short-term capital inflows, even if they were at times restricted:

–   In Thailand, the authorities approved the establishment of the Bangkok International Banking Facility (BIBF) 'which greatly eased access to foreign financing and expanded short-term inflows' (Johnston *et al.,* 1997). In 1995, the Provincial International Banking Facility was established which could extend credit in both local and foreign currencies with funding from overseas.

–   In Korea, the 1994–97 surge in short-term inflows can be attributed to acceleration in financial liberalization by allowing domestic financial institutions greater freedom in asset and liability management, in particular in borrowing from international financial markets (Park, 1998). Meanwhile, restrictions on long-term inflows were left in place, further inducing short-term inflows.

–   During the 1990s Indonesia relaxed foreign borrowing for trade finance by private entities, including sales of securities to non-residents and liberalization of FDI and portfolio investment through the stock markets (Johnston *et al.,* 1997). On the other hand, the authorities reimposed in 1991 quantitative controls on offshore borrowing by banks and state enterprises.

–   In mid-1994, Malaysia lifted reserve requirement on foreign financial institutions' accounts in Malaysian banks as well as a ban on issues of short-term securities to non residents (Folkerts-Landau *et al.,* 1995).

Concerns that financial opening in developing countries would run ahead of the financial infrastructure required to constrain financial risks have been voiced permanently since Chile's 1982 crisis (see e.g. Edwards, 1990; Fischer and Reisen, 1993). In the context of Asia's crisis countries, early warnings by IMF and World Bank staff were clear enough:

The APEC developing countries face the policy challenge of building a supervisory and regulatory infrastructure that (1) ensures the efficient allocation of bank credit, and (2) safeguards the integrity and stability of capital markets. Although many of these countries have made great strides in liberalizing and strengthening their financial systems in recent years, much remains to be done ... In many countries, banking problems have most often been the result of bad credit decisions and inept management of credit risk, including overexposure to certain types of risk, and have caused major losses. Large and relatively volatile capital flows can contribute to these problems, especially when bank balance sheets are badly structured, by causing large swings in bank liquidity that result in alternating periods of credit expansion and contraction. Two major areas of concern are the ability of the banking systems to assess, price and manage risk, and the adequacy of the supervisory frameworks to prevent and contain systemic risk, particularly in the presence of safety nets and the problem of moral hazard. (Folkerts-Landau *et al.*, 1995, p. 32)

Liberalization is inexpensive, fast and easy to implement; building institutional capacity is expensive, slow and complex. Thus many countries have done the quick and easy reforms first. However justified this sequence may be on political grounds, and even though it increases demand for a better infrastructure for finance, it undermines the stability of the financial system. (Claessens and Glaessner, 1997)

The only aspect which was underemphasized in these prophetic warnings, was the lack of corporate governance in the Asian crisis economies. More concerned with raising market share than with maximizing profits, and reluctant to issue equities as this would dilute their management control, non-bank firms greatly contributed to overborrowing by raising offshore short-term debt. As shown in Table 11.3, this problem was particularly visible in Indonesia and Korea. As in addition commercial banks imported substantial amounts of capital (rather than merely intermediating capital inflows), the heavy capital inflows contributed less to monetary–aggregate imbalances (M2/reserves) as emphasized by Calvo and Mendoza (1996a), than to increasing bank and non-bank debt imbalances.

Nevertheless, the domestic financial systems contributed heavily to weak balance sheets and financial vulnerability in Asia, not just through the excessive quantity, but also through the low quality of onlending foreign capital inflows. Table 11.4 represents the extent of risk exposure in the Asian bank systems at the outbreak of the crisis. Non-performing loans were the highest in 1997 in Korea (16 per cent of total assets), Thailand (15 per cent) and Indonesia (11 per cent); sharp increases could be expected during 1998. This compares with a non-performing loan ratio of 9.3 per cent in Mexico early 1995, where the cost of rescuing banks has been estimated at some 15 per cent of GDP on a net present value basis (Caprio and Klingebeil, 1996). As the banks, with the exception of the Philippines and possibly Malaysia, were severely under-capitalized in the Asian crisis

Table 11.4   Bank system risk exposure and financial infrastructure

	Indonesia	Korea	Malaysia	Philippines	Thailand
Bank system exposure to risk, % of assets end 1997					
– non-performing loans	11	16	8	6	15
– capital ratio	8–10	6–10	8–14	15–18	6–10
– real estate exposure	25–30	15–25	30–40	15–20	30–40
– collateral valuation	80–100	80–100	80–100	70–80	80–100
Regulatory features during the 1990s					
– bank lending to connected firms	high	high	yes	yes	yes
– government-directed bank lending	yes	yes		yes	
– bank deposit insurance	none	none	none	yes	none
– importance of state-owned banks	high			high	
– accounting standards	weak	weak	weak	weak	weak
– enforcement of existing regulations	weak	weak	weak	weak	weak
Incentives for capital flows					
– short-term inflows	limited	limited (promoted)	limited	free	promoted
– long-term inflows	limited	limited	promoted	promoted	promoted
– outflows	free	limited	limited	free	limited

Sources: Folkerts-Landau *et al.* (1995), Johnston *et al.* (1997), Corsetti *et al.* (1998).

countries (with capital to asset ratios estimated at 6–10 per cent), the non-performing loans had already wiped out the total capital of banks (on average) in Korea, Thailand and Indonesia at the end of 1997.

As previously in Latin America (see Ffrench-Davis and Reisen, 1998), excessive real estate exposure has been a prominent feature of the lending and spending boom in Asia as well. Real estate exposure is estimated at 30–40 per cent of bank assets in Indonesia, Malaysia and Thailand, while it is somewhat lower in the Philippines and in Korea (where the bad loans are concentrated with the *chaebols*). The high real estate exposure of Asian banks indicates the extent to which loans were not used to finance productive investment, but speculative demand for existing assets in fixed supply. Thus, part of the foreign inflows went into feeding speculative asset price bubbles. The excessive real estate exposure was clearly related to excessive collateral valuations; the Philippines which had the lowest real estate exposure also had the lowest collateral valuation (Table 11.4). As the asset bubble burst, the deflating values of real estate, equities and other assets, reducing the value of loan collateral, determined the extent of the non-performing loans.

In Indonesia and Korea, as in Chile in the early 1980s, balance sheet weakness in the banking system was also related to credit exposures to borrowers connected to the lending bank (Folkerts-Landau *et al.*, 1995). Although there were regulatory restrictions on bank ownership, they did not prevent banks from becoming controlled by non-bank firms. In Korea, where the use of dummy accounts was widespread, this prevented the enforcement of restrictions against concentrations of lending to the bank shareholders.

Loosening portfolio discipline and debt imbalances which were fuelled by heavy inflows can be partly traced to government intervention into bank lending and corporate finance. Folkerts-Landau *et al.* (1995) point to the fact that many APEC developing countries, in fact all five crisis victims, have regulatory requirements to allocate fixed proportions of bank loan portfolios to particular sectors (see Table 11.4). As mandated loans carry an implicit bail-out guarantee and as they are usually refinanced by the central bank at below-market interest rates, banks have little incentive to limit their credit risk. The pursuit of growing market share has led to a neglect of the cost of capital, in particular where government allocation of credit played an important role for industrial policy. 'Picking the winners' may be fairly easy during the very early stages of development, and even then it invites moral hazard and rent seeking behaviour (Vittas and Wang, 1991). Once countries have moved up the global product cycle, the chances that government-led credit allocation leads to capital waste, are increasing disproportionately. As problem loans develop as a result of mandated lending, the implicit

guarantees given by governments to the banks often obviate the need to identify such problem loans properly and to build reserves against them.

Even more endemic, it seems, are the poor accounting standards and limited disclosure requirements in the emerging markets (for Latin America, see Rojas-Suarez and Weisbrod, 1996). Inconsistent financial reporting, the limited power of auditors (or tax collectors) to examine company records, the lack of sanctions or incorrect reporting of information, the use of borrowed names and the maintenance of multiple accounts greatly diminish the reliability of reported information. Poor accounting standards imply that even detailed examination by supervisors and regulators may not reveal much information.

Another endemic shortcoming in most emerging markets is the lack of enforcement of existing regulations. In fact, the Asian crisis countries had tried to strengthen the supervisory and regulatory infrastructure during the 1980s and 1990s, partly in response to costly banking crises (such as in Indonesia and Malaysia) a decade ago (see Fischer and Reisen, 1993, for details). Bank regulators had imposed limits on bank lending, including liquidity requirements and exposure limits. Moreover, the countries now in crisis introduced risk-based capital requirements (note, however, that foreign exchange exposure was missing from the Basle accords on these requirements).

However, capital requirements are ineffective as long as accounting standards are ineffective. Inaccurate reporting on non-performing loans, with interest rate income recorded as accrued for bad loans rolled over, or unclear definitions of what can be included in capital, will show up in high capital–adequacy ratios but disguise the extent of non-performing loans. Fictitious names in bank accounts make it impossible to enforce restrictions on overexposure by banks to individual or corporate counterparts.

CONCLUSIONS FOR REDUCING THE FREQUENCY AND SEVERITY OF CURRENCY CRISES

Private spending booms, fuelled by overborrowing, have increasingly led to twin banking and currency crises in developing countries which were acclaimed as star performers until the crises erupted. Private capital inflows, attracted by financial opening and by exchange rate pegs, have repeatedly reinforced such pre-crisis booms. Domestic financial systems have tended to prove too weak as a conduit for heavy capital inflows, resulting in declining credit quality and financial fragility. As long as herding behaviour remains a prominent feature of global capital markets, developing countries with strong macroeconomic fundamentals are advised to pay close attention

to indicators of financial vulnerability, in particular to short-term debt/reserve levels as well as to currency and maturity mismatches. To avoid a rise of these indicators above critical threshold levels, several avenues can be pursued.

Some of these avenues are uncontroversial, but deceptively hard to implement, in particular in the context of developing countries' political, institutional and legal backgrounds.

–　Good accounting standards and complete, accurate and timely information disclosure are a necessary precondition for prudential regulation and supervision. Moreover, they can stabilize market expectations. This, however, requires two things, both pointed out by Alice Rivlin (1998): 'In actual fact a great deal of information usually turns out to have been available which no one ever looked at or effectively analysed. For transparency to be useful, people need to actually want to look – and too often those who are making high profits would rather not hear bad news'. And: 'A culture of transparency and timely, accurate information ... can restrain the boom by enabling investors to assess risk more accurately, and it can cushion overreaction once a downward slide begins. But such a culture cannot be built quickly, and even where it exists, has to be assiduously maintained'.

–　Only with reliable accounting systems and disclosure requirements to ensure transparency will it be possible to strengthen bank and non-bank balance-sheets and to enforce prudential regulation through serious, independent supervisory arrangements. It is safe to assume that basic ingredients for effective enforcement of prudential regulation will meet resistance from affected interest groups. Still, the basic requirements are: independent internal oversight of lending decisions by a credit review committee; vesting the supervisory agency with the authority to examine bank operations and balance sheets, close banks and establish entry criteria, define capital adequacy and exposure limits, enforce asset classification, provisioning rules and prudent collateral valuation that fully reflect the volatility of developing-country asset markets. To be sure, the 'wish list' is long, and has been lengthening (Goldstein and Turner, 1996).

These largely uncontroversial prescriptions, actively promoted since Mexico's crisis by the G10 Working Party on Financial Stability in Emerging Market Economies (with the participation of several Asian crisis countries), will take years or decades to implement and will be hard to maintain. Quick fixes will not do the job. Progress with respect to

information disclosure and strengthened public and private-sector balance sheets should determine to what extent countries can diversify the sources of capital inflows with added net benefit. First principles are the most reliable guide here, whatever the pressure from money managers.

According to the debt-cycle hypothesis, rarely validated empirically, external savings raise domestic investment and growth, which in turn stimulates savings that eventually contribute to the elimination of net foreign debt. Such a virtuous circle hides five requirements, again rarely complied with in practice (Devlin, Ffrench-Davis and Griffith-Jones, 1995):

- *First*, external capital flows should consistently augment investment, rather than be diverted to consumption;

- *Second*, the investment must be efficient;

- *Third*, the country must invest in tradables (or trade-related infrastructure) to create a trade surplus that will accommodate the subsequent switch in transfers required to service the debt;

- *Fourth*, an aggressive domestic savings effort is called for, with the marginal saving rate exceeding the average saving rate; and

- *Fifth*, the virtuous circle requires capital exporters willing to provide stable and predictable flows at terms in line with the recipient country's factor productivity.

These demanding requirements seem best fulfilled by foreign direct investment flows (Reisen, 1997). First, foreign direct investment is governed by long-term profitability expectations, it is less dependent on financial market sentiment than debt or portfolio equity flows. Second, in a largely undistorted real economy, foreign direct investment improves the host country's production function and produces positive external spillovers, comparable to agglomeration benefits. Thus, the Harberger externality does not apply to foreign direct investment.

At the other extreme, short-term debt-creating flows may have a positive role for consumption smoothing in theory (although they tend to be excessive in boom times and unavailable when a country is in a bust situation). Their contribution to growth, however, is dubious at best; that holds, in particular when short-term debt adds to high domestic savings so that marginal capital returns can be presumed to be declining fairly fast. On the other hand, short-term debt adds clearly to financial vulnerability. To avoid speculative attacks, and when the short-term debt/reserves ratio

dangerously approaches unity, this implies the need to put every dollar of increased foreign debt into official reserves to prevent the vulnerability ratio from growing. This implies borrowing at a higher rate of interest than the rate at which reinvesting it, say, into US treasury bills. The net benefit of such a swap would be clearly negative to the country.

How to influence the structure of capital inflows, then, towards long-term equity? The Latin American experience, in particular its recent experience, shows that two mutually reinforcing policies can do the trick (Ffrench-Davis and Reisen, 1998). First, keep nominal exchange rates flexible enough, and even introduce noise through central bank intervention if they are on a too-stable, appreciating trend. Managed flexibility raises the currency risk for short-term investors chasing high local returns. Second, discourage excessive inflows by an implicit tax that varies inversely with maturity. There is strong evidence that policy management can impact strongly on the composition and also overall size of flows. This is important because reducing the size of flows will contain real appreciation and the relative decline in the profitability of tradables. Biasing the composition of flows towards FDI will stimulate investment response and reduce volatility.

NOTES

1. History suggests (Kindleberger, 1978) that financial and currency crises will never be avoided altogether.

REFERENCES

Calvo, G. and E. Mendoza (1996a), 'Petty Crime and Cruel Punishment: Lessons from the Mexican Debacle', *The American Review*, Papers and Proceedings, May 1996, pp. 170–185.

Calvo, G. and E. Mendoza (1996b), 'Mexico's Balance of Payments Crisis: A Chronicle of Death Foretold', *Journal of International Economics*, Vol. 41, Nos. 3/4, pp. 235–264.

Caprio, G. and D. Klingebeil (1996), *Bank Insolvency: Bad Luck, Bad Policy, or Bad Banking?*, The World Bank, Washington, DC.

Claessens, S. and T. Glaessner (1997), *Are Financial Sector Weaknesses Undermining the East Asian Miracle?*, The World Bank, Washington, DC.

Cline, W. and K. Barnes (1997), 'Spreads and Risks in Emerging Markets Lending', *Institute for International Finance Research Paper*, No. 97-1.

Corsetti, G., P. Pesenti and N. Roubini (1998), 'What Caused the Asian Currency and Financial Crisis?', mimeo (http://www.stern.nyu.edu/~nroubini/asia/AsiaHomepage.html).

Davies, G. (1998), *Causes, Cures and Consequences of the Asian Economic Crisis*, Goldman Sachs, London.

Demirgüç-Kunt, A. and E. Detragiache (1998), 'The Determinants of Banking Crises: Evidence from Developing and Developed Countries', *IMF Staff Papers*, Vol. 45.1, pp. 81–109.

Devlin, R., R. Ffrench-Davis and S. Griffith-Jones (1995), 'Surges in Capital Flows and Development: An Overview of Policy Issues', in R. Ffrench-Davis and S. Griffith-Jones (eds), *Coping with Capital Surges: Latin American Macroeconomics and Investment*, Lynne Rienner, Boulder and London.

Edwards, S. (1990), 'The Sequencing of Economic Reform: Analytical Issues and Lessons from Latin American Experience', *The World Economy*, Vol. 13 (1), pp. 1–14.

Ffrench-Davis, R. and H. Reisen (1998), *Capital Flows and Investment Performance: Lessons from the Latin American Experience*, OECD Development Centre Studies, Paris.

Fischer, B. and H. Reisen (1993), *Liberalising Capital Flows in Developing Countries: Pitfalls, Prerequisites and Perspectives*, OECD Development Centre Studies, Paris.

Flood, R. and P. Garber (1984), 'Collapsing Exchange-Rate Regimes: Some Linear Examples', *Journal of International Economics*, Vol. 17, pp. 1–13.

Frankel, J. and A. Rose (1996), 'Currency Crashes in Emerging Markets: Empirical Indicators', *NBER Working Paper*, No. 5437.

Folkerts-Landau, D. *et al.* (1995), 'Effect of Capital Flows on the Domestic Financial Sectors in APEC Developing Countries', in M. Khan and C. Reinhart (eds), *Capital Flows in the APEC Region*, IMF Occasional Paper No. 122, pp. 31–57.

Goldstein, M. and P. Turner (1996), 'Banking Crises in Emerging Economies: Origins and Policy Options', BIS Economic Papers, No. 46.

Harberger, A. (1985), 'Lessons for Debtor-Country Managers and Policymakers', in G. Smith and J. Cuddington (eds), *International Debt and the Developing Countries*, The World Bank, Washington, DC.

Hausmann, R. and M. Gavin (1996), "Securing Stability and Growth in a Shock-Prone Region: The Policy Challenges for Latin America" in R. Hausmann and H. Reisen (eds*), Securing Stability and Growth in Latin America*, OECD, Paris.

Johnston, R., S. Darber and L. Echeverria (1997), 'Sequential Capital Account Liberalization: Lessons from the Experiences in Chile, Indonesia, Korea and Thailand', IMF Working Paper, WP/97/157.

Kaminsky, G. and C. Reinhart (1996), 'The Twin Crises: The Causes of Banking and Balance-of-Payments Problems', International Finance Discussion Paper, No. 544, Board of Governors of the Federal Reserve System, Washington, DC.

Khan, M. and C. Reinhart (1995), 'Macroeconomic Management in APEC Economies: The Response to Capital Flows', in IMF Occasional Paper No. 122, op. cit., pp. 15–30.

Kindleberger. C. (1978), *Manias, Panics and Crashes*, Basic Books, New York.

Krugman, P. (1979), 'A Model of Balance-of-Payments Crises', *Journal of Money, Credit and Banking*, Vol. 11, pp. 311–325.

Krugman, P. (1998), 'What Happened to Asia?', mimeo (http://web.mit.edu/krugman/WWW/).

McKinnon, R. and H. Pill (1996), 'Credible Liberalizations and International Capital Flows: The Overborrowing Syndrome', in T. Ito and A. Krueger (eds), *Financial Regulation and Integration in East Asia*, University of Chicago Press, Chicago.

Mishkin, F. (1996), 'Understanding Financial Crises: A Developing Country Perspective', *NBER Working Paper*, No. 5600.

Obstfeld, M. (1994), 'The Logic of Currency Crises', *Cahiers Economiques et Monetaires*, Banque de France, Vol. 43, pp. 189–213.

OECD (1997*), The World in 2020: Towards a New Global Age*, OECD, Paris.

Park, Y. (1998), 'The Financial Crisis in Korea: From Miracle to Meltdown?', mimeo.

Polak, J. (1957), 'Monetary Analysis of Income Formation and Payments Problems', *IMF Staff Papers*, Vol. 6.4, pp. 1–50.

Radelet, S. and J. Sachs (1998), 'The Onset of the East Asian Financial Crisis', mimeo (http://www.hiid.harvard.edu/).

Reisen, H. (1996), 'Managing Volatile Capital Flows: The Experience of the 1990s', *Asian Development Review*, Vol. 14.1, pp. 72–96.

Reisen, H. (1997), 'The Limits of Foreign Savings', in R. Hausmann and H. Reisen (eds*), Promoting Savings in Latin America*, IDB/OECD, Washington/Paris, pp. 233–264.

Reisen, H. (1998), 'Sustainable and Excessive Current Account Deficits', *Empirica*.

Reisen, H. and A. van Trotsenburg (1988), 'Should the Asian NICs Peg to the Yen?', *Intereconomics* (July/August), pp. 172–177.

Rivlin, A. (1998), 'Lessons Drawn from the Asian Financial Crisis', reprinted in BIS Review No. 41, 13 May.

Rodrik, D. (1998), 'Who Needs Capital Account Convertibility?', in P. Kenen (ed.), *Should the IMF Pursue Capital Account Convertibility?*, in Princeton Essays in International Finance, No. 207, Princeton, NJ.

Rojas-Suarez, L. and S. Weisbrod (1996), 'Building Stability in Latin American Financial Markets', in R. Hausmann and H. Reisen (eds), *Securing Stability and Growth in Latin America*, OECD, Paris.

Sachs, J., A. Tornell and A. Velasco (1996), 'Financial Crises in Emerging Markets: The Lessons from 1995', *NBER Working Paper*, No. 5576.

Vittas, D. and B. Wang (1991), 'Credit Policy in Japan and Korea: a Review of the Literature', World Bank Working Paper Series, No. 747.

Wolf, M. (1998), 'Flows and Blows', *Financial Times*, 3 February.

World Bank (1993), *The East Asian Miracle*, Oxford University Press, Oxford.

Wyplosz, C. (1998), 'Globalized Financial Markets and Financial Crises', mimeo (http://heiwww.unige.ch/~wyplosz/).

12. After the Great Asian Slump: Towards a Coherent Approach to Global Capital Flows[*]

The 21st century is expected to see a growing share of global output move from the rapidly ageing OECD economies to the younger developing world (OECD, 1997). This will benefit both regions. With labour forces stagnating or shrinking in the OECD area and with pension assets increasingly decumulated, returns on capital will be depressed. All the world's labour force growth will take place in the developing countries, promising higher returns on capital there (MacKellar and Reisen, 1998). This promise is reinforced by the observation that poor countries have a higher potential to grow than rich countries. These expectations, though, would not materialize without substantial global capital flows, efficiently allocated to their highest *sustainable* social rate of return. This proviso brings us back to the very end of the 20th century.

In 1998, the world witnessed the strongest financial panic since the Great Depression. Private capital flows, surging into the developing countries with unprecedented size in the years before, came to a sudden stop. What started as the Thai baht crisis in July 1997, quickly spread to other East Asian countries – Indonesia, Korea, Malaysia and to some extent the Philippines. In these worst-hit economies, income and more so consumption levels have since fallen at an alarming rate; the social costs (and political repercussions) are beginning to make themselves felt. By autumn 1998, crisis contagion had assumed global proportions, spreading to virtually all emerging markets, as investors returned to core OECD safe-haven paper. Before the 'New Global Age' can materialize, therefore, this period of historic policy challenges has given urgency to the debate on and the design of a coherent approach to financial globalization.

This Policy Brief aims at informing that debate. *First,* it sets out the importance of a coherent approach to globalizing capital flows, and the potential benefits. While these benefits have been at times oversold and certainly under-documented, a reversal from financial globalization would harm the industrial and developing countries alike. *Second,* the Policy Brief

[*] Originally published as OECD Development Centre Policy Brief No. 16, Paris, 1999.

documents the extreme economic cost of the ongoing financial crisis, and hence underlines the need for improved crisis management and crisis prevention. The following sections evaluate several suggestions to improve the management of a crisis, once it has erupted, both by global regulation and by the countries affected. The final sections are devoted to crisis prevention, evaluating what can be done, both by global and by recipient-country regulation, to reduce the frequency and severity of financial and currency crises.

THE GAINS FROM GLOBAL CAPITAL MOBILITY: MYTH OR REALITY?

With virtually all emerging-market assets on fire sale, these are very hard times to 'sell' the gains from global capital mobility. While these gains do certainly exist, the quantitative evidence is surprisingly sketchy. In principle, the benefits of global capital mobility should apply particularly in the interaction between the capital-rich, moderately-growing and fast-ageing OECD economies and the capital-poor, fast-growing and slowly-ageing emerging economies. The gains would result from a better allocation of world savings to the most productive investment opportunities, and the possibility of maintaining consumption levels in the event of adverse shocks and of demographic trends. Moreover, it is often held that open capital markets impose higher standards of economic policy on capital-recipient countries. Even with net capital flows between the OECD and non-OECD economies balanced, open capital markets can be presumed to offer sizeable diversification benefits and spillovers in the form of technology, managerial know-how, market access and competition dynamics. Differences between the two areas with respect to the exposure to country-specific shocks as well as the stage of economic and demographic maturity suggest that the diversification benefits of financial globalization will not disappear quickly.

Three major currency and financial crises in the 1990s, however, in countries with broadly sound macroeconomic fundamentals (Scandinavia 1991–93, Mexico 1994–95, now Asia), have alerted economists to the magnitude of the potential costs of open capital markets. In view of the deep economic, social and political disruptions of these crises, some countries have started to retreat towards financial autarky by imposing capital outflow controls or by unilaterally defaulting on their foreign liabilities. The events fully confirmed earlier warnings that the macroeconomic adjustment to a sudden reversal of foreign capital flows can be extremely painful. Governments and central banks had been advised (e.g. in a series of OECD Development Centre studies, originating with Fischer and Reisen, 1992) to

beware of the sustainability of capital inflows. In an address to Asian monetary authorities in the autumn of 1995, the following reasons for caution about capital flow reversals were spelled out (Reisen, 1996, p. 73):

First, it is increasingly acknowledged that global capital markets suffer from three major distortions: the problem of asymmetric information causes herd behaviour among investors and, in good times, congestion problems; the fact that some market participants are too big to fail causes excessive risk taking. It is questionable, therefore, whether the financial markets will discipline governments into better policies; even if they were to do so, the social and economic costs may be excessive.

Second, any shortfall in capital inflows will require immediate cutbacks in domestic absorption to restore external balance. The savings-investment balance is more likely to be achieved through cuts in investment than through higher savings in the short term, compromising future output levels. Current output levels fall to the extent that rigidities prevent resource reallocation, so that contractionary disabsorption effects outweigh expansionary substitution effects.

Third, the expansion of domestic credit connected with unsterilized capital inflows may not be sound enough to stand the rise in domestic interest rates and the fall in domestic asset prices that go with a reversal of these inflows. The resulting breakdown of domestic financial institutions provides incentives for monetary expansion and fiscal deficits incurred by the public bail-out of ailing banks.

The burden of proof of the gains from free capital flows has shifted to the proponents of open capital markets who are being criticized for having offered more 'banner-waving' than hard quantitative evidence on the benefits of financial globalization (Bhagwati, 1998). A look at the numbers seems to suggest that most of the gains that developing countries could reap from financial openness were obtained by *foreign direct investment* inflows:

– *First,* if foreign savings permit an acceleration of investment by augmenting (rather than crowding out) domestic savings, they typically have a positive temporary GDP growth effect of half a percentage point (Reisen, 1996). This assumes typical capital shares and capital output ratios as well as a net inflow of 3 to 4 per cent of GDP; furthermore, any externalities arising from openness are ignored.

– *Second,* foreign direct investment adds both to domestic investment and to long-term growth if the host-county is largely undistorted.[1] Borensztein, De Gregorio and Lee (1995) find that for each percentage point increase in the FDI–GDP ratio, the rate of growth in the host economy increases by 0.8 percentage points. The contribution to long-term growth results from two effects. First, foreign direct investment adds to domestic investment, as both are complementary in production

and through positive spillover effects. Second, foreign direct investment stimulates growth through the embodied transfer of technology and efficiency, provided the host country has a minimum threshold stock of human capital.

– *Third,* there is little evidence in the data that countries without capital controls have grown faster than countries with capital controls, after controlling for growth determinants such as income and education levels (Grilli and Milesi-Ferretti, 1995; Rodrik, 1998). These studies, however, do not allow for varying degrees of intensity of capital account restrictions, nor for the different growth impact of various capital-account items (Eichengreen, Mussa *et al.*, 1998). Except for foreign direct investment, the time series for private capital flows are not yet long enough to draw strong policy conclusions. In particular, there is no cross-country study that would investigate the impact of capital account liberalization, while controlling for the strength of the domestic financial system. It has been noted that none of the *developed* OECD countries maintain general capital controls, even on short-term capital (Poret, 1998). This may indicate that with mature financial systems, the benefits of free capital mobility largely outweigh any costs. It may also indicate that mature OECD economies are subject to less violent shocks in investor sentiment, and hence less disruption, than are developing countries.

The virulence of the 1997–98 contagion also reflected new financial technologies and highly leveraged assets, giving speculative currency attacks unprecedented speed and force (Summers, 1998; IMF, 1998a). Private cross-border flows have become volatile for several reasons on the supply side, notably:

– A growing proportion of long asset positions have become leveraged, most notably in the case of hedge funds; leverage (investing with borrowed funds worth a multiple of own funds) implies abrupt portfolio changes when the banks (who lend money to the hedge funds) make 'margin calls' (call in the credits as the price of the collateral drops below a specified level). OECD-based banks not only lent to hedge funds, but engaged increasingly in proprietary trading activities directed at exploiting short-term trading opportunities in the emerging markets, shorting low-coupon currencies such as the yen and taking long positions in high-coupon emerging-market paper. The technique, dubbed yen or dollar 'carry trade', relies on low interest rates in OECD

markets and stable emerging-market currencies (for detailed description, see IMF, 1998a).

– The increased availability and variety of financial derivatives in the world financial centres facilitate the evasion of emerging-market prudential regulation and supervision as well as of taxes and capital controls; and they obscure the meaning of capital account data from standard balance of payments accounts (Garber, 1998). The unwinding of the underlying positions hastens and intensifies speculative attacks on pegged currencies and exacerbates weaknesses in emerging-market systems.

– Modern risk management systems – endorsed by and imposed by industrial country regulators – have become a prime source for the contagion effects of a crisis (Folkerts-Landau and Garber, 1998; Reisen and von Maltzan, 1999). Risk control systems operating on the basis of international variance–covariance matrices of securities returns, imply that market volatility in one country will automatically generate an upward re-estimate of credit and market risk in a correlated country, triggering automatic margin calls and tightening of credit lines. Risk control systems, and in some industrial countries prudential regulations, also require that institutional and other investors hold only investment grade securities so that a downgrading of a country's credit rating leads to an immediate sell-off of the affected assets and to the closing of new funding.

THE DAMAGE DONE BY THE SUDDEN STOP: THE ASIAN SLUMP

The five countries most damaged by the Asian crisis – Indonesia, Korea, Malaysia, the Philippines and Thailand – received net private capital inflows worth 6.6 per cent of their combined GDP over the period 1995–96. The excessive optimism among international investors at that time was reflected in very low yield spreads on their debt instruments (less than 100 basis points over Eurobond yields). In the second half of 1997, there was a sudden stop. The reversal of net flows from 1996 to 1997 constituted a swing of 11 per cent of their combined GDP. The biggest swing came from commercial banks who had extended loans well into 1997, despite earlier warnings on overexposure from the Bank for International Settlements (BIS) and the Institute of International Finance (IIF). There was also an

important reversal of net portfolio investment. The only capital-account component proving its staying power – just as during Mexico's 1994–95 crisis – was foreign direct investment (Table 12.1).

Table 12.1 Net private flows to Asian countries in crisis[a] ($ billion)

	1995	1996	1997[e]	1998[f]	1999[f]
Private net flows	83.8	93.8	−6.0	−24.6	−15.1
Commercial banks	58.0	58.3	−29.0	−30.5	−17.8
Other debt (bonds)	9.9	18.1	23.3	−2.1	−3.8
Portfolio equity	11.0	11.6	−6.8	1.1	−0.9
Direct foreign investment	4.9	5.8	6.5	6.9	7.4

Notes:
a. Indonesia, Korea, Malaysia, Thailand, and the Philippines.
e = estimate, f = forecast

Source: Institute of International Finance, *Capital Flows to Emerging Market Economies*, Washington, DC, 29 September 1998.

A sudden stop in capital inflows must be met by a reduction in aggregate demand. Indeed, if depleted foreign exchange reserves have to be rebuilt, disabsorption (the cut in consumption and investment) must even exceed the reversal in flows. Between 1996 and 1998, the required switch on the current account of the five Asian countries in crisis, i.e. the difference between aggregate demand and output, was nothing less than 14.5 per cent of their GDP. The size and rapidity of the required adjustment has triggered a major economic growth crisis in the affected countries, exacerbated by weak banking systems. Used to growth rates in the 6–10 per cent range, the five Asian countries in crisis are forecast on average to shrink by 9 per cent in 1998 and a further 4 per cent in 1999 (Table 12.2). Official unemployment, traditionally lower than in OECD countries as safety nets (and claims) are absent, is expected to jump from low single-digit levels to 15 per cent in Indonesia, 13 per cent in the Philippines and 9 per cent in Thailand, according to ILO estimates (ILO, 1998).

The sharp withdrawal of private flows was reflected in tumbling exchange rates and falling local stock market prices as well as in the sovereign risk yield spreads rising to nearly prohibitive levels. The Thai baht and the Korean won lost half of their value against the dollar, and the Indonesian rupiah 80 per cent in the first months of the crisis, fanning a strong rise in non-performing loans in the local banking system and wiping out net capital for unhedged corporate borrowers. The reactive approach of the sovereign rating industry (Reisen and von Maltzan, 1999) intensified

panic by downgrading Asian borrowers from 'investment grade' to 'junk' status. The lower country ratings forced institutional investors to offload Asian assets and allowed banks to call in loans (Table 12.3).

Table 12.2 Current account balance and real GDP

	1995	1996	1997[e]	1998[f]	1999[f]
Current account (per cent of GDP)					
Asian countries in crisis[a]	−4.1	−5.1	−2.6	9.4	8.5
Emerging market economies[b]	−2.0	−1.8	−1.4	−0.9	−0.5
Real GDP (per cent change)					
Asian countries in crisis[a]	8.4	7.0	4.5	−9.1	−3.8
Emerging market economies[b]	4.4	5.0	5.0	1.2	1.4

Notes:
a. Indonesia, Korea, Malaysia, Thailand, and the Philippines.
b. 29 Major Emerging Market Economies.
e = estimate, f = forecast

Source: Institute of International Finance, *Capital Flows to Emerging Market Economies*, Washington, DC, 29 September 1998.

While there was initially a tendency to blame policy and institutional shortcomings in the Asian crisis countries for the reversal in capital flows, the widespread contagion of the crisis to other emerging markets judged fundamentally sound has strengthened the analysis of those economists who had argued that the reversal in flows, exchange rates and sovereign ratings in such a short period cannot be attributed to changes in the affected countries' fundamentals. Regardless of the ultimate causes for the Asian slump, it has worsened the economic outlook of the countries in crisis for years to come. Not least as a result of tumbling exchange rates and strong GDP contraction, the crisis countries now face a private-sector debt overhang that is estimated to exceed the 1980s Latin American proportions by far (Armstrong and Spencer, 1998). (Tables 12.4 and 12.5.) The resolution of this private debt overhang will inevitably burden government budgets, because it necessitates a large build-up in public sector debt, and it will require foreign investors to write down some of their claims. Non-performing loans, except in the Philippines, exceed bank capital by far, and discounts on external debt signal that at least some of the net present value of the debt is not expected to be repaid. Any delays in bank restructuring will raise the share of non-performing loans; any delays in foreign debt relief will lead to higher secondary market discounts; such delays can only credit-starve profitable activities and postpone the return of investor

confidence longer than necessary. For the time being, the unprecedented withdrawal of foreign capital from Asia confronts the Asian countries with a transfer problem, just as it did over the 1980s in Latin America. The lesson was then (Reisen and van Trotsenburg, 1988) that the budgetary problem was 'solved' by high inflation as regular tax receipts were insufficient to pay for the transfer and that declining export prices constituted a secondary burden as a result of many countries simultaneously trying to produce trade surpluses.

CRISIS MANAGEMENT: GLOBAL APPROACHES

Thorny policy issues arise for global crisis resolution that are difficult to balance. On the one hand, a generalized lack of confidence can only be reversed through an effective lender of last resort who could credibly commit sufficient liquidity in support of any country deemed fundamentally sound but illiquid. On the other hand, a successful rescue operation bails out (at least partly) investors who should have taken losses on their excessive risk exposure and thus is apt to encourage future excessive risk taking, in other words: moral hazard. The moral hazard argument, though, is easily exaggerated. The evidence from the Asian crisis indicates, as indeed does the evidence from Mexico's 1994–95 crisis, that equity and bond holders have experienced heavy losses. Commercial and investment banks, by contrast, can be perceived as having been bailed out during previous crises and having suffered only limited losses in the Asian crisis so far. While such perception holds for the banks' balance sheet exposure, the level of losses taken from off-balance-sheet exposures and activities (such as securities underwriting) remains to be seen.

It is now understood that the international financial institutions cannot be lenders of last resort in a world of intense capital mobility. In earlier quiet decades when capital mobility was limited, balance-of-payments crises meant imbalance on current account. Then, the phased conditional support from these institutions' resources was effective in helping countries towards payments balance. Today, with balance of payments, exchange rates and interest rates governed by the capital account, the international financial institutions need to frontload their assistance massively to have a market impact, while their involvement may feed further doubts among private investors. Official resources are, and will remain, insufficient in a world where private liquid assets are worth trillions of dollars and are virtually free to move across borders. Moreover, derivatives and leveraged positions have multiplied the market impact that the moving of these assets can exert. To the extent, therefore, that the world's leading central banks are not

prepared to assume the task of a lender of last resort, any emerging-market investment will have to reckon more downside risk than they would have had to just a few years ago. This may partly reverse financial globalization and reduce private flows to developing countries. It may, however, raise the quality of these flows as bail-out induced moral hazard is reduced.

Table 12.3 *Exchange rates, stock markets and yield spreads in Asian countries in crisis (30 September 1998)*

| | Change since July 1997, percentage | | Spreads on benchmark Eurobonds |
	Dollar exchange rate	Stock market index	(basis points)
Indonesia	−77.4	−62.1	1 397
Korea	−39.3	−59.8	810
Malaysia	−33.7	−69.5	n.a.
Thailand	−34.0	−55.0	679
The Philippines	−39.7	−55.3	821

Sources: Reuters Online; Deutsche Bank Research, *Global Emerging Markets*, Vol. 1.3, October 1998.

Table 12.4 *The foreign private debt overhang^a in Asian countries in crisis, 1998 (30 September 1998)*

	Foreign debt, $bn	Discount, %	Debt overhang, $bn	% GDP
Indonesia	79	55	44	40.0
Korea	83	36	30	9.6
Malaysia	39	36	14	18.7
Thailand	79	35	28	17.5
The Philippines	24	41	10	15.4

Notes:
a. The discount is calculated as the change in the market price of the debt since 30 June 1997. The debt refers to estimated market-based debt (total minus estimated official). The debt overhang is estimated by applying the discount to all commercial external debt.

Source: Deutsche Bank Research, *Global Emerging Markets*, Vol. 1.3, October 1998.

Table 12.5 *The domestic private debt overhang in Asian countries in crisis, 1998*

| | Non-performing loans | | Loan losses | |
	% of loans	% of GDP	$bn	% of bank capital
Indonesia	70	19.0	20.8	1 088
Korea	35	17.2	53.0	196
Malaysia	35	20.3	15.1	145
Thailand	45	26.5	41.6	347
The Philippines	20	6.5	4.1	86

Source: Deutsche Bank Research, *Global Emerging Markets*, Vol. 1.3, October 1998.

The limited resources of the international financial institutions can be given some leverage, however. In October 1998, the first successful issue of a Thai bond since the crisis erupted was made possible, despite the country's junk credit-rating status, because of a World Bank guarantee that lifted the bond to investment grade. By providing guarantees instead of money, the international financial institutions can use their funds more productively and help selected countries to re-enter capital markets. In order to reduce the risk of default on these bonds, only countries with considerable reform progress should be considered; the guarantee should also be tied to specific projects rather than balance-of-payments finance. This latter proviso clearly, however, limits their scope in the resolution of the current crisis.

The G22 Working Group on International Financial Crises, which published its recommendations for managing future crises in October 1998 (stating explicitly that the recommendations should not be considered as an agenda for the resolution of the 1998 crisis), acknowledges that 'the scale of private capital flows significantly exceeds the resources that can reasonably be provided by the official community.' (Summary of Reports, p. 21). With official resources insufficient, this implies that the Asian foreign debt overhang documented in Table 12.4 will not be resolved without some debt relief. While the G22 report favours voluntary debt reduction, it concedes that 'a purely voluntary approach may be impractical. In particular, it might consume so much time that it would lead to an erosion of confidence that would be contrary to the collective interest of creditors and debtors in a co-operative and equitable workout' (Summary of Reports, p. 22). Indeed, this is precisely what the 1980s debt crisis has taught us and what the rising yield spreads on Asian sovereign bonds are telling us now.

The 1980s Latin American debt crisis showed that debt rescheduling alone provides little relief in the presence of insolvency or severe illiquidity problems. This was finally recognized by the 1989 Brady debt reduction initiative after secondary market discounts on Latin American liabilities had continuously risen to an average of 70 per cent. Likewise, while during the early months of the current Asian crisis fairly stable yield spreads reflected the market perception that the crisis was a temporary liquidity problem, the growing awareness of insolvency and default risk fuelled a rise in secondary market discounts to 40 per cent, on average, for the five Asian countries in crisis (see Table 12.4). As emphasized by Armstrong and Spencer (1998) of Deutsche Bank Research, there has been very little external debt reduction in Asia so far, as interbank debt rescheduling arrangements resulted in no reduction of the debt stocks and as the Indonesia plan for corporate debt had no voluntary contributors.

Co-ordination failures essentially prevent voluntary debt reductions, as these fail to address the 'free-rider problem'. By voluntarily writing off a part of its claim, a creditor produces an externality to all other creditors because the price of the remaining outstanding debt will rise. Since the one making the voluntary write-off cannot 'internalize' the rise in securities prices, and thus it favours all other creditors (and investors), too little of the 'public good' of debt relief will occur on a voluntary basis. Debt reduction, in order to be effective in stimulating Asia's recovery, needs a centrally co-ordinated approach. So far, this is not even on the policy agenda. Leadership is required to avoid the protracted round of negotiations between debtors, creditors and their respective governments that proved so devastating in Latin America during the 1980s.

Table 12.6 Possible debtor–creditor relationships

Debtor	Creditor	
	Private banks	Private non-banks (Bond markets)
Public sector	*Case No. 1:* London Club	*Case No. 2:* Mexico 1995
Private banks	*Case No. 3:* Korea, Thailand	*Case No. 4:* –
Private non-banks	*Case No. 5:* Essentially Indonesia	*Case No. 6:* Partially Indonesia

Note: Creditor–debtor relationships shown for individual countries represent the situation at the start of the crisis.

Source: Regling (1999).

Table 12.6 explains why co-ordinated debt reduction will be very difficult to organize. The 1980s was characterized by one debtor – the public sector – and a fairly homogeneous group of syndicated bank creditors (Case No. 1). International banks used the London Club as a forum for rescheduling and reducing public sector debt. Case No. 2 largely reflects Mexico in 1995 where the public-sector debtor was confronted with a heterogeneous group of bondholders. The co-ordination problem was overcome by a then unprecedented IMF loan and by swift US support, leading to Mexico's quick recovery. Mexico's bail-out, however, has been held responsible by some for encouraging moral hazard by international investors in subsequent years and, ultimately, the current global financial crisis (e.g. Regling, 1999). Cases 3, 5 and 6 represent the current situation for the Asian countries in crisis, where essentially private-sector debtors and creditors are involved. With a large number of debtors and creditors on both

sides, it is hard to start negotiations and even harder to find agreement among the participants.

It is encouraging that Group of Ten (1996) recommendations for the resolution of sovereign liquidity crises, spelled out in the aftermath of Mexico's 1994–95 crisis, but not followed by co-ordinated policy actions since then, are now being actively pursued in order to bail foreign creditors in, rather than out (Group of Twenty Two, 1998):

–   Debt holders are to be induced to participate actively in the resolution of debt crises through debt contracts that would (1) provide for the collective representation of debt holders in the event of crises; (2) allow for qualified majority voting to alter the terms and conditions of debt contracts; and (3) require the sharing of assets received from the debtor.

–   The IMF Executive Board has agreed that the Fund should extend the 1989 decision on 'lending into arrears' in order to provide support for debtor countries with sovereign arrears to private creditors (including bond holders), and members with non-sovereign arrears to private creditors. The 'lending into arrears' could signal confidence in the debtor countries' policies and prospects as well as hasten creditors in concluding debt rescheduling or reduction deals.

These provisions, however, should be more effective in reducing the frequency and severity of future crises than in resolving the current emerging-market crisis.

If unilateral debt moratoria are to be avoided, a partial socialization of distressed foreign private sector debt by the Asian crisis countries in return for respective concessions by foreign creditors in terms of pricing, maturity and principal of their claims has to be envisaged. Debt socialization results from granting of government guarantees (as in Korea late 1997) on private sector debt, its legal assumption or its conversion into public debt. This moves the Asian borrowers back to Cases No. 1 and 2 in Regling's table.

The *quid pro quo* must come from foreign lenders. They, however, can afford to wait (with sizeable provisions already made in most cases), in the hope that foreign aid flows and funding from international financial institutions will raise the market value of their claims. Creditor country governments are therefore well advised to induce the private sector, and their home banks in particular, into financial rescue operations, not only to reduce moral hazard in *future* private sector lending but also to encourage Asia's recovery now. A model of how the complex underlying co-ordination and negotiation problems can be solved, was provided by the Brady plan (Reisen, 1994; Dooley, 1994; Cline, 1995). The Brady plan

became possible only after debtor and creditor governments forced creditor banks to participate in the deal; in turn, a broad menu of options to creditors, allowing the resulting deals to combine debt reduction, rescheduling and the provision of new money, raised the attractiveness of the plan to creditor participation. The Brady plan also showed that only a part of the debt overhang had to be written off to make the remaining debt sustainable, as the post-relief market price of debt rose.

HOW (NOT) TO RECOVER FROM THE DOMESTIC DEBT OVERHANG

The domestic debt overhang (see Table 12.5) – primarily bank obligations which can no longer be serviced – in the Asian countries in crisis is larger than both their external debt overhang (except in Indonesia and the Philippines) and than that witnessed in prior financial and currency crises in Latin America and Scandinavia. Whatever the external financial and trade conditions, the resolution of Asia's domestic debt problem must be the overriding policy concern for Asian governments. The write-down of claims on insolvent corporate borrowers crystallizes the losses on the banks' balance sheets. Without resolving the non-performing loan problem and recapitalizing the domestic financial systems, there will be no sustained recovery. But without economic recovery, Asia's financial systems and corporate sectors will be further impaired, as fiscal imbalances ultimately needed for bank crisis resolution would become unsustainable.

Banking and currency woes are costly. A recent study by the IMF (1998b), covering 50 crisis episodes over the 1975–97 period, indicates that the cumulative loss in output is severe – on average some 14–15 per cent of GDP. Average recovery came sooner in emerging market economies (2.8 years) than in industrial countries (4.1 years), though the cumulative output loss was larger, on average, for emerging market economies than for industrial countries. Such historical evidence, in view of the size of the domestic debt overhang in the Asian crisis economies, warns against being too relaxed about Asia's potential to grow out of its problems. Basing policy responses on overly optimistic scenarios makes it difficult to develop policies against worse outcomes, thus exacerbating the downturn.

A case in point is Japan's experience over the 1990s. It was hoped that banks would 'grow out of' their problems with a magic mix of wider intermediation spreads (imposing rescue costs on borrowers and depositors), relaxation of prudential regulations and lower funding rates. But with low levels of capitalization, Japanese banks proved unwilling to lend; with

Pensions, Savings and Capital Flows

declining collateral values, good credit risk evaporated. The failure to address the consolidation of the domestic financial system led to a decade of stagnation (Posen, 1998).

The recent stabilization of currencies and drop in money market rates, and the dramatic turnaround in trade balances in the Asian crisis countries can be, and indeed often has been, interpreted as a first solid sign of 'bottoming out'; they have also underpinned optimistic growth projections already for the closing months of 1998. However, the Asian currencies have been supported by official flows (with relatively little more to follow); moreover, having undershot equilibrium levels so drastically at the start of the crisis (Davies, 1998), a gradual real appreciation was widely expected to materialize. Relying on a gradual drop in money market rates to stimulate growth ignores the economics of banking crises. While the drop in money rates may just reflect rising demand for risk-less cash balances, the cost of capital is still higher than domestic private-sector credit growth (except for Indonesia), implying tight rather than easy credit conditions. Finally, the trade adjustment has been achieved through import compression, as export growth has been flat or falling. Unless trade is redirected away from intra-regional orientation (roughly 50 per cent now), unless exporters cease to be credit-starved and unless Asia recovers there will not be much export-led growth (Table 12.7).

Table 12.7 Cost of debt, credit growth and trade (annual percentage change)

	Cost of debt[a], %		Private dom. credit[b]		Exports, $		Imports, $	
	1997Q2	1998Q2	1997Q2	1998Q2	1997[e]	1998[f]	1997[e]	1998[f]
Indonesia	15.4	41.0	25.4	104.1	12.2	−1.3	4.5	−31.6
Korea	9.6	18.6	21.3	8.7	6.6	−7.1	−2.1	−36.2
Malaysia	7.8	12.3	n.a.	10.3	0.9	−9.3	1.5	−15.3
Thailand	20.4	23.1	16.2	15.2	4.2	−0.4	−13.8	−28.7
Philippines	12.6	22.6	33.1	12.6	22.9	15.9	14.1	−9.9

Notes:
a. Six months local interbank rates (Korea, six months implied offshore rates) and corporate spread over local interbank rates.
b. End of period.
e = estimate; f = forecast

Sources: Deutsche Bank Research, *Global Emerging Markets*, Vol. 1.3, October 1998; JP Morgan, *World Financial Markets*, Fourth Quarter 1998.

Tumbling exchange rates and high interest rates have driven corporate balance-sheet losses beyond equity values in a large number of firms in Indonesia, Korea and Thailand. According to this criterion, the World Bank (1998) assesses two out of three listed firms as bankrupt in Indonesia, two out of five in Korea, and one out of four in Thailand. Even very loose fiscal and monetary policies will fail to stimulate a recovery, unless restructuring and debt workouts are carried out upfront. The domestic debt overhang is mirrored in a systemic banking crisis as, with rising default, banks become unwilling to provide new loans and prefer to accumulate risk-less assets in order to regain capital adequacy standards.

As a large share of the financial and corporate sectors have been rendered technically insolvent by the new exchange rate/debt cost combination, governments have to assume a strong leadership role in revitalizing the private sector. The OECD (1998) and the World Bank (1998) draw the following core lessons from successful restructuring experiences:

– Early and comprehensive evaluation (distinguishing between viable and bankrupt banks);

– Transfer of non-performing loans from the banks' balance sheets to a separate loan recovery agency;

– Provision of capital only to viable banks during restructuring;

– Enforcement of exit policies for firms (bankruptcy codes, asset sales);

– Requirement for loan workouts to recover part of the fiscal cost of restructuring and to send signals to delinquent borrowers.

Beyond this list, the attraction of foreign banking capital is a further option to recapitalize banks (and improve banking standards). Before the crisis, foreign banks had relatively little penetration of Asia's domestic markets. The IMF (1998a) warns, however, that this may further weaken domestic banks (which stay with the 'lemons', i.e. bad credit risk). While the Asian crisis countries now have mostly lifted bank entry restrictions, only Thailand has so far attracted new capital (worth roughly 5 per cent of GDP) into the banking system.

Market observers agree that Korea and Thailand have progressed more on banking sector reform than Malaysia and Indonesia (the Philippines, as shown, does not have a banking crisis as the preceding credit boom started relatively late there). As shown in Table 12.8, the weakest banks have been closed down and been liquidated in auctions, some banks have been

nationalized with the intention of later privatization, and mergers have been forced. Moreover, restructuring agencies and bankruptcy laws have been established, and stricter loan provisioning, asset classification and income recognition requirements have been introduced. Despite such progress, the fear of causing further bankruptcies in the corporate sector and the implicit fiscal cost have limited and delayed the solution of banking and non-performing loan problems (see Table 12.9).

Table 12.8 Bank crisis resolution in Asia, 1998

	Indonesia	Korea	Malaysia	Thailand
Number of institutions				
Original	240	169	89	132
Closed	23	21	0	56
Nationalized	47	2	0	13
Merged	0	5	61	13
Bought by foreigners	0	0	0	4

Source: JP Morgan, *World Financial Markets*, Fourth Quarter 1998.

Table 12.9 The fiscal impact of banking and currency crises, 1990s

	Years	Non-performing loans percentage of total loans at peak	Fiscal and quasi-fiscal cost[a] percentage of GDP	Public revenues percentage of GDP
Finland	1991–93	9	8–10	33
Norway	1991–93	9	4	40
Sweden	1991–93	11	4–5	39
Mexico	1994–95	11	12–15	15
Indonesia	1998	70	17	11
Korea	1998	35	16	20
Malaysia	1998	35	15	23
Thailand	1998	45	18	20

Notes:
a. Lower estimates include costs of funds, credit, and bonds injected directly into the banking system; higher estimates include other fiscal costs, such as exchange rate subsidies.

Sources: IMF, *World Economic Outlook 1998*; IMF, *International Financial Statistics*, various issues; Deutsche Bank Research, *Global Emerging Markets*, Vol. 1.3, October 1998.

Delay in bank restructuring to ease the fiscal burden involved and to allow continuing expansion of bank credit to non-viable borrowers will only raise the ultimate costs of financial system reform; this lesson has been brought home clearly by Latin America's experiences in the 1980s (World Bank, 1998) and Japan's in the 1990s (Posen, 1998). While for speedy recovery it is primordial to restore credit to exporters and to viable investment, delay of reform will provide perverse incentives to under-capitalized or bankrupt banks. Either, to stem the decline in risk-weighted capital ratios, banks will increase their exposure to government liabilities and other zero-risk weighted assets. Or, banks will engage in activities (such as derivatives) with a high risk–return profile in a gamble to earn their way out of difficulties. Good risks, by contrast, are underfinanced and growth prospects undermined as long as the banking crisis is not fully and quickly addressed.

There is a clear trade-off, however, between cleaning up the banking system aggressively to eliminate a major obstacle to growth, and weakening the government's fiscal position. This trade-off has never been stronger than it is for the Asian countries in crisis. Not only are the loan losses in the Asian crisis countries much higher than in earlier episodes of banking and currency crises, but they also imply fiscal costs that must be met from much lower public revenue levels than ever before (Table 12.9). The fiscal costs stem mostly from the need for the government to take over non-performing assets by issuing a corresponding amount of new debt. In the Asian crisis countries, the interest costs alone on the new government debt represent a very large share of government revenues; further fiscal burdens arise from direct equity stakes.

Given these strong policy dilemmas, there are some tempting but short-sighted and ineffective policy prescriptions for reducing the fiscal cost of cleaning up the debt overhang. Notably, the imposition of controls on capital outflows or unilateral debt default clearly damage other emerging markets.

On 1st September 1998, Malaysia imposed strong controls on outflows. As a crisis measure, its main rationale is to lower the fiscal cost of bank restructuring by lowering the local interest rate without leading to further currency depreciation which would in turn nurture more losses in the banking system and in unhedged corporate balance sheets. The developing-country evidence, however, is not good for outflow controls (Dooley, 1995). They generally help delay reform, allow extending further credit to favoured borrowers and hence are likely to deepen the non-performing loan problem in the local banking system, thus raising the ultimate cost of bank restructuring. There is a danger that Malaysia will closely follow this script. Outflow controls effectively discourage inflows, including foreign direct

investment that has helped Malaysia to grow in the past. The absence of inflows in turn lowers the equilibrium exchange rate, and with the nominal exchange rate fixed by decree, raises the black market premium. A rising premium intensifies incentives to evade the outflow controls through overinvoicing of imports or underinvoicing of exports or through stimulating purchases of real commodities such as gold.

Two weeks prior to the Malaysian announcement, Russia not only imposed outflow controls but also defaulted by announcing a 90-day moratorium on its private obligations (involving both foreign and domestic creditors). Latin America's 1980s experiences with (often temporary) default have been extremely costly and thus short-lived (Reisen, 1989). The costs include: loss of market access reflected in skyrocketing sovereign yield spreads; the transfer of official reserves to avoid seizure; support for foreign affiliates of domestic banks that are being precluded from interbank business; private capital flight resulting from lost confidence of domestic and foreign investors; and, last but not least, the cut off from trade-related credit lines. Moreover, as domestic banks are often important (captive) lenders to their government and as default dries up market liquidity, banks will see their capital further depleted.

Other policies to reduce the fiscal cost of bank crisis resolution also have serious side effects (see Reisen, 1989). Chile, for example, recapitalized the banking system in the early 1980s by issuing central bank debt rather than government debt. While this leaves public budgets unaffected by the crisis resolution, the quasi-fiscal costs are high. Ultimately, the government had to recapitalize the central bank; but, admittedly, breathing space was gained in the meantime. A more transparent way is to follow the Scandinavian practice of establishing independent loan recovery agencies. These were mandated to maximize the recovery value of non-performing assets by either immediate closure and sale of the underlying collateral or by trying to recapitalize illiquid borrowers to improve repayment prospects.

Another option is to tax government bond returns. This raises the tax base by the amount of public interest outlays on government debt; but, if there is perfect foresight and if assets are perfect substitutes, taxing interest payments has no effect on government budgets. Changes in tax rates on any assets bring about an equal change in their equilibrium returns, and hence leave after-tax yields unaltered.

Yet another policy option to be explored is the concept of debt/equity swaps, which were an important element to the solution of Chile's debt overhang (both domestic and foreign) in the early 1980s. A debt/equity swap improves the structure of corporate liabilities by reducing current debt service requirements while allowing creditors (the bank or the government, after the transfer of bad loans) to reap the benefits of foregoing current debt

service claims by sharing in future corporate profits. However, swaps are difficult to implement on a large scale, in view of problems in loan valuation, equity pricing and corresponding free-rider problems similar to those discussed above.

More importantly, the inevitable fiscal cost in Asia's restructuring process must – and can – be supported by growth-oriented fiscal adjustment and easy monetary policy. With extremely high domestic interest rates, banks will not start lending again; they would rather invest money in high-interest public paper. The private corporate sector, obviously, can not operate at interest rates that are 30–50 per cent in inflation-adjusted terms. With negative or zero real growth, issuing government debt at these rates will lead to explosive debt dynamics and government insolvency – with default or hyperinflation as ultimate policy alternatives.

The fact that exchange rates have undershot their equilibrium levels by far can be exploited by monetary policy. As shown by Ize and Ortiz (1987) for Mexico's 1980s debt overhang, real interest rates on domestic debt can fall, in an open economy, provided that the exchange rate initially overshoots in reaction to a debt and currency crisis. If the initial depreciation gives rise to expectations of future appreciation, hence creating a wedge between returns in domestic and foreign currencies, this would allow debt servicing on local currency debt to fall. A more accommodating monetary policy can thus be part of continued restructuring in corporate and banking sectors, without compromising exchange rate stability, as confidence is restored.

Fiscal adjustment to cope with the banking woes should not be sought at the cost of output growth, as it is very likely to be disrupted by social and political resistance. Fiscal adjustment also has to contain tax-induced capital flight. This implies that the focus in Asian public finance has to be on tax-base broadening rather than on non-interest spending cuts. Effective tax ratios are low in the Asian debtor countries, and there are non-distortionary ways to increase them. While keeping marginal tax rates low to discourage capital flight and encourage business, tax bases need broadening by eliminating exemptions and special incentives. Low tax rates should raise compliance and enforcement of taxation, helped by high credible penalties on outright avoidance and abolition of discretionary elements in tax legislation. The tax base can also be broadened and the public revenue ratio raised, through introducing effective withholding schemes on wages, dividends and interest and through strengthening tax administration to cross-check different tax sources.

GLOBAL APPROACHES TO CRISIS PREVENTION

The global 1997–98 financial crisis has presented complex and unprecedented regulatory challenges to the international policy community. Attention has increasingly shifted from policy failures in emerging-market economies to the structural weaknesses of the international financial system, 'from the follies of borrowers to the follies of lenders' (Laura D'Andrea Tyson, 1998). US Deputy Treasury L.H. Summers (1998) has described the self-fulfilling flight of private capital out of the emerging-market economies as analogous to bank runs on entire economies. The G22 Report of the Working Group on International Financial Crises has aimed at identifying policies to 'prevent' international financial crises (and to facilitate their orderly resolution).

History suggests (Kindleberger, 1978) that financial and currency crises will never be prevented altogether. Whatever regulatory changes the authorities might find the vision, determination and leadership to bring forward, these changes can at best reduce the frequency, severity and contagion of financial crises; they cannot preclude them altogether. In the absence of 19th century 'gunboat' diplomacy and in the absence of enforceable global bankruptcy legislation, capital flows between private or public entities of sovereign nations will remain prone to moral hazard, adverse selection and changes in investor sentiment. Progress, however, towards a less crisis-prone international financial system has been made since late 1997, as official thinking has rapidly evolved.

Some proposals for a 'new global financial architecture' have widespread agreement among policymakers in both industrial and developing countries. The need for more transparency and accountability is generally accepted. The G22 Working Group on Transparency and Accountability has attached particular importance to enhancing the relevance, reliability, comparability and understandability of information disclosed by the private sector; the Group sees also a need for broad, frequent and timely data on international exposures of investment banks, hedge funds and other institutional investors. The public sectors need to provide better information disclosure on foreign exchange reserves, external debt and financial-sector soundness. An increasing number of countries have committed themselves to the IMF's Special Data Dissemination Standard, and BIS recording of the maturity, sectoral and national distribution of interbank lending comes in with broader country and risk coverage and quarterly frequency.

Good accounting standards and complete, accurate and timely information disclosure are not only a necessary precondition for prudential regulation and supervision. They also can help stabilize market

expectations. To be sure, better information is a necessary, not a sufficient condition, to prevent crises. 'The Asian experience makes this very clear: In spite of the ready availability of BIS data showing the increasing vulnerability of some of these countries to a sudden withdrawal of short-term international bank loans, the volume of these loans simply kept on rising', notes the BIS in its 1998 Annual Report. To stabilize market expectations, points out Alice Rivlin (1998) 'people need to actually want to look – and too often those who are making profits would rather not hear bad news'.

Table 12.10   Basle Capital Accord: risk weights by selected category of on-balance-sheet assets

Risk weight	Category
0 per cent	• Claims on central governments and central banks denominated and funded in national currency • Other claims on OECD central governments and central banks
20 per cent	• Claims on multilateral development banks • Claims on banks incorporated in the OECD • Claims on banks outside the OECD with a residual maturity of up to one year
100 per cent	• Claims on banks outside the OECD with a residual maturity of over one year • Claims on the private sector • Claims on governments outside the OECD, unless denominated in national currency

Source: IMF, *International Capital Markets*, September 1998.

It is also widely agreed that cross-border bank lending faces regulatory distortions through the 1988 Basle Accord, the capital adequacy regime imposing different risk weights by category of bank lending. Table 12.10 provides a selective overview of the current risk-weighting scheme for on-balance-sheet assets. Most importantly, short-term bank credit to non-OECD banks of up to one year carries a low 20 per cent risk weight, while long-term credit to non-OECD banks (over one year) is discouraged by a 100 per cent risk weight. A lower risk weight reduces borrowing costs, as banks have to acquire less capital relative to their risk-weighted assets. Similar distortions are created by the fact that claims on banks carry a 20 per cent risk weight, while claims on the private sector carry a 100 per cent risk weight. This encourages cross-border interbank lending, which has been described as the 'Achilles' heel' of the international financial system (Greenspan, 1998). It further implies that there is a greater incentive for

banks to lend to unregulated hedge funds (indirectly through interbank lending) than to even the bluest of the world's blue-chip companies. Note also that OECD-based banks and governments receive a more lenient treatment in the Basle Accord, even if they constitute sovereign risks equivalent or inferior to non-OECD emerging markets. Finally, the fixed 8 per cent minimum capital assigned to risk-weighted assets works in a pro-cyclical way: At the peak of the cycle, when asset prices are up, the capital buffer may be insufficient in light of the higher downside price risk of collateralized assets; at the trough of a cycle, by contrast, the Basle Accord may well intensify credit starvation.

The Asian crisis has also demonstrated that the recent shift in bank supervision from rules-based to risk-focused methods is unlikely to tame volatile bank lending behaviour. The growing competition from other institutional investors, the globalization of banking, new technologies (such as the Internet) and the proliferation of new financial instruments have lowered the potential franchise value of banks and pushed them into assuming new market, credit and liquidity risks (BIS, 1998). The regulatory framework, illustrated by the recent amendment to the Basle Capital Accord, has tried to catch up with the increasing complexity of financial markets by permitting the use of internal models for evaluating market risk. The state of the art risk management methodology – the value at risk (VAR) approach, an outgrowth of portfolio theory – has been shown to have first encouraged excessive bank lending and then intensified the global contagion of crisis. Bank lending to emerging markets was overly encouraged by VAR models, which establish backward looking variance–covariance matrices on daily asset returns, and hence failed to signal the true extent of losses that certain long or short asset positions could inflict (not surprisingly, the same model was used at the near-bankrupt Long Term Capital Management hedge fund). Contagion was intensified as a volatility event in one country automatically generated an upward re-estimate of credit and market risk in a correlated country. This triggered automatic margin calls and tightening of credit lines, as the VAR method encourages a defined net asset position (through, e.g., limiting net exposure to emerging markets by going long *and* short on highly correlated currencies, bonds or stock markets). The application of internal risk control methods may also explain why Russia's default and Malaysia's controls had such a deep impact on other emerging markets (Folkerts-Landau and Garber, 1998).

Banks have also increasingly engaged in proprietary trading activities directed at exploiting short-term trading opportunities in the emerging markets; moreover, they have increasingly lent to unregulated hedge funds[2] whose lack of transparency masks the banks' ultimate exposure to risk. The winding and unwinding of the underlying positions, often leveraged to high

multiples in order to enhance returns, has strongly destabilizing effects in the shallow asset markets of developing countries. This not only generates boom–bust cycles in the flow-recipient countries; it also raises counterparty risk so that banks and hedge funds can no longer be closed rapidly by regulators without posing a wider economic threat. It follows that the Basle capital adequacy requirements would have to raise the cost of proprietary trading and of bank lending to hedge funds. It has to be reckoned, however, that the sprawling derivatives facilitate the evasion of prudential regulation and supervision, unless extremely tight and sophisticated (Garber, 1998). As regulations containing the onshore use of derivatives just makes them move offshore, international co-operation between OECD and developing countries has to be fostered to bring offshore markets under the umbrella of supervision.

The recent emerging market crises have brought the moral hazard of commercial and investment bank lending to developing countries to the forefront. The evidence from the Mexican and the Asian crises indicates that equity, long-term bond and local-currency investors have suffered heavy losses. By contrast, banks have been the main beneficiaries of the Mexican bailout and have so far rarely suffered large losses on their exposure to Asia (IMF, 1998a). This may also have distorted the structure of capital flows from equity to debt, from long to short term and from local to foreign currency. While precise evidence on such interactions has not and cannot be established, recent events have shown that moral hazard of foreign investors cannot be eliminated cheaply.

The Russian unilateral moratorium, partly triggered by the refusal of the international community to provide further external assistance, was a clear first warning that 'governments limit the scope and clarify the design of guarantees that they offer' (G22, 1998, p. 3). In the presence of modern risk-control methods (discussed above), the failure to bail Russia out once again has clearly spread contagion to other emerging markets (and beyond). Regardless of fundamentals, risk premia rose for all emerging markets. The rise may also have reflected investors' perception that the suggestions floated in the policy community on how to bail in creditors may actually raise default risk.

Some policy options to reduce the trade-off between exorcizing moral hazard from foreign lending and intensifying crisis contagion exist, however. The G22 suggests a standing, privately funded mechanism to provide new credits in the event of a crisis or payments suspension. A prototype has been provided by Argentina and Mexico, both of which have set up standby credit lines with banks which will lend in times of crisis. How these agreements work out in practice remains to be (stress) tested.

Other suggestions are all based on extending insurance or contingent-loan facilities to countries which prequalify for such support by pursuing 'sound' policies or by fulfilling defined banking standards. The attractiveness of such plans lies in the restoration of a genuine lender of last resort for international assistance, since the club of potential beneficiaries and likelihood that they will succumb to financial crises is reduced. Such pre-defined liquidity support might rapidly establish market confidence in times of panic. The important drawback of such proposals, however, is that they would cement the world into a class society where some can count on support and others cannot. The experience of strings attached to liquidity support, designed to reduce moral hazard in official lending, has amply shown that the definition of eligibility for support becomes easily politicized.

A lot of attention has been given to the problem of how to correct the underpricing of risk and hence excessive risk-taking by banks. Relatively little thought has been devoted to how to prevent crises by inducing a rise in stable flows to developing countries. Long-term contractual savings institutions – pension funds and insurance companies – command a reliable long-term liability structure on their balance sheets and they pool large assets. These institutions have a great capacity to absorb risk, but regulation has often prevented them from investing in higher-risk assets, such as those in below investment-grade emerging markets. The reactive downgrading of Asian sovereign ratings from investment-grade to 'junk' status reinforced the region's crisis in many ways, e.g. by forcing institutional investors to offload Asian assets as they were required to maintain portfolios only in investment-grade securities. Rating agencies have also reinforced global crisis contagion in a self-fulfilling way by justifying the downgrading of Latin American assets with risks of contagion rather than fundamentals. The reactive (rather than preventive) approach of rating agencies can be explained by the fact that the information content of sovereign risk ratings and the nature of sovereign risk provide only little room for rating agencies to acquire advance knowledge or superior information on emerging market economies (Reisen and von Maltzan, 1999). Regulators should therefore reconsider the role of sovereign ratings that they stipulate when institutional investors hold emerging market assets. The removal of investment rating requirements might attenuate the boom–bust cycle in emerging-market lending by forcing banks and investors to rely on their own judgement rather than moving like herds on rating signals.

CRISIS PREVENTION: WHAT HOST COUNTRIES CAN DO

Private spending booms, fuelled by overborrowing, have increasingly led to twin banking and currency crises in developing countries, even in countries with a reputation for sound macroeconomic fundamentals (IMF, 1998b). Private capital inflows, attracted by exchange rate pegs and (often 'disorderly') financial opening, have repeatedly reinforced such pre-crisis booms. Domestic financial systems have tended to prove too weak as a conduit for heavy capital inflows, resulting in declining credit quality and financial fragility (Reisen, 1998b).[3]

The speculative currency attacks of the 1990s have challenged traditional crisis models that view them as a result of the government's inability to achieve fiscal and monetary discipline. The vulnerability to attacks was driven by private bank and non-bank borrowing, resulting in rising stock imbalances between real cash balances, short-term debt and official reserves (Calvo and Mendoza, 1996), as well as in currency and maturity mismatches. Once short-term foreign debt exceeds official reserves, a run on a country's liquid assets is intensified by the investor knowledge that there are not enough liquid reserves to restore confidence (Radelet and Sachs, 1998). Short-term debt poses special problems for the maintenance of financial stability, as its rapid withdrawal can trigger sovereign default, a systemic banking and payments crisis and large-scale corporate defaults (Eichengreen, Mussa *et al.,* 1998).

In order to reap the benefits of global capital flows without falling victim to their inherent risks, host countries have two broad policy sets at their disposal, macroeconomic discipline assumed. One set of policies serves to strengthen bank and non-bank balance sheets, so that capital inflows are intermediated and allocated efficiently. The other set aims to raise the quality of these inflows. Neither of these two policy sets, however, can be a substitute for the country's strong determination to maintain stability and to address instability should it arise.

Some of the avenues to strengthen a country's balance sheets are uncontroversial; but they are deceptively hard to implement, in particular in the historical context of developing countries' political, legal and institutional backgrounds. The recommendations of the G22 Working Groups on 'Transparency and Accountability' and 'Strengthening Financial Systems' point to a long list of ingredients deemed critical for lessening the probability of financial imbalances:

- Good accounting standards and complete, accurate and timely information disclosure are a necessary precondition for prudential regulation and supervision. Moreover, they can stabilize market expectations by improving risk assessment during the boom and by cushioning panic during a downturn, including crisis contagion. Transparency helps to promote accountability – by creating pressure on private and public decision-makers to explain their acts and to assume responsibility. Public policy can help to create the appropriate environment by mandating the proper use of accounting, auditing and reporting rules. Moral hazard in the allocation of capital within countries, particularly relevant in the presence of connected and directed lending, has to be exorcized by abolishing guarantees and through forcing banks and other lenders to assume capital loss for ill-assessed credit risk.

- Only with reliable accounting systems and disclosure requirements to ensure transparency will it be possible to strengthen bank and non-bank balance sheets and to enforce prudential regulation through serious, independent supervisory arrangements. It is safe to assume that basic ingredients for effective enforcement of prudential regulation will meet resistance from affected interest groups. Nonetheless, the basic requirements are: independent internal oversight of lending decisions by a credit review committee; vesting the supervisory agency with the authority to examine bank operations and balance sheets, close banks and establish entry criteria, define capital adequacy and exposure limits, enforce asset classification, provisioning rules and prudent collateral valuation that fully reflect the volatility of developing-country asset markets.

- The Asian crises, particularly in Indonesia and Korea, have also shown the importance of sound practices in the area of corporate governance (Millstein, 1998). More concerned with raising market share than with maximizing profits, and reluctant to issue equity as this would dilute their management control, non-bank firms greatly contributed to overborrowing and currency mismatches by raising offshore short-term debt. This has created systemic risk to entire economies, as large-scale default resulting from currency devaluation threatens the stability of the banking system. Corporate risk management and risk control, notably the management of liquidity and foreign exchange risk, are central to avoiding financial instability arising from access to global markets.

These prescriptions, while largely uncontroversial and emphasized by official thinking in both industrial and emerging countries, will take time to implement and will be hard to maintain. In fact, the Asian crisis countries had tried to strengthen the supervisory and regulatory infrastructure during the 1980s and 1990s, partly in response to costly banking crises (such as in Indonesia and Malaysia) a decade ago. What matters is the enforcement of prudential regulation.

Because the institutional capacity for durably strengthening balance sheets is not built overnight, appropriate policies have to be formulated. Where the required manpower is in short supply, allowing free entry by foreign banks and financial service providers can speed up capacity building. Importing rather than building expertise strengthens accounting practices, disclosure standards and risk management practices as they are shaped by more demanding requirements in the foreign banks' home countries. This, however, requires an orderly exit policy for ailing domestic banks as foreign bank entry squeezes profit margins and encourages ailing domestic banks into high-risk bets for survival. It also requires free entry of financial-sector experts and supervisors, as otherwise scarce supervisory personnel may be drawn to the entrant banks, as happened in Thailand.

A second set of policies to dampen the risk from excessive short-term debt, less emphasized by official thinking, aims at raising the quality of capital inflows. Such policies can be grouped under the headings of (a) appropriate exchange rate management; (b) prudential and control measures to contain short-term flows into the country, and (c) promotion of long-term inflows, not least through orderly sequenced capital account liberalization.

The excessive reliance on short-term borrowing can be discouraged by flexible exchange rates. By contrast, exchange rate pegs, in combination with high interest rates, typical in developing countries for structural reasons, tend to reinforce bank lending and spending booms (Reisen, 1998a). They constitute an incentive for leveraged investors to exploit interest differentials as well as for offshore borrowing by creditworthy banks and non-banks to tap seemingly cheap sources of finance. Central bank intervention on the foreign exchange market to peg the currency in the face of net inflows, unless sterilized fully, is intermediated into the domestic banking system. The exchange rate peg provides the incentive to allocate those funds disregarding currency and maturity risks, as these are being implicitly transferred to the central bank (Calvo and Mendoza, 1996). Keeping nominal exchange rates flexible, even introducing 'noise' through central bank intervention when it is seen to be on a too-stable, appreciating trend during inflow periods, improves the mix of inflows towards longer

maturities and encourages banks and firms to hedge their foreign-currency exposures.

Most mutual funds, pension funds and life insurers impose penalties for early withdrawal by investors. Chile, with its one-year unremunerated reserve requirement gradually extended to all inflows except foreign direct investment, has done likewise, as has Colombia (Ffrench-Davis and Reisen, 1998). Such capital inflow restrictions provide policymakers with a policy instrument in the policy trilemma that free capital flows, an independent monetary policy and pegged exchange rates are mutually inconsistent. They also extend the range of prudential regulation measures to limit the winding-up and unwinding of foreign-currency short-term positions, which have devastated emerging-market banking systems and economies in the past, including Chile's in 1982.

It has been argued that Chile's reserve requirements amount to a distortion that does not allow capital to flow to uses that offer the highest rate of return. To the extent, however, that these flows pose an exogenous distortion to returns (e.g. when high flows with multiple leverage drive asset prices up and down) or that the structure of foreign capital supply is distorted (e.g. by the Basle adequacy regimes, discussed above) capital restrictions on short-term inflows can be seen as correcting rather than creating a distortion. Finally, when the short-term debt/reserves ratio dangerously approaches unity, avoiding a speculative attack implies the need for the central bank to put every dollar of increased debt into official reserves to prevent the vulnerability ratio from growing. For developing countries, this means borrowing at a higher rate of interest than the rate at which funds are reinvested, say, into US Treasury Bills. Such a swap clearly constitutes a negative externality to the country, hence the rational to restrict short-term borrowing at the source.

Are caps on short-term inflows effective in improving the structure of inflows? After all, the high degree of integration in trade, production and financial services opens up many ways of circumventing controls. One reason that capital controls in most OECD countries were abolished in the 1980s was the perception that they were increasingly ineffective. Restrictions on inflows, but also prudential regulations on open foreign currency positions, are difficult to enforce as banks can use offshore subsidiaries or derivatives to evade them (Garber, 1998).[4] Authoritative studies from Chile's Central Bank do show that Chile's measures to regulate capital flows have been effective in providing a degree of monetary autonomy and in influencing the size and mix of capital inflows (Box 12.1).

Box 12.1 Banco Central de Chile studies on the effectiveness of the country's measures to regulate capital flows

The Chilean prudential framework, including capital inflow restrictions, has featured prominently in policy discussion on how best to deal with volatile capital inflows. Chile's authorities followed two main policy targets in view of a surge in capital inflows during the 1990s: First, to maintain a tight monetary policy without hindering export competitiveness resulting from unwarranted exchange rate appreciation. Second, to control the composition of inflows by discouraging short-term capital so as to limit the short-term foreign debt and foreign currency exposure of both bank and non-bank entities. In 1991, the central bank imposed a one-year unremunerated reserve requirement (*encaje*) on foreign loans. Subsequently, the rate of the *encaje* was increased to 30 per cent and its coverage extended to cover virtually all foreign inflows except foreign direct investment. The one-year minimum holding period effectively implied a tax on inflows, inversely tied to their maturity. Prudential regulation complemented these curbs on inflows. Except for trade credits, banks cannot lend domestically in foreign currency. And maximum open foreign exchange positions are set at 20 per cent of banks' capital and reserves. As short-term flows dried up in 1998, the *encaje* was reduced to 0 per cent, but not abolished.

As it is difficult to quantify the intensity of inflow restrictions and to control for prudential regulations, macroeconomic policies and other conditions that impact on capital inflows, the effectiveness of Chile's measures is being hotly debated. The Banco Central de Chile has provided the OECD Development Centre with a set of unpublished internal studies on the impact of the *encaje*.[a] These authoritative studies do show that the *encaje* has been effective in providing some monetary autonomy and in influencing the mix of capital inflows. Eyzaguirre and Schmidt-Hebbel (1997) set up a model for analysing and estimating the dynamic effects of the *encaje* on capital inflows. The model predicts an intensification of the *encaje* to result in higher domestic interest rates, diminished net foreign debt and a depreciation of the exchange rate. These predictions are borne out by calibrating the model with monthly data for the period January 1991 to June 1996. It is also shown that the *encaje*, with a lag of one year, modifies the composition of inflows by reducing the share of short-term flows in favour of longer maturities. The paper does not explore, however, to what extent the improved mix of inflows represents relabeling in order to escape the implicit tax on short-term flows. Le Fort and Sanhueza (1997) also provide evidence for 1990–96 that Chilean capital controls have been effective in keeping domestic interest rates above international rates, and that the effectiveness has not been eroded over time. Moreover, each time the coverage of the *encaje* has been extended, the newly taxed inflows have been reduced without a full substitution towards tax-free flow items. However, while the study is empirical, it does not provide an econometric analysis of the degree of effectiveness. Soto (1997) ran a vector autoregression analysis on capital flows, interest rates and the real exchange rate for June 1991 to June 1996. He found that capital controls had the desired effect of reducing capital inflows, maintaining higher interest rates and a lower real exchange rate, and reducing the share of short-term capital inflows. However, the magnitude of these effects was fairly small. One explanation for the small impact of the *encaje* on the dependent variable may be that the implicit tax of the inflow controls are smaller than assumed in most studies. Considering the positive option value of closing the investment position or staying invested in Chile once the investment has been done, reduces the implicit tax on a one-year investment from 2.50 to 1.25 per cent (Herrera and Valdés, 1997).

Note:

a. The author gratefully acknowledges the co-operation of Klaus Schmidt-Hebbel, Head of Research at the Banco Central de Chile.

But the impact has been weak, and regulatory measures in Chile have been supported by a culture of transparency and enforcement as well as by a set of macroeconomic policies (balanced budgets, wide target zones for exchange rates) consistent with raising the share of long-term inflows (Ffrench-Davis and Reisen, 1998). These conditions have not always been present in other emerging economies.

While Chile's controls were designed to tax short-term inflows without hindering long-term portfolio and direct investment, financial opening in the worst-hit Asian economies was 'disorderly' (Poret, 1998; Reisen, 1998b). Often the result of discretionary authorization granted to selected sectors, the opening process implicitly encouraged short-term inflows in the pre-crisis years. While tight quantitative ceilings were maintained on non-resident purchases on the stock market and on foreign direct investment (notably in Korea), financial opening eased access to short-term foreign borrowing. Table 12.11 may be indicative of the lessons to be drawn: the rise in short-term debt can be contained through 'orderly' liberalization (as in Colombia and Chile); but disorderly liberalization (as in the Asian crisis countries) encourages financial vulnerability, in particular if a strongly enforced supervisory framework is not yet in place.

Table 12.11   Maturity structure of foreign debt in selected countries (per cent of short-term in foreign debt, end-June 1997)

Country	Short-term debt
Colombia	39.4
Chile	43.3
Malaysia	56.4
The Philippines	58.8
Indonesia	59.0
Thailand	65.7
Korea	67.9

Source: Bank for International Settlements, *The Maturity, Sectoral and Nationality Distribution of International Bank Lending*, Basle, May 1988.

These observations reinforce the need for a capacity-building sequence of liberalizing capital inflows, as has indeed been advocated since the early 1990s (Fischer and Reisen, 1992). Foreign direct investment and trade-related finance, while a necessary ingredient for development even at the earliest stage, are unlikely to cause trouble for macroeconomic management and financial sector stability. They are early candidates for liberalization,

while other capital flows confront the authorities with more complicated issues. In view of the considerable time needed to establish a sound domestic financial system – accounting, auditing, disclosure, regulation and supervision – the required infrastructure should be built without delay and be enhanced by liberalizing the entry of financial-market expertise. This requires a clear and durable solution of prior bad-loan problems in the banking sector. The next candidates for liberalization are portfolio equity and long-term bond investments, which should be fostered in parallel with building the infrastructure for domestic stock, corporate debt and mortgage instruments. This will deepen domestic money markets, which allow authorities to smooth shocks to domestic liquidity. Deepened domestic financial markets pave the way for dismantling controls on short-term borrowing by banks and non-banks, assuming a tough supervisory regime is in place. Financial opening has the best chance to achieve its ultimate objective, to raise efficiency and growth without compromising stability, when combining a sequential opening process with building the prerequisite institutions.

NOTES

1. Capital inflows can be shown to be 'immiserising' (Brecher and Diaz-Alejandro, 1997), if they magnify welfare losses due to distorted consumption and production patterns by stimulating capital accumulation in protected sectors and by attracting foreign capital into these sectors.
2. The impact of hedge funds on the Asian crisis is difficult to determine with any precision. Eichengreen and Mathieson (1998) find little evidence that hedge funds led the crisis. The BIS (1998), by contrast, reports strong credit demand from offshore financial centres (where these funds are mostly incorporated). Market participants (Garber, 1998; Howell, 1998) maintain that the absence of data on hedge fund transactions, such as over-the-counter (OTC) contracts written by investment banks, clearly leads to underestimation of their impact.
3. To add another narrative to the large literature on the domestic causes of the Asian crisis, is beyond the scope of this Brief. See in particular IMF (1998a), Davies (1998), Corsetti *et al.* (1998), Radelet and Sachs (1998) and Reisen (1998b).
4. The BIS (1998) suggests in its 1998 annual report that the withdrawal of rights of establishment for banks from jurisdictions with inadequate prudential standards might have to be contemplated.

REFERENCES

Armstrong, A. and M. Spencer (1998), 'Will the Asian Phoenix Rise Again?', *Global Emerging Markets*, Vol. 1.3, Deutsche Bank Research, London.
Bank for International Settlements (1998), *68th Annual Report 1997/98.*
Bhagwati, J. (1998), 'The Capital Myth', *Foreign Affairs*, Vol. 77.3.
Borensztein, E., J. de Gregorio and J.-W. Lee (1995), 'How Does Foreign Direct Investment Affect Economic Growth?', *NBER Working Paper*, No. 5057.
Brecher, R.A. and C.F. Diaz-Alejandro (1997), 'Tariffs, Foreign Capital and Immiserizing Growth', *Journal of International Economics*, Vol. 7.4.

Calvo, G. and E. Mendoza (1996), 'Petty Crime and Cruel Punishment: Lessons from the Mexican Debacle', *American Economic Review*, Papers and Proceedings.

Cline, W. (1995), *International Debt Reexamined*, Institute for International Economics, Washington, DC.

Corsetti, G., P. Pesenti and N. Roubini (1998), 'What Caused the Asian Currency and Financial Crisis?', mimeo (http://www.stern.nyu.edu/~nroubini/asia/AsiaHomepage.html).

D'Andrea Tyson, L. (1998), 'The Global Meltdown: What To Do Next', *Business Week*, 26 October.

Davies, G. (1998), *Causes, Cures and Consequences of the Asian Economic Crisis*, Goldman Sachs, London.

Dooley, M. (1994), 'A Retrospective on the Debt Crisis', *NBER Working Paper*, No. 4963.

Dooley, M. (1995), 'A Survey of Academic Literature on Controls over International Capital Transactions', *NBER Working Paper*, No. 5352.

Eichengreen, B. and D. Mathieson (1998), 'Hedge Funds and Financial Market Dynamics', IMF Occasional Paper, No. 166.

Eichengreen, B., M. Mussa *et al.* (1998), 'Capital Account Liberalization: Theoretical and Practical Aspects', IMF Occasional Paper, No. 172.

Eyzaguirre, N. and K. Schmidt-Hebbel (1997), 'Encaje a la entrada de capitales y ajuste macroeconomico', Banco Central de Chile, mimeo.

Ffrench-Davis, R. and H. Reisen (1998), *Capital Flows and Investment Performance: Lessons from Latin America*, ECLAC, Santiago and OECD Development Centre, Paris.

Fischer, B. and H. Reisen (1992), *Towards Capital Account Convertibility*, Policy Brief No. 4, OECD Development Centre, Paris.

Folkerts-Landau, D. and P. Garber (1998), 'Capital Flows From Emerging Markets in a Closing Environment', *Global Emerging Markets*, Vol. 1.3, Deutsche Bank Research, London.

Garber, P. (1998), 'Derivatives in International Capital Flows', *NBER Working Paper*, No. 6623.

Greenspan, A. (1998), *Remarks by Alan Greenspan, Chairman, Board of Governors of the Federal Reserve System*, at the 34th Annual Conference on Bank Structure and Competition of the Federal Reserve Bank of Chicago, May 7.

Grilli, V. and G. Milesi-Ferretti (1995), 'Economic Effects and Structural Determinants of Capital Controls', *IMF Staff Papers*, Vol. 42.3.

Group of Ten (1996), 'The Resolution of Sovereign Liquidity Crises: A Report to the Ministers and Governors', Basle.

Group of Twenty-Two (1998), 'Summary of Reports on the International Financial Architecture', Washington, DC.

Herrera, L. and R. Valdés (1997), 'Encaje y autonomia monetaria en Chile', Banco Central de Chile, mimeo.

Howell, M. (1998), *Asia's 'Victorian' Financial Crisis*, Cross Border Capital, London.

ILO (1998), *The Social Impact of the Asian Financial Crisis*, ILO, Geneva.

IMF (1998a), *International Capital Markets: Development, Prospects and Key Policy Issues*, Washington, DC.

IMF (1998b), *World Economic Outlook*, Washington, DC.

Ize, A. and G. Ortiz (1987), 'Fiscal Rigidities, Public Debt and Capital Flight', *IMF Staff Papers*, Vol. 34.2.

Kindleberger, C. (1978), *Manias, Panics and Crashes*, Basic Books, New York.

Le Fort, G. and G. Sanhueza (1997), 'Flujo de capitales y encaja en la experienza chilena de los 90', Banco Central de Chile, mimeo.

MacKellar, L. and H. Reisen (1998), *A Simulation Model of Global Pension Fund Investment*, Technical Paper No. 137, OECD Development Centre, Paris; forthcoming, *Journal of Economic Policy Modelling*.

Millstein, I. (1998), 'Corporate Governance: Improving Competitiveness and Access to Capital in Global Markets – A Report to the OECD', OECD, Business Sector Advisory Group on Corporate Governance, Paris.

OECD (1997), *The World in 2020: Towards a New Global Age*, Paris.

OECD (1998), *OECD Economic Outlook*, No. 63, Paris.

Poret, P. (1998), 'Liberalising Capital Flows: Lessons from Asia', *OECD Observer*, No. 214.

Posen, A. (1998), *Restoring Japan's Economic Growth*, Institute for International Economics, Washington, DC.

Radelet S. and J. Sachs (1998), 'The Onset of the East Asian Financial Crisis', mimeo (http://www.hiid.harvard.edu/).

Regling, K. (1999), 'Financial Liberalisation in Asia: Analysis and Prospects', in M. Queisser (ed.), *Financial Liberalisation in Asia: Analysis and Prospects*, ADB/OECD.

Reisen, H. (1989), 'Public Debt, External Competitiveness, and Fiscal Discipline in Developing Countries', *Princeton Studies in International Finance*, No. 66.

Reisen, H. (1994), 'The Brady Plan and Adjustment Incentives', in H. Reisen, *Debt, Deficits and Exchange Rates: Essays on Financial Interdependence and Development*, Edward Elgar Publishing Ltd, Aldershot, UK.

Reisen, H. (1996), 'Managing Volatile Capital Inflows: The Experience of the 1990s', *Asian Development Review*, Vol. 14.1.

Reisen, H. (1998a), *Excessive and Sustainable Current Account Deficits*, Technical Paper No. 132, OECD Development Centre, Paris, published in *Empirica*, Vol. 25.2.

Reisen, H. (1998b), *Domestic Causes of Currency Crises: Policy Lessons for Crisis Avoidance*, Technical Paper No. 136, OECD Development Centre, Paris.

Reisen, H. and A. van Trotsenburg (1988), *Developing Country Debt: The Budgetary and Transfer Problem*, OECD Development Centre Studies, Paris.

Reisen, H. and J. von Maltzan (1999), 'Boom and Bust and Sovereign Ratings', *International Finance*, Vol. 1.3.

Rivlin, A. (1998), 'Lessons Drawn from the Asian Financial Crisis', reprinted in *BIS Review*, No. 41, 13 May.

Rodrik, D. (1998), 'Who Needs Capital Account Convertibility?', in P. Kenen (ed.), *Should the IMF Pursue Capital Account Convertibility?*, Princeton Essays in International Finance, No. 207.

Soto, C. (1997), 'Controles a los movimentos de capital: evaluación empirica del caso chileno', Banco Central de Chile, mimeo.

Summers, L. (1998), 'Building an International Financial Architecture for the 21st Century', Remarks to the Cato Institute, 22 October.

World Bank (1998), *East Asia's Road to Recovery*, Washington, DC.

Index